2017 EDITION

Gree

AMERICAN FLYER®

POCKET PRICE GUIDE

Edited by Roger Carp

Kalmbach Books
21027 Crossroads Circle
Waukesha, Wisconsin 53186
www.kalmbach.com/books

Published in 2016
Thirtieth Edition

Manufactured in the United States of America

ISBN: 978-1-62700-286-8

Front cover photo: American Flyer no. 405 Silver Streak Alco PA,
model courtesy John Heck

Back cover photo: American Flyer no. 799 Talking Union Station

We constantly strive to improve Greenberg's Pocket Price Guides. I
you find missing items or detect misinformation, please contact us
Send your comments, new information, or corrections via e-mail
to books@kalmbach.com or by mail to Lionel Pocket Price Guide
Editor at the address above.

Library of Congress Control Number: 2016931491

CONTENTS

INTRODUCTION

The latest and greatest guide

Welcome to the latest edition of what hobbyists regard as the most authoritative and trusted price guide to the trains and accessories produced by the leading S gauge firms of the past 69 years. Whether you're a longtime S gauge enthusiast or a newcomer to the toy train hobby, in this guide, you'll find the information you need to identify and evaluate the thousands of items made by various S gauge manufacturers between 1946 and 2017. Most of all, you will have at your fingertips the most up-to-date prices for locomotives, freight cars, passenger cars, stations, tunnels, signals, track sections, transformers, and catalogs.

Over the years, hundreds of enthusiasts have contributed extensive research to each edition of the *American Flyer Pocket Price Guide*. This 2017 edition represents the culmination of tremendous effort by many contributors. As a result, this 30th edition contains information on just about every toy train product marketed by the A.C. Gilbert Co. for its American Flyer line between 1946 and 1966. Also collected between the two covers of this guide are complete listings of all the S gauge trains put out by Lionel (using Gilbert tooling as well as its own), American Models S-Helper Service, and MTH.

What is listed and what isn't

When the first editions of this pocket price guide were published, the only S gauge products included were the classic trains and accessories developed by the A.C. Gilbert Co. for its American Flyer line. You'll still find those terrific models listed in **Section 1**, which includes locomotives, freight cars, and passenger cars cataloged between 1946 and 1966. Also included are American Flyer accessories, track sections, and transformers.

Gilbert released its final, abbreviated line of American Flyer trains in 1966 and declared bankruptcy a year later. In one of those "who'd-a-thunk-it?" scenarios, Lionel, which dominated the toy train industry in the postwar era, acquired the tools and dies that Gilbert had used to mass-produce American Flyer trains and related items.

Finally, in 1979, Lionel brought out a selection of Flyer trains and accessories. Ever since, thanks to old and new tooling, Lionel has been cataloging train sets, locomotives, cars, and accessories for its revamped American Flyer line.

Section 2 covers items that Lionel has produced or sponsored for that line since 1979. The vast majority of these items represent postwar models that Lionel has updated with different paint and lettering schemes and improved motors. Popular operating accessories have been revived, much to the delight of S gauge hobbyists as well as O gauge operators, who agree that particular freight loaders, light towers, and other accessories work equally well on their layouts. Other Lionel-produced models appear as uncataloged items offered by toy train collecting associations, museums, and other organizations for promotional purposes.

Section 3 covers every set, locomotive, and car made and marketed by American Models since the company entered the toy train field in 1981. Over the past 36 years, this firm has offered S gauge collectors and operators a wide range of popular electric-profile and diesel locomotives and, more recently, steam locomotives and tenders. The types of freight and passenger cars American Models has developed are impressive in terms of their variety and decoration. Also part of the company's S gauge line are sections of track and remote control switches.

Section 4 features the S gauge trains of MTH Electric Trains. MTH purchased the tooling of S-Helper Service's Showcase Line. MTH used this tooling to reintroduce and add to the freight cars and locomotives of S-Helper Service. Its locomotives include Proto-Sound, MTH's sound and control system.

Section 5 covers locomotives and cars made by S-Helper Service from 1994, when production began, through 2012, when its owners retired. The number of items this manufacturer put out is breathtaking—more than 1,500 train sets, diesel and steam locomotives, freight and passenger cars, switches, trucks, and couplers. Its locomotives and rolling stock feature an incredible array of railroad names.

Section 6 features a listing of the catalogs and other paperwork that A.C. Gilbert put out for consumers and dealers.

About the only notable American Flyer items not included in Section 1 are the boxed train sets that Gilbert cataloged. These S gauge sets are omitted from this guide because, to be considered complete, they must have all the items, including ancillary ones, that Gilbert packed with them. In addition, they should be in their original boxes. The level of completeness demanded for American Flyer sets puts them beyond the scope of this guide.

Also left out of the *American Flyer Pocket Price Guide* are rare items that have surfaced. These unique pieces include mock-ups of products that were assembled by members of Gilbert's Engineering Department. They also include models created for company executives to evaluate different paint and lettering schemes. These items, some of which are one of a kind, are so scarce that values cannot be assigned to them.

The guide's focus on S gauge trains of the post-World War II years explains other omissions. You won't find mention of the O gauge trains that Gilbert cataloged between 1939 and 1942 or the HO scale trains that it offered after the war. For the same reason, information on the Wide and O gauge trains produced by American Flyer Manufacturing is also absent.

How values are determined

Every user of the *American Flyer Pocket Price Guide* wants to know how the values are ascertained. There's nothing mysterious or arbitrary about the process. Over the years, we at Kalmbach Publishing Co. have gained the cooperation of many dealers and hobbyists, some of whom serve on our national review panel. These knowledgeable individuals share information about the trains and accessories they have bought and sold. They report on transactions conducted at meets across the United States, in retail outlets, and at live and online auctions. The editors of this guide study the information and supplement it with data from the publications of hobby groups that relates to buying and selling S gauge trains.

The values presented here are an averaged reflection of prices for items bought and sold across the country over the year prior to the publication of this edition. These values are offered as guidelines and should be viewed as starting points that buyers and sellers can use to begin informed and reasonable negotiations.

Values for individual items may differ from what is listed in this price guide due to a few key factors. Where collectible trains are scarce and demand outruns supply, actual values may exceed what is shown. Values may also rise where certain items are especially popular, often because of their road names. And as with all collectibles, national and local economic conditions will impact values, which tend to drop when times are tough and demand falls.

Another factor influencing what a toy train is worth relates to the venue in which it is being sold. Antiques dealers generally ask more for an item than do folks putting it out at a garage sale. Mail-order and retail outlets tend to charge more for trains than do individuals at shows because they need to be compensated for the additional costs generated by operating a store, compiling and distributing price lists, and packing and shipping trains. Of course, the cost of any item can balloon far beyond its listed value when two or more people compete for it at a live or online auction.

HOW TO READ THIS GUIDE

Number	Description	Condition——Good	Exc	
24067	Keystone Line Boxcar, *60* u	1350	2425	___
24076	Union Pacific Stock Car, *57–60*			
	(A) Knuckle couplers	32	85	___
	(B) Pike Master couplers	28	71	___

Reading an entry

Each section is arranged in numerical order by catalog numbers. Every item is listed by the product's catalog number or other number assigned by its manufacturer. A catalog number often appears on the product as its road number.

A basic description of the model follows the number. It gives the type of product, lists the name of any railroad identified with it, and includes identifying characteristics, such as color or lettering. If the item has a road number that differs from its catalog number, that number is shown in quotation marks. Abbreviations used in the descriptions, including those of railroad names, are found at the back of the price guide.

Next, you'll find the year or years during which that item was cataloged. The years are shown in italics. If one is followed by a *u*, then this item was uncataloged, most likely a promotional item and not part of the manufacturer's cataloged line.

In the American Models section, items are continually manufactured, so no years are listed. MTH and S-Helper Service products are also undated. Some entries show an asterisk (*) after the year. This mark indicates that a reproduction of the item has been made.

Some entries feature variations, each indicated by a separate letter (A, B, and so forth). Variations amount to slight yet noteworthy differences in appearance that distinguish models that otherwise seem identical. These differences can relate to color, lettering, and details that were added or deleted. For items having many variations, an entry may not include every variation.

An entry concludes with an indication of the item's value for several common conditions.

Condition

American Flyer and S gauge enthusiasts should be familiar with the condition and grading standards established by the Train Collectors Association, which are used as the basis for evaluating the condition of toy trains and accessories:

C-10 **Mint:** brand new—all original, unused, and unblemished.

C-9 **Factory New:** same condition as Mint but with evidence of factory rubs or slight signs of handling, shipping, and being test run at the factory.

C-8 **Like New:** complete and all original with no rust or no missing parts; may show effects of being displayed or signs of age and may have been run.

C-7 **Excellent:** all original and may have minute scratches and paint nicks; no rust, no missing parts, and no distortion of component parts.

C-6 **Very Good:** has minor scratches, paint nicks, or minor spots of surface rust; is free of dents and may have minor parts replaced.

C-5 **Good:** shows evidence of heavy use and signs of play wear—small dents, scratches, minor paint loss, and minor surface rust.

C-4 **Fair:** shows evidence of heavy use—scratches and dents, moderate paint loss, missing parts, and surface rust.

C-3 **Poor:** requires major body repair and is a candidate for restoration; major rust, missing parts, and heavily scratched.

C-2 **Restoration:** needs to be restored.

C-1 **Junk:** parts value only.

In this guide, Gilbert American Flyer trains are evaluated in Good (C-5) and Excellent (C-7) conditions. Lionel-produced trains are assessed in Mint (C-10) condition. American Models, MTH, and S-Helper items are listed with their last suggested retail price.

You may also see NRS listed as a value in the guide. NRS (No Reported Sales) refers to an item for which no adequate pricing data is available. Typically, these items are so scarce that only a handful have been reported.

Gilbert catalogs and paper items are evaluated in Good (P-5) and Excellent (P-7) conditions according to the following paper grading standards established by the Train Collectors Association:

P-10 **Mint:** Brand new, complete, all original as manufactured, and unused. Free of all flaws. Original folds are crisp with no signs of damage, and individual pages appear to have never been opened. No rusty staples, creases, tears, fading, or wear marks.

P-9 **Store New:** Complete, all original, and unused. Item may have merchant additions such as store stamps and price tags. May have been handled since leaving the original factory, but original folds are crisp without signs of wear.

P-8 **Like New:** Complete and all original. There is evidence of light use and aging. Item may have notations (discrete) added since leaving the manufacturer.

P-7 **Excellent:** Complete and all original. Item can show signs of moderate use, but it is completely intact. Original paper folds can show minute signs of damage including evidence of bending and folding. Item may have rusty staples that have not affected the paper.

P-6 **Very Good:** Complete and all original. Item shows signs of usage such as minor abrasions and creases. It is completely intact, but original paper folds show signs of damage. All printing is legible; however, there may be weathering, slight fading, pencil or ink marks, and soiling from rust, grease, or oil. Pages may have tears.

P-5 **Good:** Item shows substantial wear which can include moderate abrasions, creases, and folds. All existing printing is legible; however, the item is severely worn. Colors may be extensively faded, and original folds and edges may be damaged, Rusty staples may have stained pages. (Any paper having been repaired cannot be graded above P-5.)

P-4 **Fair:** Shows heavy damage but printing is generally legible. Paper may be brittle or have been repaired. Could have grease, oil, or water damage.

S GAUGE MARKETPLACE

When to consult this guide

Many readers of the *American Flyer Pocket Price Guide* use it after the fact. They already have some trains and accessories and now want to identify and evaluate those items. The *American Flyer Pocket Price Guide* can also help you think about what to acquire in the future. That's really when the fun begins! Once you have a general idea of how to enjoy this hobby, you can make informed decisions about which trains you want.

Postwar trains and accessories

This is an interesting time to be concentrating on postwar American Flyer. On the one hand, serious collectors are paying record prices for Like New and Mint items, boxes are escalating in value, and demand for original and complete sets, top-of-the-line locomotives, and scarce variations continues to rise.

On the other hand, the need that operators once felt to acquire postwar pieces to run on their S gauge layouts has all but vanished. The selection of realistic steam and diesel locomotives and colorful freight and passenger cars becomes greater each year.

As a result, folks who want to run trains can choose from models that promise superior performance and outstanding detail. Few S gauge enthusiasts can say that the postwar line from Gilbert surpassed what is available today, which is why operators are devouring new catalogs and paying less attention to what was offered 50 years ago.

Anyone who wants Good and even Excellent trains to display or operate will find that all but the most deluxe and exotic models are available in abundant supply and at affordable prices. Collectors with deep pockets and high standards may turn up their noses at common pieces as well as notable ones because those items are graded below Like New or do not come with all their original packaging.

So collectors willing to forgo a box and accept a scratch or paint chip may find items available that they once thought were beyond their aspirations. They may also benefit from the shift of operators away from postwar trains to contemporary ones. Operating cars, especially those models and road names that are considered fairly common, deserve more attention. In contrast, passenger cars continue to dazzle serious collectors, and so their prices have stayed at the same level or even climbed.

Demand for certain items in the higher grades seems stronger, which means that those same trains in Good or possibly Excellent condition may be overlooked. For example, the big steam locomotives, sleek PA diesels, realistic boxcars, and impressive tank cars that Gilbert cataloged in the 1950s continue to gain strength on the collector market. The same can be said of different freight loaders, figures, and stations. Originals draw more attention, probably because reproductions have flooded the market.

Modern trains and accessories

Flip through Sections 2 through 5 and you'll come across S gauge models of many of the best-known diesel locomotives and any kind of freight or passenger car imaginable. Railroads, large and small, prominent and forgotten, are represented.

Increasing numbers of S gauge enthusiasts are jumping on the contemporary bandwagon and buying trains of recent vintage to operate. They have found dozens of locomotives to run, including the EMD diesels and GG1 electrics that Gilbert never made as well as a variety of steamers.

When it comes to cars for any of these powerful, detailed locomotives, hobbyists have a selection of rolling stock that overshadows what was available in the 1950s and 1960s. Lionel and other current manufacturers have brought out superb models of vintage and contemporary boxcars, tankers, refrigerator cars, and covered hoppers. The array of loads carried on flatcars is amazing, and the range of caboose styles and road names continues to grow.

Kleer-Pak

In 1960, the following items came packaged in a Kleer-Pak, which significantly increases its value if found in the Kleer-Pak.

23743	Track Maintenance Car
24029	BAR State of Maine Boxcar
24055	Gold Belt Line Boxcar
24065	NYC Boxcar
24067	Keystone Line Boxcar
24125	Bethlehem Steel Gondola
24216	Union Pacific Hopper
24221	C&EI Hopper
24225	Santa Fe Hopper
24323	Baker's Chocolate Tank Car (white ends)
24425	BAR Reefer
24426	Rath Packing Reefer
24533	AFL Track Cleaning Car
24549	Erie Floodlight Car
24557	U.S. Navy Flatcar with jeeps
24565	FY&PRR Flatcar with cannon
24574	U.S. Air Force Flatcar with rocket fuel tanks
24575	National Car Co. Flatcar
24577	Illinois Central Flatcar with jet engine
24579	Illinois Central Flatcar
25046	Rocket Launcher Car
25057	TNT Exploding Boxcar
25515	U.S. Air Force Flatcar with rocket sled

		Good	Exc
____1	Transformer, 25 watts, *49–52*	2	4
____1	Transformer, 35 watts, *56*	4	9
____1A	Transformer, 40 watts, *57 u*	3	10
____1B	Transformer, 50 watts, *56*	1	5
____1½	Transformer, 45 watts, *53*	1	5
____1½	Transformer, 50 watts, *54–55*	1	5
____1½ B	Transformer, 50 watts, *56*	1	5
____2	Transformer, 75 watts, *47–53*	3	13
____2B	Transformer, 75 watts, *47–48*	3	29
____3	Transformer, 50 watts, *46 u*	1	6
____4B	Transformer, 100 watts, *49–56*	10	19
____4B-EX	Transformer, 100 watts, made for export, *49–56*	20	95
____5	Transformer, 50 watts, *46*	1	6
____5A	Transformer, 50 watts, *46*	1	6
____5B	Transformer, 50 watts, *46*	3	6
____6	Transformer, 75 watts, *46*	1	8
____6A	Transformer, 75 watts, *46*	1	7
____7	Transformer, 75 watts, *46 u*	2	9
____7B	Transformer, 75 watts, *46*	2	9
____8B	Transformer, 100 watts, *46–52*	11	43
____8B-EX	Transformer, 100 watts, made for export, *46–52*	20	95
____9B	Transformer, 150 watts, *46*	18	33
____10	DC Inverter, *46*	6	17
____11	Circuit Breaker, *46*	3	23
____12B	Transformer, 250 watts, *46–52*	35	93
____13	Circuit Breaker, *52–55*	4	10
____14	Rectiformer, *47, 49*	9	94
____15	Rectifier, *48–52*	5	26
____15B	Transformer, 110 watts, *53*	13	66
____16	Rectiformer, *50*	10	41
____16B	Transformer, 175 watts, *54–56*	23	82
____16B	Transformer, 190 watts, *53*	30	80
____16C	Transformer, 35 watts, *58*	6	17
____17B	Transformer, 190 watts, *52*	33	69
____18	Filter, *50 u*		NRS
____18B	Transformer, 175 watts, *54–56*	27	115
____18B	Transformer, 190 watts, *53*	33	120
____18B-EX	Transformer, 175 watts, made for export, *54–56*	35	140
____19B	Transformer, 300 watts, *52–55*	60	129
____21	Imitation Grass, *49–50*	15	35
____21A	Imitation Grass, *51–56*	15	35
____22	Scenery Gravel, *49–56*	13	21
____23	Artificial Coal, *49–56*	14	34
____24	Rainbow Wire, *49–56*	3	11
____25	Smoke Cartridge, *47–56*	5	19
____26	Service Kit, *52–56*	8	36

		Good	Exc
27	Track Cleaning Fluid, *52–56*	2	9____
28	Track Ballast, *50*	5	16____
28A	Track Ballast, *51–53*	5	24____
29	Imitation Snow, *50*	45	247____
29A	Imitation Snow, *51–53*	50	294____
30	Highway Signs, *49*	81	115____
30A	Street Signs, *51–52*	70	140____
30B	Transformer, 300 watts, *53–56*	70	137____
31	Railroad Signs, *49–50*	100	181____
31A	Railroad Signs, *51–52*	75	252____
32	City Street Equipment, *49–50*	55	206____
32A	Park Set, *51*	55	200____
33	Passenger and Train Figure Set, *51–52*	75	404____
34	Railway Figure Set, *53*	105	802____
35	Brakeman with lantern, *50–52*	71	171____
40	Smoke Set, *53–56*	2	4____
50	District School, *53–54*	90	171____
91½ B	Transformer, 50 watts, made for export, *56*	20	95____
160	Station Platform, *53*	263	590____
161	Bungalow, *53*	115	240____
162	Factory, *53*	80	195____
163	Flyerville Station, *53*	130	311____
164	Red Barn, *53*	105	513____
165	Grain Elevator, *53*	105	182____
166	Church, *53*	95	427____
167	Town Hall, *53*	108	284____
168	Hotel, *53*	120	276____
247	Tunnel, *46–48*	20	42____
248	Tunnel, *46–48*	20	45____
249	Tunnel, *47–56*	14	43____
270	News and Frank Stand, light or dark blue, *52–53*	55	124____
271	Whistle Stop Set, 3 pieces, *52–53*	65	227____
271-1	Waiting Station, brown, *52–53*	21	60____
271-2	Refreshment Booth, white, *52–53*	21	60____
271-3	Newsstand, green, *52–53*	21	60____
272	Glendale Station and Newsstand, *52–53*	64	202____
273	Suburban Railroad Station, *52–53*	65	262____
274	Harbor Junction Freight Station, *52–53*	55	250____
275	Eureka Diner, *52–53*	49	296____
282	C&NW 4-6-2 Pacific Locomotive, *52–53*		
	(A) AF tender, plastic or metal, *52*	34	62____
	(B) AF or AFL tender with coal pusher, *53*	44	99____
283	C&NW 4-6-2 Pacific Locomotive, *54–57*	32	70____
285	C&NW 4-6-2 Pacific Locomotive, *52*	52	111____
287	C&NW 4-6-2 Pacific Locomotive, *54*	21	79____
289	C&NW 4-6-2 Pacific Locomotive, *56 u*	332	451____
290	American Flyer 4-6-2 Pacific Locomotive, *49–51*	38	105____
293	NYNH&H 4-6-2 Pacific Locomotive, *53–58*		
	(A) Reverse in tender, *53–57*	77	119____
	(B) Reverse in cab, *58 u*	150	390____
295	American Flyer 4-6-2 Pacific Locomotive, *51*	95	155____

		Good	Exc
____**296**	NYNH&H 4-6-2 Pacific Locomotive, *55 u*	90	391
____**299**	Reading 4-4-2 Atlantic Locomotive, *54 u*	72	186
300	Reading 4-4-2 Atlantic Locomotive, *46–47, 52*		
____	(A) Reading, *46–47*	19	52
____	(B) Other variations, *47, 52*	15	33
300AC	Reading 4-4-2 Atlantic Locomotive, *48–51*		
____	(A) 4-piece boiler, *48*	20	63
____	(B) Other variations, *49–51*	15	34
301	Reading 4-4-2 Atlantic Locomotive		
____	(A) Metal tender, *46*	15	46
____	(B) Plastic tender, *53*	15	34
302	Reading 4-4-2 Atlantic Locomotive, *48, 51–53*		
____	(A) Smoke in boiler	18	46
____	(B) Plastic boiler	17	35
302AC	Reading 4-4-2 Atlantic Locomotive, *48, 50–52*		
____	(A) 4-piece boiler	17	48
____	(B) Other variations	18	37
____**303**	Reading 4-4-2 Atlantic Locomotive, *54–56*	17	41
____**307**	Reading 4-4-2 Atlantic Locomotive, *54–57*	18	58
____**308**	Reading 4-4-2 Atlantic Locomotive, *56*	24	72
310	PRR 4-6-2 Pacific Locomotive		
____	(A) Pennsylvania, *46 u*	92	156
____	(B) PRR-AFL, *47 u*	40	84
312	PRR 4-6-2 Pacific Locomotive, *46–48, 51–52*		
____	(A) Pennsylvania, s-i-t, *46*	55	145
____	(B) Other variations	65	121
____**312AC**	PRR 4-6-2 Pacific Locomotive, *49–51*	55	84
313	PRR 4-6-2 Pacific Locomotive, *55–57*		
____	(A) Small motor, *55*	75	164
____	(B) Large motor, *56–57*	95	215
314AW	PRR 4-6-2 Pacific Locomotive, *49–50*		
____	(A) Die-cast trailing truck, *49*		292
____	(B) One-piece trailing truck and drawbar assembly, *50*		223
____**315**	PRR 4-6-2 Pacific Locomotive, *52*	75	240
____**316**	PRR 4-6-2 Pacific Locomotive, *53–54*	77	213
320	NYC 4-6-4 Hudson Locomotive, *46–47*		
____	(A) New York Central, *46*	50	245
____	(B) NYC-AFL, *47*	45	137
321	NYC 4-6-4 Hudson Locomotive		
____	(A) New York Central, s-i-t, *46*	75	303
____	(B) NYC-AFL, *47*	50	185
322	NYC 4-6-4 Hudson Locomotive, *46–49*		
____	(A) New York Central, s-i-t, *46*	90	134
____	(B) American Flyer Lines, s-i-t or s-i-b, *47–49*	38	102
____**322AC**	NYC 4-6-4 Hudson Locomotive, *49–51*	44	123
____**324AC**	NYC 4-6-4 Hudson Locomotive, *50*	70	145
____**325AC**	NYC 4-6-4 Hudson Locomotive, *51*	60	145
K325	NYC 4-6-4 Hudson Locomotive, *52*		
____	(A) Early coupler riveted to truck	155	400
____	(B) Other variations	55	181

No.	Description	Good	Exc
326	NYC 4-6-4 Hudson Locomotive, *53–57*		
	(A) Small motor, *53–54*	60	144____
	(B) Large motor, *54–57*	138	242____
332	UP 4-8-4 Northern Locomotive, *46–49*		
	(A) AC, Union Pacific, s-i-t, *46*		NRS____
	(B) AC, American Flyer Lines, s-i-t, *47*	1050	2800____
	(C) DC, American Flyer Lines, s-i-t, *47*	1300	3000____
	(D) AC, American Flyer Lines, *47–48*	170	382____
	(E) DC, American Flyer Lines, *48–49*	170	542____
332AC	UP 4-8-4 Northern Locomotive, *51*	170	402____
332DC	UP 4-8-4 Northern Locomotive, *49*	155	416____
334DC	UP 4-8-4 Northern Locomotive, *50*	170	415____
K335	UP 4-8-4 Northern Locomotive, *52*	210	356____
336	UP 4-8-4 Northern Locomotive, *53–56*		
	(A) Small motor, *53*	170	429____
	(B) Large motor	248	500____
342	NKP 0-8-0 Switcher, *46–48, 52*		
	(A) Nickel Plate Road, s-i-t, *46*	500	1875____
	(B) American Flyer Lines, s-i-t, *47*	115	477____
	(C) Same as (B), but DC	110	428____
	(D) American Flyer Lines, *48*	95	253____
	(E) American Flyer, *52*	105	238____
342AC	NKP 0-8-0 Switcher, *49–51*	100	263____
342DC	NKP 0-8-0 Switcher, *48–50*	100	263____
343	NKP 0-8-0 Switcher, *53–58*		
	(A) Reverse in tender, *53–54*	115	289____
	(B) Reverse on motor, *55–57*	135	378____
346	NKP 0-8-0 Switcher, *55*	205	442____
350	Royal Blue 4-6-2 Pacific Locomotive, *48, 50*		
	(A) Wire handrails, *48*	85	133____
	(B) Cast handrails, *50*	43	87____
	(C) Cast handrails, Royal Blue on tender, *50*	750	1300____
353	AF Circus 4-6-2 Pacific Locomotive, *50–51*		
	(A) Wire handrails, *50*	125	513____
	(B) Cast handrails, *51*	150	513____
354	Silver Bullet 4-6-2 Pacific Locomotive, *54*	100	249____
355	C&NW Baldwin Locomotive, *56–57*		
	(A) Unpainted green plastic	68	88____
	(B) Green-painted plastic	115	196____
356	Silver Bullet 4-6-2 Pacific Locomotive, *53*		
	(A) Chrome finish	65	134____
	(B) Satin silver-painted	80	160____
360/61	Santa Fe PA/PB Diesel Set, *50–51*		
	(A) Chrome finish, *50*	85	307____
	(B) Chrome finish with handrails, *50*	120	585____
	(C) Chrome finish with warbonnet, *50*	110	600____
	(D) Silver-painted with warbonnet, *51*	75	233____
360/64	Santa Fe PA/PB Diesel Set, *50–51*		
	(A) Silver-painted, Santa Fe, *50*	75	217____
	(B) Other variations		NRS____
370	AF GM GP7 Diesel, *50–53*		
	(A) Link coupler bars, *50–52*	60	106____
	(B) Knuckle couplers, *53*	65	142____

		Good	Exc
____371	AF GM GP7 Diesel, *54*	105	147
372	Union Pacific GP7 Diesel, *55–57*		
____	(A) Built by Gilbert	115	214
____	(B) Made by American Flyer	135	216
374/75	Texas & Pacific GP7 Diesel, *54–55*		
____	(A) Sheet metal frame, *54*	175	422
____	(B) Die-cast frame, *55*	160	346
____375	AF GM GP7 Diesel, *53*	490	1398
____377/78	Texas & Pacific GP7 Diesel, *56–57*	175	383
405	Silver Streak PA Diesel, red stripe, *52*		
____	(A) Chrome finish	95	225
____	(B) Marblized chrome finish	110	290
____440	Lamp	1	5
____441	Lamp	1	5
____442	Lamp	1	5
____443	Lamp	1	10
____444	Lamp	1	5
____451	Lamp	1	5
____452	Lamp	1	5
453	Lamp, *46–48*		
____	(A) Single bulb	1	5
____	(B) 3 bulbs	1	6
____455	Bulbs, 3 pieces	2	5
____460	Bulbs, *51, 53–54*	34	233
____461	Lamp	2	7
466	AFL Comet PA Diesel, *53–55*		
____	(A) Chrome finish, *53*	103	164
____	(B) Silver-painted, decal, *54–55*	75	121
____	(C) Silver-painted, heat-stamped letters	90	203
____	(D) Silver-painted over Santa Fe lettering	85	203
____	(E) Silver-painted over Rocket lettering	90	250
____467	AFL Comet PB Diesel, *55**		NRS
470/71/73	SF PA/PB/PA Diesel Set, *53–58*		
____	(A) Chrome finish, metal steps, *53*	135	389
____	(B) Silver-painted, metal steps, *54–57*	120	376
____	(C) Silver-painted, cast plastic steps	245	705
____472	Santa Fe PA Diesel, *56*	110	203
474/75	Rocket PA/PA Diesel Set, *53–55*		
____	(A) Chrome finish, *53*	140	383
____	(B) Silver-painted, *54–55*	120	355
____476	Rocket PB Diesel, *55**		NRS
477/78	Silver Flash PA/PB Diesel Set, *53–54*		
____	(A) Chrome finish, *53*	175	470
____	(B) Silver-painted, *54*	232	510
____479	Silver Flash PA Diesel, *55*	80	257
____480	Silver Flash PB Diesel, *55**	600	2146
____481	Silver Flash PA Diesel, *56*	136	374
____484/85/86	Santa Fe PA/PB/PA Diesel Set, *56–57*	215	584
____490/91/93	Northern Pacific PA/PB/PA Diesel Set, *56**	340	765
____490/92	Northern Pacific PA/PA Diesel Set, *57*	200	497
____494/95	New Haven PA/PA Diesel Set, *56*	250	525
____497	New Haven PA Diesel, *57*	105	233

		Good	Exc
499	New Haven GE Electric, *56–57*	120	329____
500	AFL Combination Car, *52 u*		
	(A) Satin silver-painted	140	425____
	(B) Chrome finish	108	287____
501	AFL Coach, *52 u*		
	(A) Satin silver-painted	150	396____
	(B) Chrome finish	110	299____
502	AFL Vista Dome Car, *52 u*		
	(A) Satin silver-painted	145	428____
	(B) Chrome finish	110	303____
503	AFL Observation Car, satin silver-painted, *52 u*	155	515____
520	Knuckle Coupler Kit, *54–56*	1	7____
521	Knuckle Coupler Kit		26____
525	Knuckle Coupler Trucks		31____
526	Knuckle Coupler Trucks		45____
529	Knuckle Coupler Trucks		48____
530	Knuckle Coupler Trucks		45____
531	Knuckle Coupler Trucks		45____
532	Knuckle Coupler Trucks		45____
541	Fuses, *46*		NRS____
561	Billboard Horn, *55–56*		
	(A) Santa Fe Freight Train in Desert	50	60____
	(B) Santa Fe Alco with Steam Engine on Bridge	51	63____
	(C) Santa Fe Alco with Steam Engine on Bridge, green base	51	65____
	(D) Santa Fe Freight Train in Desert, green base	55	65____
566	Whistling Billboard, *51–55*	16	42____
568	Whistling Billboard, *56*	18	38____
571	Truss Bridge, *55–56*	11	35____
573	American Flyer Talking Station Record		NRS____
577	Whistling Billboard, *46–50*		
	(A) Circus, *46–47*	21	72____
	(B) Fox Mart, *47*	500	2650____
	(C) Trains, *50*	24	40____
578	Station Figure Set, *46–52*	55	244____
579	Single Street Lamp, green or silver, *46–49*	10	25____
580	Double Street Lamp, green or silver, *46–49*	18	37____
581	Girder Bridge, *46–56*	11	33____
582	Blinker Signal, *46–48*	55	120____
583	Electromatic Crane, *46–49*	65	105____
583A	Electromatic Crane, *50–53*	65	145____
584	Bell Danger Signal, *46–47*	250	860____
585	Tool Shed, *46–52*	23	118____
586F	Wayside Station, *46–56*	33	97____
587	Block Signal, *46–47*	70	314____
588	Semaphore Block Signal, *46–48*	650	3725____
589	Passenger and Freight Station, *46–56*		
	(A) Green-painted roof	17	36____
	(B) Black-painted roof	15	61____
590	Control Tower, *55–56*	26	87____
591	Crossing Gate, *46–48*	25	81____
592	Crossing Gate, *49–50*	24	39____

		Good	Exc
____592A	Crossing Gate, *51–53*	27	66
____593	Signal Tower, *46–54*	41	146
____594	Animated Track Gang, *46–47**	662	2130
____596	Operating Water Tank, *46–56*	35	60
____598	Talking Station Record, *46–56*	10	18
____599	Talking Station Record, *56*	11	42
____600	Crossing Gate with bell, *54–56*	30	67
____605	American Flyer Lines Flatcar, silver or gray, *53*	11	24
____606	American Flyer Lines Crane, *53*	25	44
____607	AFL Work and Boom Car, gray base, *53*	9	35
____609	American Flyer Lines Flatcar, *53*	10	25
____612	Passenger and Freight Station with crane, *46–51, 53–54*	55	109
____613	Great Northern Boxcar, *53*	21	62
____620	Southern Gondola, *53*	22	60
____622	General American Boxcar, *53**	16	40
____623	Illinois Central Reefer, *53**	11	22
____625	Shell Tank Car, *46–50*		
____	(A) Orange tank, plastic or painted	370	682
____	(B) Black tank	10	19
____	(C) Silver tank	6	22
____625	Gulf Tank Car, *51–53*	8	20
____625G	Gulf Tank Car, *51–53 u*	9	20
____627	AFL Flatcar, die-cast base, *50*	14	24
____627	C&NW Flatcar, plastic base, *46–50*	10	88
____628	C&NW Flatcar, *46–53*		
____	(A) Metal or plastic	8	31
____	(B) Pressed wood	13	40
____629	Missouri Pacific Stock Car, *46–53*	15	25
____630	Reading Caboose, *46–52*	6	33
____630	American Flyer Caboose, *52*	12	36
____630	American Flyer Lines Caboose, *53*	8	23
____631	Texas & Pacific Gondola, *46–53*		
____	(A) Unpainted green plastic	8	12
____	(B) Unpainted dark gray, *48 u*	85	295
____	(C) Red-painted, *52 u*	31	164
____	(D) Green-painted, *46–52*	4	19
____632	Virginian Hopper, gray or blue-gray, die-cast, *46*	30	108
____632	Lehigh New England Hopper, *46–53*		
____	(A) Gray-painted, die-cast, *46*	30	170
____	(B) Black plastic, *46*	8	33
____	(C) Gray plastic, *47–49*	4	20
____	(D) White plastic, *50*	33	99
____	(E) Gray-painted plastic, *53*	9	30
____	(F) Black plastic, red filled circle in logo		250
____633	Baltimore & Ohio Boxcar, *46–52*	10	25
____633	Baltimore & Ohio Reefer, *46–52*		
____	(A) Red, *52 u*	41	159
____	(B) Tuscan, *52 u*	51	260
____633F	G. Fox & Co. Boxcar, *47* u*	990	1825

		Good	Exc	
634	C&NW Floodlight Car "42597," *46–49, 53*			
	(A) Plastic base, *46*	20	71	___
	(B) Die-cast base, *47–49*	11	27	___
635	C&NW Crane, plastic base, *46*	15	56	___
635	C&NW Crane, metal base, *47–49*			
	(A) Yellow cab	11	34	___
	(B) Red cab	123	300	___
	(C) Black roof		580	___
636	Erie Flatcar, *48–53*			
	(A) AF, die-cast frame	13	30	___
	(B) AFL, die-cast frame	50	235	___
	(C) Pressed-wood frame, *53*	65	290	___
637	MKT Boxcar, yellow-painted or yellow plastic, *49–53**	8	24	___
638	American Flyer Caboose, *49–52*	6	10	___
638	American Flyer Lines Caboose, *53*	5	10	___
639	American Flyer Boxcar, *49–52*			
	(A) Unpainted yellow plastic	7	12	___
	(B) Tuscan-painted	16	83	___
	(C) Red-painted		555	___
	(D) Yellow-painted	10	26	___
639	American Flyer Reefer, *51–52*			
	(A) Yellow-painted or unpainted yellow plastic	6	10	___
	(B) Unpainted cream plastic	64	219	___
639	American Flyer Reefer, yellow-painted, *50–51*	10	19	___
640	Wabash Hopper, *53*	10	15	___
640	American Flyer Hopper, *49–53*			
	(A) Gray plastic body, white lettering	4	11	___
	(B) Gray plastic body, black lettering	4	10	___
	(C) White plastic body, black lettering	14	47	___
641	American Flyer Gondola, *49–52*			
	(A) Red-painted or unpainted red plastic	10	15	___
	(B) Unpainted gray plastic, *51 u*	143	283	___
641	Frisco Gondola, *53*	11	20	___
642	American Flyer Boxcar, *51–52*	10	16	___
642	American Flyer Reefer, *52 u*			
	(A) Unpainted red plastic	7	15	___
	(B) Red-painted	10	20	___
	(C) Tuscan-painted	25	27	___
642	Seaboard Boxcar, *53*	11	24	___
643	American Flyer Circus Flatcar, *50–53**			
	(A) Yellow, metal, with door guides for load, *50*	100	525	___
	(B) Yellow, metal	75	250	___
	(C) Yellow, pressed wood	90	346	___
	(D) Red, metal	120	1009	___
	(E) Metal car, no load	29	35	___
644	American Flyer Crane Car, *50–53*			
	(A) Red cab, black boom, *50*	35	96	___
	(B) Red cab, green boom, *50*	22	66	___
	(C) Tuscan-painted cab, green boom, *50–51*	27	77	___
	(D) Black cab, black boom	20	39	___

GILBERT PRODUCTION 1946-1966

			Good	Exc
____ **645**	AF Work and Boom Car, *50*		16	52
____ **645A**	AF or AFL Work and Boom Car, *51–53*		16	29
646	Erie Floodlight Car, *50–53*			
____	(A) Green-painted, die-cast generator, *50*		47	177
____	(B) Red or green plastic generator		15	32
____	(C) Red or green painted generator		15	33
____ **647**	Northern Pacific Reefer, *52–53*		13	33
____ **648**	American Flyer Flatcar, red or tuscan, *52–54*		11	21
649	AF Circus Coach, *50–52*			
____	(A) Unpainted yellow plastic		23	35
____	(B) Yellow-painted		55	161
650	New Haven Pullman Car, *46–53*			
____	(A) Red or green, plastic frame		21	80
____	(B) Red or green, die-cast frame		22	48
____	(C) Red or green, sheet metal frame		15	25
651	New Haven Baggage Car, *46–53*			
____	(A) Red or green, plastic frame		12	56
____	(B) Red or green, die-cast frame		12	32
____	(C) Red or green, sheet metal frame		11	31
652	Pullman Car, *46–53*			
____	(A) Red or green, long trucks		65	300
____	(B) Red, tuscan, or green, short trucks		41	120
____	(C) Red, maroon, or green, Pikes Peak		48	143
653	Pullman Car, *46–53*			
____	(A) Red or green, long trucks		65	208
____	(B) Red or green, short trucks		40	90
654	Pullman Observation Car, *46–53*			
____	(A) Red or green, long trucks		60	234
____	(B) Red or green, short trucks		41	88
655	AFL Coach, *53*			
____	(A) Red-painted		22	66
____	(B) Green-painted		32	62
655	Silver Bullet Coach, *53*			
____	(A) Chrome finish		25	63
____	(B) Satin silver-painted		20	139
660	AFL Combination Car, *50–52*			
____	(A) Aluminum body		18	49
____	(B) Chrome finish, plastic body		27	118
661	AFL Coach, *50–52*			
____	(A) Aluminum body		52	74
____	(B) Chrome finish, plastic body		44	78
____	(C) Satin silver-painted, plastic body		50	263
662	AFL Vista Dome Car, *50–52*			
____	(A) Aluminum body		22	70
____	(B) Chrome finish, plastic body		30	77
____ **663**	AFL Observation Car, aluminum, *50–52*		22	79
____ **668**	Manual Switch, left hand, *53–55*		5	9
____ **669**	Manual Switch, right hand, *53–55*		5	9
____ **670**	Track Trip, *55–56*		2	13
____ **678**	Remote Control Switch, left hand, *53–56*		7	19
____ **679**	Remote Control Switch, right hand, *53–56*		6	16
____ **690**	Track Terminal, *46–56*			4

		Good	Exc
691	Steel Pins, *46–48*		1____
692	Fiber Pins, *46–48*		3____
693	Track Locks, dozen, *48–56*		5____
694	Couplers, Trucks, Wheels, and Axles, *46–53*	2	18____
695	Reverse Loop Relay, *55–56*	26	106____
695	Track Trip, *46*	6	14____
696	Track Trip, *55–57*		
	(A) Plastic shoe	10	16____
	(B) Die-cast shoe	10	26____
697	Track Trip, *50–54*	4	15____
698	Reverse Loop Kit, *49–50, 52–54*	17	66____
700	Straight Track, *46–56*		2____
701	Straight Track, half section, *46–56*		2____
702	Curved Track, *46–56*		2____
703	Curved Track, half section, *46–56*		2____
704	Manual Uncoupler, *52–56*		5____
705	Remote Control Uncoupler, *46–47*	1	5____
706	Remote Control Uncoupler, *48–56*	1	6____
707	Track Terminal, *46–59*		2____
708	Air Chime Whistle Control, *51–56*	3	11____
709	Lockout Eliminator, *50–55*	2	19____
710	Automatic Track Section, *46–47*	1	9____
710	Steam Whistle Control, *55–56*	10	190____
711	Mail Pickup, *46–47*	9	22____
712	Special Rail Section, *47–56*		1____
713	Special Rail Section with mail bag hook, *47–56*	8	30____
714	Log Unloading Car, *51–54*	16	45____
715	American Flyer Lines Flatcar, *46–54*		
	(A) Tootsietoy armored car	37	132____
	(B) Manoil coupe	25	46____
	(C) Tootsietoy racer		49____
716	American Flyer Lines Hopper, *46–51*		
	(A) Between-rail pickup, *46*	6	40____
	(B) Outside rail pickup, *47–51*	6	27____
717	American Flyer Lines Flatcar, *46–52*	15	31____
718	AFL Mail Pickup Car, *49–54*		300____
718	New Haven Mail Pickup Car, *46–54*		
	(A) Red body, red pickup arm	155	468____
	(B) Red or green body	31	112____
	(C) Maroon body		NRS____
719	CB&Q Hopper Dump Car, *50–54*		
	(A) Tuscan-painted	25	57____
	(B) Red plastic	34	82____
720	Remote Control Switches, *46–49*	19	55____
720A	Remote Control Switches, *50–56*	23	47____
722	Manual Switches, *46–51*	10	24____
722A	Manual Switches, *52–56*	9	18____
725	90-degree Crossing, *46–56*	3	14____
726	Straight Rubber Roadbed, *50–56*	1	5____
727	Curved Rubber Roadbed, *50–56*	1	3____
728	Re-railer, *56*	3	33____

		Good	Exc
730	Bumper, *46–56*		
____	(A) Green plastic	11	19
____	(B) Red, *51*	35	95
____	(C) Green-painted	23	90
____**731**	Pike Planning Kit, *52–56*	11	24
732	AF Operating Baggage Car, *51–54*		
____	(A) Unpainted red or green	29	77
____	(B) Green-painted	34	100
734	American Flyer Operating Boxcar, *50–54*		
____	(A) Red plastic	20	48
____	(B) Red painted	25	80
____	(C) Tuscan painted	20	48
____	(D) Tuscan painted, AFL	30	92
____**735**	NH Animated Station Coach, *52–54*	32	78
____**736**	Missouri Pacific Stock Car, *50–54*	10	34
740	AFL Motorized Handcar, *52–54*		
____	(A) No decals, no vent holes, black lettering, *52*	33	123
____	(B) Shield decal with stripes, *52*	20	54
____	(C) Shield decal with vent holes, no stripes	17	69
____**741**	AFL Handcar and Shed, motorized, *53–54*	75	123
____**742**	AFL Reversing Handcar, *55–56*	41	84
____**743**	Track Maintenance Car		2750
____**747**	Cardboard Trestle Set	7	22
____**748**	Girder, Trestle, and Tower Bridge, *58 u*	22	50
748	Overhead Foot Bridge, *51–52*		
____	(A) Gray/aluminum	17	32
____	(B) Bluish silver	28	51
____**749**	Street Lamp Set, *50–52*	6	26
750	Trestle Bridge, *46–56*		
____	(A) Black-painted	16	54
____	(B) Silver-painted	16	90
____	(C) Bluish gray-painted	25	110
____**751**	Log Loader, *46–50*	69	158
____**751A**	Log Loader, *52–53*	47	97
____**752**	Seaboard Coaler, *46–50*	100	135
____**752A**	Seaboard Coaler, *51–52*	115	165
____**753**	Mountain Tunnel and Pass Set, *60 u*	17	127
____**753**	Single Trestle Bridge, *52*	16	54
____**754**	Double Trestle Bridge, *50–52*	50	98
755	Talking Station, *48–50*		
____	(A) Green roof	50	70
____	(B) Blue roof	60	145
____**758**	Sam the Semaphore Man, *49*	29	55
____**758A**	Sam the Semaphore Man, *50–56*	36	113
____**759**	Bell Danger Signal, *53–56*	22	46
____**760**	Highway Flasher, *49–56*	9	29
____**761**	Semaphore, *49–56*	22	108
____**762**	Two-in-One Whistle, *49–50*	35	94
____**763**	Mountain Set, *49–50*	46	140
____**764**	Express Office, *50–51*	47	204
____**766**	Animated Station, *52–54*	68	134

		Good	Exc
K766	Animated Station, *53–55*	55	142____
767	Roadside Diner, *50–54*		
	(A) Yellow plastic	40	75____
	(B) Yellow-painted	50	138____
768	Oil Supply Depot, *50–53*		
	(A) Shell	40	116____
	(B) Gulf	60	190____
769	Aircraft Beacon, *50*	16	37____
769A	Aircraft Beacon, *51–56*	19	55____
770	Girder Trestle Set, *60 u*	4	18____
770	Loading Platform, *50–52*	31	85____
771	Operating Stockyard, *50–54*	46	59____
K771	Stockyard and Car, *53–56*	50	84____
772	Water Tower, *50–56*		
	(A) Small tank	30	59____
	(B) Small tank, with workman, *50*	207	505____
	(C) Large checkerboard tank, metal shack	49	122____
773	Oil Derrick, *50–52*		
	(A) American Flyer, *50*	48	76____
	(B) Gulf logo		775____
774	Floodlight Tower, *51–56*		
	(A) Red base, gray tower and platform	18	63____
	(B) Red base, gray tower and platform, with workman	80	324____
775	Baggage Platform with boxcar, link couplers, *53–55*	24	78____
K775	Baggage Platform with boxcar, knuckle couplers, *53–55*	35	131____
778	Street Lamp Set, *53–56*	11	29____
779	Oil Drum Loader, *55–56*		
	(A) Tan plastic base	55	120____
	(B) Gray-painted base	75	211____
780	Trestle Set, *53–56*		
	(A) Black, *53*	15	26____
	(B) Orange	10	28____
781	Abutment Set, *53*	22	122____
782	Abutment Set, *53*	17	121____
783	Hi-Trestle Sections, *53–56*	6	46____
784	Hump Set, *55*	75	354____
785	Coal Loader, *55–56*	141	206____
787	Log Loader, *55–56*	73	142____
788	Suburban Station, *56*	11	56____
789	Station and Baggage Smasher, *56–57*	93	168____
790	Trainorama, *53 u*	48	189____
792	Terminal, *54–56*	65	137____
793	Union Station, *55–56*	16	83____
794	Union Station, *54*	32	129____
795	Union Station and Terminal, *54*	110	352____
799	Talking Station, *54–56*	35	174____
801	Baltimore & Ohio Hopper, *56–57*	11	14____
802	Illinois Central Reefer, *56–57**		
	(A) Orange plastic	16	21____
	(B) Orange-painted	100	242____

			Good	Exc
____	803	Santa Fe Boxcar, tuscan, unpainted, *56–57*	17	24
____	804	Norfolk & Western Gondola, *56–57*	6	14
____	805	Pennsylvania Gondola, tuscan, *56–57*	7	13
____	806	American Flyer Lines Caboose, *56–57*	7	10
	807	Rio Grande Boxcar, *57*		
____		(A) Unpainted, nonopening door	19	28
____		(B) Opening door		NRS
____		(C) White-painted, nonopening door		415
____	900	NP Combination Car, *56–57**	100	238
____	901	NP Coach, *56–57**	100	242
____	902	NP Vista Dome Car, *56–57**	100	242
____	903	NP Observation Car, *56–57**	100	235
____	904	AFL Caboose, *56*	11	18
____	905	AFL Flatcar, gray or blue-gray, *54*	11	34
____	906	AFL Crane, gray or blue-gray, *54*	16	43
____	907	AFL Work and Boom Car, *54*	13	36
____	909	AFL Flatcar, gray or blue-gray, *54*	11	30
____	910	Gilbert Chemical Tank Car, *54**	70	210
	911	C&O Gondola, *55–57*		
____		(A) Silver pipes, black-painted or black body	10	39
____		(B) Brown pipes, black-painted body, *55*	39	195
	912	Koppers Tank Car, *55–57*		
____		(A) Die-cast frame	38	58
____		(B) Plastic frame	25	59
	913	Great Northern Boxcar, *53–58*		
____		(A) Decal goat logo	14	36
____		(B) Painted goat logo	14	30
____	914	American Flyer Lines Flatcar, *53–57*	17	59
	915	American Flyer Lines Flatcar, *53–57*		
____		(A) Black and red, yellow ramp, with TootsieToy racer	12	66
____		(B) gray, brown ramp, with Renwal gas truck	12	81
____	916	Delaware & Hudson Gondola, *55–56*	9	34
	918	American Flyer Lines Mail Car, *53–58*		
____		(A) American Flyer Lines	29	79
____		(B) New Haven	35	162
____	919	CB&Q Dump Car, *53–56*	41	83
____	920	Southern Gondola, *53–56*	14	31
____	921	CB&Q Hopper, *53–56*	8	27
	922	General American Boxcar, *53–57**		
____		(A) Decal	15	31
____		(B) Stamped	15	59
____	923	Illinois Central Reefer, *54–55**	13	17
____	924	Jersey Central Hopper, *53–56*	9	23
	925	Gulf Tank Car, *52–57*		
____		(A) Early knuckle coupler, *52*	28	176
____		(B) Die-cast frame	15	33
____		(C) Plastic frame	10	20
	926	Gulf Tank Car, *55–57*		
____		(A) Die-cast frame	10	48
____		(B) Plastic frame	10	43

		Good	Exc
928	C&NW Flatcar, *52–54*		
	(A) Pressed-wood base, *52*	24	87____
	(B) Die-cast base, *53–54*	9	23____
928	New Haven Log Car, *56 u*	17	32____
928	New Haven Lumber Car, *56–57*	11	32____
929	Missouri Pacific Stock Car, *52–57*		
	(A) Closed slats, tuscan or red	10	31____
	(B) Open slats, tuscan, *57*	100	900____
	(C) Early knuckle coupler, *52*	75	243____
930	American Flyer Caboose, *52*		
	(A) Early knuckle coupler	28	112____
	(B) Red	15	37____
	(C) Tuscan	9	28____
930	American Flyer Lines Caboose, *53–57*		
	(A) Type I or II body	22	46____
	(B) Type III body	28	119____
931	T&P Gondola, green, *52–55*		
	(A) Riveted couplers, *52*		1000____
	(B) Nonriveted couplers	5	18____
933	B&O Boxcar, *53–54*	19	43____
934	American Flyer Lines Caboose, *54 u*	16	39____
934	C&NW Floodlight Car "42597," gray or blue-gray, *53–54*	10	26____
934	Southern Pacific Floodlight Car, *54 u*	14	32____
935	AFL Bay Window Caboose, *57*	21	58____
936	Erie Flatcar, *53–54*	12	43____
936	Pennsylvania Flatcar, *55–57*	40	127____
937	MKT Boxcar, *53–58**		
	(A) All yellow	10	40____
	(B) Yellow and tuscan	10	34____
938	American Flyer Lines Caboose, *54–55*	5	16____
940	Wabash Hopper, *53–56*	7	17____
941	Frisco Lines Gondola, *53–56*	7	21____
942	Seaboard Boxcar, *54*	9	17____
944	American Flyer Crane, *52–57*		
	(A) Gray die-cast body, black cab	22	47____
	(B) Blue-gray die-cast body, black cab	30	63____
945	AF or AFL Work and Boom Car, *52–57*		
	(A) Die-cast base, *52–56*	10	41____
	(B) Plastic base, *57*	15	39____
946	Erie Floodlight Car, *53–56*		
	(A) Red or green painted generator	13	41____
	(B) Red, green, or yellow plastic generator	13	41____
947	Northern Pacific Reefer, *53–58*	16	30____
948	AFL Flatcar, *53–57*	11	30____
951	AFL Baggage Car, *53–57*		
	(A) Red or maroon	15	62____
	(B) Green	18	58____
952	AFL Pullman Car, *53–58*		
	(A) No silhouettes, maroon or green	36	152____
	(B) Silhouettes, maroon	50	176____

			Good	Exc
953		AFL Combination Car, *53–58*		
____		(A) No silhouettes, maroon or green	56	105
____		(B) Silhouettes, maroon	55	160
954		AFL Observation Car, *53–56*		
____		(A) No silhouettes, maroon or green	36	109
____		(B) Silhouettes, maroon	105	160
955		AF or AFL Coach, *54–55*		
____		(A) Satin silver-painted	30	81
____		(B) Green-painted	31	64
____		(C) Maroon-painted, silhouettes, "955"	21	80
____		(D) Maroon-painted, silhouettes, white-outlined windows	29	90
____	**956**	Monon Flatcar, *56*	21	57
____	**957**	Erie Operating Boxcar, *57 u*	47	557
____	**958**	Mobilgas Tank Car, plastic or metal frame, *57 u*	23	90
	960	AFL Columbus Combination Car, *53–56*		
____		(A) Satin silver	30	92
____		(B) Blue, green, or red band	56	114
____		(C) Chestnut band	75	182
____		(D) Orange band	50	131
____		(E) Chrome finish	50	114
	961	AFL Jefferson Pullman Car, *53–58*		
____		(A) Satin silver	40	272
____		(B) Green or red band	45	115
____		(C) Chestnut band	108	256
____		(D) Orange band	65	159
____		(E) Chrome finish	50	108
	962	AFL Hamilton Vista Dome Car, *53–58*		
____		(A) Satin silver	40	114
____		(B) Blue, green, or red band	41	110
____		(C) Chestnut band	90	238
____		(D) Orange band	65	164
____		(E) Chrome finish	50	113
	963	AFL Washington Observation Car, *53–58*		
____		(A) Satin silver	40	107
____		(B) Blue, green, or red band	36	123
____		(C) Chestnut band	85	223
____		(D) Orange band	65	157
____		(E) Chrome finish	50	110
	969	Rocket Launcher Flatcar, *57 u*		
____		(A) Black plastic	20	55
____		(B) Black-painted	80	285
____	**970**	Seaboard Operating Boxcar, *56–57*	48	90
	971	Southern Pacific Lumber Unloading Car, *56–57*		
____		(A) Tuscan plastic	39	105
____		(B) Tuscan-painted plastic	50	620
____	**973**	Gilbert's Operating Milk Car, *56–57*	65	117
____	**974**	AFL Operating Boxcar, *53–54*	27	102
____	**974**	Erie Operating Boxcar, *55*	48	151
____	**975**	AFL Operating Coach, *54–55*	29	75
____	**976**	MP Operating Cattle Car, *53–62*	25	46

		Good	Exc	
977	AFL Caboose, metal or rubber man, *55–57*	26	46	___
978	AFL Grand Canyon Observation Car, *56–58*	130	401	___
979	AFL Bay Window Caboose, *57*	62	104	___
980	Baltimore & Ohio Boxcar, *56–57*	35	81	___
981	Central of Georgia Boxcar, *56–57*			
	(A) Shiny black paint	44	90	___
	(B) Dull black paint	70	201	___
982	BAR Boxcar, *56–57*	42	91	___
983	MP Boxcar, *56–57*	48	96	___
984	New Haven Boxcar, *56–57*	30	64	___
985	B&M Boxcar, *57*	55	91	___
988	ART Reefer, *56–57*	49	78	___
989	Northwestern Reefer, *56–58*	73	125	___
994	Union Pacific Stock Car, *57*	62	162	___
C1001	White's Discount Centers Boxcar, *61* * *u*	345	1578	___
1023A	Trestle Set		220	___
1-1024A	Trestle Set, *52 u*	10	44	___
C2001	Post Boxcar, *62 u*	13	22	___
L2001	Game Train 4-4-0 Locomotive, *63*	15	42	___
L2002	Burlington Route 4-4-0 Locomotive, *63 u*	50	295	___
L2004	Rio Grande F9 Diesel, *62*	80	190	___
C2009	Texas & Pacific Gondola, *62–64*			
	(A) Unpainted dark green or dark green-painted		2000	___
	(B) Unpainted light green	7	20	___
21004	PRR 0-6-0 Switcher, *57 u*	115	344	___
21005	PRR 0-6-0 Switcher, *57–58*	125	381	___
21084	C&NW 4-6-2 Pacific Locomotive, *57 u*	41	154	___
21085	C&NW or CMStP&P 4-6-2 Pacific Locomotive, *58–65*			
	(A) Plastic drivers	32	58	___
	(B) Metal drivers	32	68	___
21088	FY&P Franklin 4-4-0 Locomotive, red, black, or green, *59–60*	53	86	___
21089	FY&PRR Washington 4-4-0 Locomotive, *60–61*	65	206	___
21095	NYNH&H 4-6-2 Pacific Locomotive, *57*		NRS	___
21099	NYNH&H 4-6-2 Pacific Locomotive, *58*	192	482	___
21100	Reading 4-4-2 Atlantic Locomotive, *57 u*	14	31	___
21105	Reading 4-4-2 Atlantic Locomotive, *57–60*			
	(A) Aluminum drive wheels	100	200	___
	(B) Die-cast wheels with white tires	40	67	___
	(C) Black plastic drive wheels	20	41	___
21106	Reading 4-4-2 Atlantic Locomotive, *59 u*	105	253	___
21107	PRR or BN 4-4-2 Atlantic Locomotive, *64–66 u*	10	20	___
21115	PRR 4-6-2 Pacific Locomotive, *58*	215	1120	___
21129	NYC 4-6-4 Hudson Locomotive, *58*	318	1354	___
21130	NYC 4-6-4 Hudson Locomotive, *59–60*	140	335	___
21139	UP 4-8-4 Northern Locomotive, *58–59*	353	1428	___
21140	UP 4-8-4 Northern Locomotive, *60*	525	2014	___
21145	NKP 0-8-0 Switcher, *58*	165	1060	___
21155	0-6-0 Switcher, *58*	90	285	___
21156	0-6-0 Switcher, *59*	75	200	___
21158	0-6-0 Switcher, *60 u*	41	80	___
21160	Reading 4-4-2 Atlantic Locomotive, *58–60 u*	15	26	___

		Good	Exc
21161	Reading 4-4-2 Atlantic Locomotive, *60 u*		
____	(A) American Flyer Lines	11	22
____	(B) Prestone Car Care Express	83	287
____**21165**	Erie 4-4-0 Locomotive, *61–62, 65–66 u*	10	26
21166	Burlington Route 4-4-0 Locomotive, *63–65*		
____	(A) White letters in black box	10	32
____	(B) Black letters in white box	85	204
21168	Southern 4-4-0 Locomotive, *61–63*		
____	(A) Knuckle coupler, *61*	25	64
____	(B) Pike Master couplers, *62–63*	10	44
21205/-1	B&M Twin F9 Diesels, *61–62 u*		
____	(A) Twin A units	110	252
____	(B) Single unit	75	149
____**21206/-1**	SF Twin F9 Diesels, *61–62 u*	105	352
____**21207/-1**	GN Twin F9 Diesels, *63–64*	100	333
____**21210**	Burlington F9 Diesel, *61*	65	262
____**21215/-1**	UP Twin F9 Diesels, *61–62*	95	298
____**21215/16**	UP Twin F9 Diesels, *61*		2100
21234	Chesapeake & Ohio GP7 Diesel, *59–61*		
____	(A) Long steps	145	411
____	(B) Short steps	165	694
21551	Northern Pacific PA Diesel, *58*		
____	(A) Plastic steps, portholes filled in	135	298
____	(B) Sheet-metal steps, portholes open	135	373
21561	New Haven PA Diesel, *57–58*		
____	(A) Plastic steps	125	226
____	(B) 1-rivet metal steps	125	328
21573	New Haven GE Electric, *58–59*		
____	(A) Shiny black, *58*	145	355
____	(B) Dull black, *59*	200	450
____**21720**	Santa Fe PB Diesel, *58 u*	275	1135
21801	C&NW Baldwin Locomotive, *57–58*		
____	(A) Unpainted	42	109
____	(B) Painted	70	320
21801-1	C&NW Baldwin Locomotive, *58 u*		
____	(A) Unpainted	70	172
____	(B) Painted	85	290
____**21808**	C&NW Baldwin Locomotive, *58 u*	61	97
____**21812**	Texas & Pacific Baldwin Locomotive, *59–60*	75	127
____**21813**	M&StL Baldwin Locomotive, *58 u, 60 u*	190	646
21831	Texas & Pacific GP7 Diesel, *58*		
____	(A) American Flyer Lines	150	323
____	(B) Texas & Pacific	185	541
____**21910/-1/-2**	SF PA/PB/PA Diesel Set, *57–58*	370	811
____**21918/-1**	Seaboard Baldwin Locomotive, *58*	320	484
____**21920**	Missouri Pacific PA Diesel, *63–64*	185	527
____**21920/-1**	Missouri Pacific PA/PA Diesel Set, *58**	340	1032
____**21922/-1**	Missouri Pacific PA/PA Diesel Set, *59–60*	275	852
____**21925/-1**	Union Pacific PA/PA Diesel Set, *59–60**	235	889
____**21927**	Santa Fe PA Diesel, *60–62*	110	206
____**22004**	Transformer, 40 watts, *59–64*	2	10
____**22006**	Transformer, 25 watts, *63*	2	9

GILBERT PRODUCTION 1946-1966

		Good	Exc
22020	Transformer, 50 watts, *57–64*	2	8____
22030	Transformer, 100 watts, *57–64*	4	21____
22033	Transformer, 25 watts, *65*	2	5____
22034	Transformer, 50 watts, *65*	4	12____
22035	Transformer, 175 watts, *57–64*	16	78____
22040	Transformer, 110 watts, *57–58*	5	18____
22050	Transformer, 175 watts, *57–58*	12	42____
22060	Transformer, 175 watts, *57–58*	12	39____
22080	Transformer, 300 watts, *57–58*	34	195____
22090	Transformer, 350 watts, *59–64*	63	173____
23021	Imitation Grass, *57–59*	6	22____
23022	Scenery Gravel, *57–59*	6	22____
23023	Imitation Coal, *57–59*	5	17____
23024	Rainbow Wire, *57–64*	4	10____
23025	Smoke Cartridges, *57–59*	4	25____
23026	Service Kit, *59–64*	6	30____
23027	Track Cleaning Fluid, *57–59*	1	4____
23028	Smoke Fluid Dispenser, *60–64*	2	17____
23032	Equipment Kit, *60–61*	33	105____
23036	Money Saver Kit, *60, 62, 64*	32	295____
23040	Mountain Tunnel and Pass Set, *58*		140____
23249	Tunnel, *57–64*	9	48____
23561	Billboard Horn, *57–59*	10	43____
23568	Whistling Billboard, *57–64*	11	73____
23571	Truss Bridge, *57–64*	7	30____
23581	Girder Bridge, *57–64*	8	35____
23586	Wayside Station, *57–59*	25	113____
23589	Passenger and Freight Station, *59 u*	15	55____
23590	Control Tower, *57–59*	20	110____
23596	Water Tank, *57–58*	25	103____
23598	Talking Station Record, *57–59*	5	19____
23599	Talking Station Record, *57*	9	36____
23600	Crossing Gate with bell, *57–58*	13	105____
23601	Crossing Gate, *59–62*	13	83____
23602	Crossing Gate, *63–64*	13	69____
23743	Track Maintenance Car, *60–64*	90	156____
23750	Trestle Bridge, *57–61*	26	75____
23758	Sam the Semaphore Man, *57*	29	85____
23759	Bell Danger Signal, *56–60*	12	105____
23760	Highway Flasher, *57–60*	9	42____
23761	Semaphore, *57–60*	22	68____
23763	Bell Danger Signal, *61–64*	11	92____
23764	Flasher Signal, *61–64*	12	42____
23769	Aircraft Beacon, *57–64*	13	75____
23771	Stockyard and Car, *57–61*	29	113____
23772	Water Tower, *57–64*	20	150____
23774	Floodlight Tower, *57–64*	16	109____
23778	Street Lamp Set, *57–64*	8	39____
23779	Oil Drum Loader, *57–61*	55	198____
23780	Gabe the Lamplighter, *58–59*		
	(A) Dark green base	294	563____
	(B) Light green base	650	900____
23785	Coal Loader, *57–60*	130	216____

			Good	Exc
____	23786	Talking Station, *57–59*	60	104
____	23787	Log Loader, *57–60*	90	253
____	23788	Suburban Station, *57–64*	10	60
____	23789	Station and Baggage Smasher, *58–59*	55	217
____	23791	Cow on Track, black/white or brown/white, *57–59*	26	100
____	23796	Sawmill, *57–64*	105	216
____	23830	Piggyback Unloader, *59–60*	39	88
	24003	Santa Fe Boxcar, *58*		
____		(A) Unpainted tuscan plastic	14	41
____		(B) Tuscan-painted		713
____	24006	Great Northern Boxcar, *57–58*		2500
____	24016	MKT Boxcar, *58*	260	803
____	24019	Seaboard Boxcar, *58, 61 u*	18	35
____	24023	Baltimore & Ohio Boxcar, *58–59*	34	119
____	24026	Central of Georgia Boxcar, *58*	32	144
	24029	BAR State of Maine Boxcar		
____		(A) Knuckle couplers, *57–60*	58	94
____		(B) Pike Master couplers, *61*	100	180
	24030	MKT Boxcar, *60 u*		
____		(A) Unpainted yellow plastic	10	17
____		(B) Yellow-painted plastic	50	607
____	24033	Missouri Pacific Boxcar, *58*	48	131
____	24036	New Haven Boxcar, *58–60*	24	88
	24039	Rio Grande Boxcar, *59*		
____		(A) Unpainted white plastic	18	66
____		(B) Unpainted ivory plastic	10	41
____		(C) White-painted		228
____	24043	Boston & Maine Boxcar, *58–60*	33	93
____	24045	MEC Boxcar		NRS
____	24047	Great Northern Boxcar, *59*	55	185
____	24048	M&StL Boxcar, *59–62*	62	121
	24052	UFGE Boxcar, *61*		
____		(A) Unpainted yellow plastic	11	19
____		(B) Yellow-painted	150	208
	24054	Santa Fe Boxcar, *62–64, 66*		
____		(A) Red-painted plastic, *62–64*	20	54
____		(B) Unpainted red plastic, *66*	9	34
	24055	Gold Belt Line Boxcar, *60–61*		
____		(A) Opening with door	14	52
____		(B) Opening without door	14	35
	24056	Boston & Maine Boxcar, *61*		
____		(A) Blue-painted black plastic	70	283
____		(B) Unpainted blue plastic	27	136
	24057	Mounds Boxcar, *62*		
____		(A) White	5	11
____		(B) Ivory	9	19
	24058	Post Boxcar, white or ivory, *63–64*		
____		(A) Cereal	8	27
____		(B) Cereals	11	20
____	24059	Boston & Maine Boxcar, *63*	48	189

		Good	Exc
24060	M&StL Boxcar, *63–64*	39	130____
24065	NYC Boxcar, *60–64*		
	(A) Knuckle couplers	41	174____
	(B) Pike Master couplers	30	75____
24066	L&N Boxcar, blue-painted, *60*	80	165____
24067	Keystone Line Boxcar, *60* * u	1350	2425____
24068	Planters Peanuts Boxcar, *61* * u		NRS____
24076	Union Pacific Stock Car, *57–60*		
	(A) Knuckle couplers	32	85____
	(B) Pike Master couplers	28	57____
24077	Northern Pacific Stock Car, *59–62*		
	(A) Knuckle couplers	85	313____
	(B) Pike Master couplers	60	152____
24103	Norfolk & Western Gondola, black plastic, *58, 63–64*	7	20____
24106	Pennsylvania Gondola, *60 u*		
	(A) Unpainted tuscan plastic	7	19____
	(B) Tuscan-painted	43	160____
24109	C&O Gondola with pipes, *57–60*		
	(A) Silver plastic or cardboard pipes	24	63____
	(B) Orange cardboard pipes	45	125____
24110	Pennsylvania Gondola, *59 u*		
	(A) Unpainted tuscan plastic	5	12____
	(B) Tuscan-painted	20	60____
24113	Delaware & Hudson Gondola, *57–59*	14	28____
24116	Southern Gondola, *57–60*	19	102____
24120	Texas & Pacific Gondola, *60 u*		
	(A) Unpainted green plastic	14	58____
	(B) Green-painted	100	300____
24124	Boston & Maine Gondola, *63–64*		
	(A) Unpainted blue	5	16____
	(B) Dark blue-painted	72	222____
24125	Bethlehem Steel Gondola, *60–66*		
	(A) Gray-painted with rail load	24	121____
	(B) Unpainted gray without load	9	21____
24126	Frisco Gondola, tuscan, *61*	33	136____
24127	Monon Gondola, *61–65*		
	(A) Knuckle couplers	5	14____
	(B) Pike Master couplers	4	11____
24130	Pennsylvania Gondola, *60 u*		
	(A) Pike Master couplers	9	18____
	(B) Fixed or operating knuckle couplers	4	12____
24203	Baltimore & Ohio Hopper, *58, 63–64*		
	(A) Unpainted black, *58*	20	30____
	(B) Black-painted, *58*	150	275____
	(C) Marbleized, *58*	150	275____
	(D) PM trucks and couplers, *63–64*	17	52____
24206	CB&Q Hopper, *58*	35	110____
24209	Jersey Central Hopper, *57–60*	27	121____
24213	Wabash Hopper, *58–60*	15	29____
24216	Union Pacific Hopper, *58–60*	22	66____

GILBERT PRODUCTION 1946-1966

			Good	Exc
___24219	Western Maryland Hopper, *58–59*		42	130
___24221	C&EI Hopper, *59–60*		35	128
___24222	Domino Sugar Hopper, *63–64**		138	383
24225	Santa Fe Hopper, *60–65*			
___	(A) Red-painted, knuckle couplers		15	43
___	(B) Red-painted, PM couplers		9	37
___	(C) Unpainted red plastic, PM couplers		25	42
24230	Peabody Hopper, *61–64*			
___	(A) Knuckle couplers		21	75
___	(B) Pike Master couplers		21	58
___24309	Gulf Tank Car, *57–58*		4	34
___24310	Gulf Tank Car, *58–60*		8	22
24313	Gulf Tank Car, *57–60*			
___	(A) Full tank		21	50
___	(B) Open-bottom tank			692
24316	Mobilgas Tank Car, *57–61, 65–66*			
___	(A) Knuckle couplers, complete tank		20	52
___	(B) Knuckle couplers, open-bottom tank		70	240
___	(C) Pike Master couplers		5	28
___24319	PRR Salt Tank Car, *58**		155	407
24320	Deep Rock Tank Car, *60–61*			
___	(A) Complete tank, *60*		50	331
___	(B) Open-bottom tank, *61*		100	459
___24321	Deep Rock Tank Car, *59*		20	82
24322	Gulf Tank Car, *59*			
___	(A) Full tank		15	21
___	(B) Open-bottom tank		25	99
24323	Baker's Chocolate Tank Car, *59–60**			
___	(A) Type II frame white, white ends		480	1476
___	(B) Type II frame white, gray-painted ends		118	358
___	(C) Type III frame white, open-bottom tank			2100
___24324	Hooker Tank Car, *59–60*		31	131
24325	Gulf Tank Car, *60*			
___	(A) Type II plastic frame		6	17
___	(B) Type III plastic frame, open-bottom tank		15	143
24328	Shell Tank Car, *62–66*			
___	(A) Yellow plastic		7	22
___	(B) Yellow-painted		300	450
___24329	Hooker Tank Car with platform, *61*		10	38
24329	Hooker Tank Car, no platform or number, *62–65 u*		9	27
___24330	Baker's Chocolate Tank Car, *61–62*		54	117
24403	Illinois Central Reefer			
___	(A) Unpainted orange plastic		18	23
___	(B) Orange-painted			300
___24409	Northern Pacific Reefer, *58*		355	1322
___24413	ART Reefer, *57–60*		38	141
___24416	Northwestern Reefer, *58*		680	2027
___24419	Canadian National Reefer, *58–59*		112	280
___24420	Simmons Reefer, *58** *u*		660	1321
___24422	Great Northern Boxcar, *63–65, 66 u*		50	148

		Good	Exc
24422	Great Northern Reefer, *63–65, 66 u*		
	(A) Unpainted green plastic, non-opening door	12	18____
	(B) Green-painted plastic, opening door	65	193____
	(C) Green-painted plastic, non-opening door	60	192____
24425	BAR Reefer, *60*		
	(A) Knuckle couplers	175	639____
	(B) Pike Master couplers	200	473____
24426	Rath Packing Reefer, *60–61*	200	303____
24516	New Haven Flatcar, *57–59*	12	40____
24519	Pennsylvania Flatcar, *58*	265	1008____
24529	Erie Floodlight Car, *57–58*	10	52____
24533	AFL Track Cleaning Car, *58–66*	10	31____
24536	Monon Flatcar, *58*	385	1705____
24537	New Haven Flatcar, *58 u*	10	33____
24539	New Haven Flatcar, *58–59, 63–64*		
	(A) Silver plastic or cardboard pipes, *58–59*	12	30____
	(B) Orange cardboard pipes, *63–64*	17	50____
	(C) Orange pipes, no number, *63–64*	25	57____
24540	New Haven Flatcar, *60 u*	44	305____
24543	American Flyer Lines Crane, *58*	11	44____
24546	AFL Work and Boom Car, *58–64*	10	55____
24547	Erie Floodlight Car, *58*	265	939____
24549	Erie Floodlight Car, *58–66*		
	(A) Yellow generator, knuckle couplers	15	47____
	(B) Red generator, PM couplers	12	25____
	(C) Yellow generator, PM couplers	8	21____
24550	Monon Flatcar, *59–64*	23	88____
24553	Rocket Transport Flatcar, *58–60*	22	85____
24556	Rock Island Flatcar, *59*	22	52____
24557	U.S. Navy Flatcar with jeeps, *59–61*	29	107____
24558	Canadian Pacific Flatcar with trees, *59–60*	102	462____
24559	New Haven Flatcar, *59 u*	80	245____
24561	American Flyer Lines Crane, *59–61*		
	(A) Gray-painted frame, knuckle couplers, *59*	10	40____
	(B) Unpainted gray frame, PM couplers, *60–61*	8	26____
24562	New York Central Flatcar, *60*	14	35____
24564	New Haven Flatcar, *60 u*		
	(A) Silver-gray plastic pipes	9	38____
	(B) Orange cardboard pipes	25	60____
24565	FY&PRR Flatcar with cannon, *60–61**	38	177____
24566	National Car Flatcar, *61–65*	26	86____
24566	New Haven Flatcar, *61–64*		
	(A) Unpainted black body, blue or red tractor	27	147____
	(B) Unpainted gray body, *61*	300	892____
24569	AFL Crane, *62–66*	11	25____
24572	U.S. Navy Flatcar with 2 jeeps, *61*		
	(A) Gray plastic or painted, knuckle couplers	38	110____
	(B) Gray plastic, Pike Master couplers	75	189____
24574	U.S. Air Force Flatcar with rocket fuel tanks, *60–61*		
	(A) Knuckle couplers	40	163____
	(B) Pike Master couplers	39	130____

		Good	Exc
____ **24575**	Borden's Milk Flatcar, unmarked, *66 u*	9	37
24575	National Car Co. Flatcar, *60–66*		
____	(A) Knuckle couplers	17	68
____	(B) Pike Master couplers	17	47
24577	Illinois Central Flatcar with jet engine, *60–61, 63–64*		
____	(A) Knuckle couplers	48	251
____	(B) Pike Master couplers	42	175
____ **24578**	New Haven Flatcar with Corvette, *62–63*	113	248
24579	Illinois Central Flatcar, *60–61*		
____	(A) Silver pipes, knuckle couplers	45	177
____	(B) Orange pipes, PM couplers	50	210
24603	AFL Caboose, *57–58*		
____	(A) Unpainted red plastic	5	13
____	(B) Painted red plastic		NRS
____ **24610**	AFL Caboose, *58–60 u*	5	18
____ **24619**	AFL Bay Window Caboose, *58*	20	132
____ **24626**	AFL Caboose, *58*	9	29
____ **24627**	AFL Caboose, *59–60*	4	17
____ **24630**	AFL Caboose, *59–61 u*	4	18
24631	AFL Caboose, yellow-painted, *59–61, 63–65*		
____	(A) Knuckle couplers, stripe, *59–61*	8	34
____	(B) Pike Master couplers, stripe, *63–65*	6	29
____	(C) Pike Master couplers, no stripe, *65*	80	165
____ **24632**	American Flyer Lines Caboose, *59*	28	62
____ **24633**	AFL Bay Window Caboose, *59–62*	19	87
24634	AFL Bay Window Caboose, *63–66*		
____	(A) Unpainted red plastic, illuminated	20	36
____	(B) Red-painted, illuminated	20	62
____	(C) Nonilluminated, plastic wheels	8	20
24636	American Flyer Lines Caboose, *60–66*		
____	(A) Red plastic	6	16
____	(B) Yellow-painted	150	470
____	(C) Red-painted		500
____ **24638**	AFL Bay Window Caboose, *62*	27	68
24720	FY&PRR Coach, *59–61*		
____	(A) Unpainted yellow	23	42
____	(B) Yellow-painted	29	56
24730	FY&PRR Overland Express Baggage Car, *59–60*		
____	(A) Unpainted yellow	20	35
____	(B) Yellow-painted	29	56
____ **24733**	AFL Pikes Peak Coach, *57*	145	611
____ **24739**	AFL Niagara Falls Combination Car, *57*		NRS
____ **24740**	Baggage Express Combination Car, *60*	28	41
____ **24750**	FY&PRR Combination Car, *60–61*	123	187
____ **24773**	AFL Columbus Combination Car, *57–58, 60–62*	65	152
____ **24776**	AFL Columbus Combination Car, *59*	60	157
____ **24793**	AFL Jefferson Coach, *57–58, 60–62*	70	193
____ **24794**	AFL Jefferson Coach, *59*		1700
____ **24813**	AFL Hamilton Vista Dome Car, *57–58, 60–62*	60	140
____ **24816**	AFL Hamilton Vista Dome Car, *59*	60	160
____ **24833**	AFL Washington Observation Car, *57–58, 60–62*	60	127
____ **24836**	AFL Washington Observation Car, *59*	60	121

		Good	Exc
24837	Union Pacific Combination Car, *59–60**	85	245 ____
24838	Union Pacific Coach, *59–60**	90	347 ____
24839	Union Pacific Vista Dome Car, *59–60**	95	330 ____
24840	Union Pacific Observation Car, *59–60**	95	311 ____
24843	Northern Pacific Combination Car, no lights, *58*	90	255 ____
24846	Northern Pacific Coach, no lights, *58*	90	305 ____
24849	Northern Pacific Vista Dome Car, no lights, *58*	90	301 ____
24853	Northern Pacific Observation Car, no lights, *58*	90	240 ____
24856	MP Eagle Hill Combination Car, *58, 63–64**	125	325 ____
24859	MP Eagle Lake Coach, *58, 63–64**	130	435 ____
24863	MP Eagle Creek Coach, *58, 63–64**	120	443 ____
24866	MP Eagle Valley Observation Car, *58, 63–64**	120	385 ____
24867	AFL Combination Car, no lights, *58 u, 60 u*	46	177 ____
24868	AFL Observation Car, no lights, *58 u, 60 u*	50	213 ____
24869	AFL Coach, no lights, *58 u, 60 u*	50	185 ____
24963	Car Assortment, *58*		NRS ____
25003	American Flyer Log Car, *57–60*		
	(A) Number and lettering on bin	85	388 ____
	(B) No number or lettering on bin	20	55 ____
25005	Mail Car, *57*		NRS ____
25016	Southern Pacific Flatcar, *57–60*	44	125 ____
25019	Operating Milk Car, *57–60*	65	255 ____
25025	CB&Q Dump Car, *58–60*	75	271 ____
25031	AFL Caboose, *58*		NRS ____
25042	Erie Operating Boxcar, *58*	70	215 ____
25045	Rocket Launcher Flatcar, *57–60*	16	60 ____
25046	Rocket Launcher Car, *60*	14	94 ____
25049	Rio Grande Boxcar, *58–60*	85	243 ____
25052	AFL Bay Window Caboose, *58*	53	137 ____
25056	USM Boxcar and Rocket Launcher Flatcar, *59*	125	319 ____
25057	TNT Exploding Boxcar, *60*	70	269 ____
25058	Southern Pacific Flatcar, *61–64*	48	152 ____
25059	Rocket Launcher Flatcar, *60–64*	21	82 ____
25060	CB&Q Dump Car, *61–64*	80	283 ____
25061	TNT Exploding Boxcar, *61*	100	365 ____
25062	Mine Carrier Exploding Boxcar, *62–64*		
	(A) Silver roof and ends	125	703 ____
	(B) Tuscan roof and ends	125	539 ____
25071	AF Tie-Jector Car, *61–64*	7	23 ____
25081	NYC Operating Boxcar, *61–64*	15	56 ____
25082	New Haven Operating Boxcar, *61–64*	11	68 ____
25515	U.S. Air Force Flatcar, black, *60–63*		
	(A) Unpainted yellow sled	78	204 ____
	(B) Yellow-painted sled	200	885 ____
26101	Curved Track Panel, *65–66*	3	25 ____
26121	Straight Track Panel, *65–66*	4	35 ____
26122	Straight Panel with whistle, *65–66*	7	50 ____
26141	Switch Panel, right hand, *65–66*	7	54 ____
26142	Switch Panel, left hand, *65–66*	7	54 ____
26151	Crossover Panel, *65–66*	7	45 ____
26261	Curved Snow Panel		94 ____
26262	Straight Snow Panel		94 ____

		Good	Exc
_____26263	Snow Switch, right hand		144
_____26264	Snow Switch, left hand		144
_____26265	Crossover Snow Panel		94
_____26300	PM Straight Track, *61–64*		1
_____26301	PM Straight Track, *61–64*		1
_____26302	PM Straight Track with uncoupler, *61–64*		2
_____26310	PM Curved Track, *61–64*		1
_____26320	PM Remote Switch, right hand, *61–64*	6	13
_____26321	PM Remote Switch, left hand, *61–64*	7	12
_____26322	PM 90-degree Crossing, *61–64*	1	3
_____26323	PM Manual Switch, right hand, *61–64*	1	5
_____26324	PM Manual Switch, left hand, *61–64*	1	5
_____26340	PM Steel Track Pins, *61–64*		1
_____26341	PM Insulating Pins, *61–64*		8
_____26342	PM Adapter Pins, *61–64*		4
_____26343	PM Track Locks, *61–64*		8
_____26344	PM Track Terminal, *61–64*		1
_____26415	Track Assortment, *60, 62*		NRS
_____26419	Accessory Package	4	15
_____26421	Accessory Package, *60*		403
_____26425	Track Assortment Pack, *60*	6	11
_____26426	Accessory Package, *60–61*		242
_____26428	Accessory Pack with box, *58 u*		410
_____26520	Knuckle Coupler Kit, *57–64*	1	5
_____26521	Knuckle Coupler Kit, *57–58*		12
_____26601	Fiber Roadbed, *59–62*		1
_____26602	Fiber Roadbed, *59, 61–62*		1
_____26611	4-Level Trestle Display, *59–61*		600
_____26670	Track Trip, *57–58*	4	16
_____26671	Track Trip, *59*	3	23
_____26672	Track Trip, *60*	2	22
_____26673	Track Trip, *61–64*	2	26
_____26690	Track Terminal, with envelope, *57–59*	1	2
_____26691	Steel Pins, *57–60, 64*		1
_____26692	Fiber Pins, *57–60, 64*		1
_____26693	Track Locks, dozen, *57–60, 64*	2	6
_____26700	Straight Track, *57–64*		1
_____26704	Manual Uncoupler		1
_____26708	Horn Control, *57–58*	4	9
_____26710	Straight Track, half section, *57–64*		1
_____26718	Remote Control Switch, left hand, *57*	6	17
_____26719	Remote Control Switch, right hand, *57*	6	17
_____26720	Curved Track, *57–64*		1
_____26722	Curved Track, dozen	6	11
_____26726	Straight Rubber Roadbed, half section, *58*	1	2
_____26727	Rubber Roadbed, half section, *58*	1	2
_____26730	Curved Track, half section, *57–64*		1
_____26739	Whistle Control, *57–58*	13	40
_____26742	Remote Control Switches, pair, *57*	9	50
_____26744	Manual Switches, pair, *57–58*	4	16
_____26745	Railroad Crossing, *57–64*	1	21
_____26746	Rubber Roadbed, *57–64*		2

GILBERT PRODUCTION 1946-1966

		Good	Exc
26747	Rubber Roadbed, *57–64*		2____
26748	Re-railer, *57–64*	3	22____
26749	Bumper, *57–60*	2	18____
26751	Pike Planning Kit, *57–59*	8	24____
26752	Remote Control Uncoupler, *57–58, 60–61*	1	15____
26756	Bumper, *61–64*	5	17____
26760	Remote Control Switches, pair, *58–64*	11	41____
26761	Remote Control Switch, left hand, *58–64*	7	17____
26762	Remote Control Switch, right hand, *58–64*	7	17____
26770	Manual Switches, pair, *59–64*	4	15____
26781	Trestle Set, *57*	10	33____
26782	Trestle Set, *58–60*	4	24____
26783	Hi-Trestles, *57*	8	41____
26790	Trestle Set, *61–64*	13	30____
26810	Pow-R-Clips, *60–64*		6____
27441	Lamps, 3 bulbs, red	1	4____
27443	Lamps, 3 bulbs, green	1	3____
27458	Lamps, 3 bulbs, clear	1	4____
27460	Lamp Assortment, *59, 64*	10	100____

Unnumbered Items

	Good	Exc
Buffalo Hunt Gondola, *63–64*	4	14____
Freight Ahead Caboose, *63*	3	7____

Mint

____ **0700**	Boxcar (NASG), *81 u*	113
____ **2300**	Oil Drum Loader, *83–87*	69
____ **2321**	Operating Sawmill, *84, 86–87*	90
____ **8150/52**	Southern Pacific Alco PA1 Diesel AA Set, *81*	363
____ **8151**	Southern Pacific Alco PA1 Diesel B Unit, *82*	185
____ **8153/55**	Baltimore & Ohio Alco PA1 Diesel AA Set, *81, 83*	275
____ **8154**	Baltimore & Ohio Alco PA1 Diesel B Unit, *81, 83*	100
____ **8251/53**	Erie Alco PA1 Diesel AA Set, *82*	250
____ **8252**	Erie Alco PA1 Diesel B Unit, *82*	151
____ **8350**	Boston & Maine GP7 Diesel, *83*	300
____ **8458**	Southern GP9 Diesel, *84*	208
____ **8459**	Chessie System GP20 Diesel, *84*	271
____ **8551**	Santa Fe GP20 Diesel, *86*	205
____ **8552**	New York Central GP9 Diesel, *86*	188
____ **9000**	B&O Flatcar with trailers, *81, 83*	44
____ **9002**	B&M Flatcar with logs, *83*	85
____ **9004**	Southern Flatcar with trailers, *84*	42
____ **9005**	NYC Flatcar with trailers, *86*	33
____ **9100**	Gulf 1-D Tank Car, *79*	60
____ **9101**	Union 76 1-D Tank Car, *80*	35
____ **9102**	B&O 1-D Tank Car, *81, 83*	27
____ **9104**	B&M 3-D Tank Car, *83*	92
____ **9105**	Southern 3-D Tank Car, *84*	28
____ **9106**	NYC 3-D Tank Car, *86*	26
____ **9200**	Chessie System Hopper with coal, *79*	38
____ **9201**	B&O Covered Hopper, *81, 83*	32
____ **9203**	Boston & Maine Hopper, *83*	78
____ **9204**	Southern Hopper, *84*	24
____ **9205**	Pennsylvania Covered Hopper, *84*	35
____ **9206**	New York Central Covered Hopper, *84*	29
____ **9207**	B&O Covered Hopper, *86*	30
____ **9208**	Santa Fe Covered Hopper, *86*	27
____ **9209**	New York Central Hopper, *86*	29
____ **9300**	Burlington Gondola, *80*	27
____ **9301**	B&O Gondola with canisters, *81, 83*	23
____ **9303**	Southern Gondola with canisters, *84*	27
____ **9304**	NYC Gondola with canisters, *86*	25
____ **9400**	Chessie System Bay Window Caboose, *80*	34
____ **9401**	B&O Bay Window Caboose, *81, 83*	31
____ **9402**	B&M Bay Window Caboose, *83*	68
____ **9403**	Southern Bay Window Caboose, *84*	35
____ **9404**	NYC Bay Window Caboose, *86*	34
____ **9405**	Santa Fe Bay Window Caboose, *86*	38
____ **9500**	Southern Pacific Combination Car, *81*	90
____ **9501**	Southern Pacific Coach, *81*	130
____ **9502**	Southern Pacific Vista Dome Car, *81*	123
____ **9503**	Southern Pacific Observation Car, *81*	90
____ **9504**	Erie Combination Car, *82*	55
____ **9505**	Erie Coach, *82*	75
____ **9506**	Erie Vista Dome Car, *82*	72
____ **9507**	Erie Observation Car, *82*	55

Mint

9700	Santa Fe Boxcar, *79*	
	(A) Door nibs	108____
	(B) No door nibs	64____
9701	Rock Island Boxcar, *80*	31____
9702	B&O Sentinel Boxcar, *81, 83*	52____
9703	Boston & Maine Boxcar, *83*	95____
9704	Southern Boxcar, *84*	38____
9705	Pennsylvania Boxcar, *84*	46____
9706	New York Central Pacemaker Boxcar, *84*	80____
9707	Railbox Boxcar, *84*	57____
9708	Conrail Boxcar, *84*	43____
9709	Baltimore & Ohio Boxcar, *86*	32____
9710	Santa Fe Boxcar, *86*	33____
9711	Southern Pacific Boxcar, *86*	31____
9712	Illinois Central Gulf Boxcar, *86*	34____
9713	New York Central Boxcar, *86*	35____
22678	B&M Baked Beans Boxcar (NETCA), *10*	45____
22997	Oil Drum Loader, *99*	113____
24213	Universal Lockon for S Gauge Track, *10*	4____
41000	Sierra Beer Boxcar (TTOS), *13*	90____
41001	Marathon Motors Boxcar (NASG), *12*	75____
41003	Aluminum Ore Covered Hopper (TCA), *13*	70____
41009	Milwaukee Road Boxcar (NASG), *14*	90____
41018	Candy Cane Tank Car (TTOS Cal-Stewart), *14*	65____
41021	BNSF Boxcar (NASG), *15*	70____
41024	Forest Service/Smokey Bear Gondola (TTOS), *15*	55____
41025	Monsanto Chemical Tank Car, *15*	65____
41023	G. Fox & Co. Boxcar (NETCA)	138____
41942	Youngstown Steel "Spirit of '76" Baldwin Diesel Switcher, *14*	290____
42169	KCS SD70ACe Diesel Locomotive "4042," CC, *12*	480____
42173	KCS SD70ACe Diesel Locomotive "4022," gray, *12*	480____
42500	UP "Building America" SD70ACe Diesel "8348," CC, *12*	460____
42501	UP "Building America" SD70ACe Diesel, nonpowered, *12*	240____
42502	UP "Building America" SD70ACe Diesel "8461," CC, *12*	480____
42504	KCS SD70ACe Diesel "4042," CC, *12*	480____
42505	BNSF SD70ACe Diesel "9344," CC, *12*	480____
42506	CSX SD70ACe Diesel "4847," CC, *12*	480____
42507	KCS SD70ACe Diesel "4847," gray, *12*	480____
42508	SP UP Heritage SD70ACe Diesel "1865," CC, *12*	480____
42509	D&RGW UP Heritage SD70ACe Diesel "1870," CC, *12*	480____
42510	C&NW UP Heritage SD70ACe Diesel "1859," CC, *12*	480____
42511	MP UP Heritage SD70ACe Diesel "1851," CC, *12*	480____
42512	Santa Fe U33C Diesel "8525," CC, *12–13*	480____
42513	D&H U33C Diesel "761," CC, *12–13*	480____
42514	IC U33C Diesel "5057," CC, *12*	480____
42515	PC U33C Diesel "6560," CC, *12–13*	480____
42516	Milwaukee Road U33C Diesel "5705," CC, *12–13*	480____
42519	CNJ NS Heritage SD70ACe Diesel "1071," CC, *12*	480____
42520	CNJ NS Heritage SD70ACe Diesel "1834," nonpowered, *12*	240____
42521	DL&W NS Heritage SD70ACe Diesel "1074," CC, *12*	480____
42522	DL&W NS Heritage SD70ACe Diesel "1856," nonpowered, *12*	240____
42523	Erie NS Heritage SD70ACe Diesel "1068," CC, *12*	480____

		Mint
42524	Erie NS Heritage SD70ACe Diesel "1835," nonpowered, *12*	240
42525	Illinois Terminal NS Heritage SD70ACe Diesel "1072," CC, *12*	480
42526	Illinois Terminal NS Heritage SD70ACe Diesel "1899," nonpowered, *12*	240
42527	NYC NS Heritage SD70ACe Diesel "1066," CC, *12*	480
42528	NYC NS Heritage SD70ACe Diesel "1834," nonpowered, *12*	240
42529	PC NS Heritage SD70ACe Diesel "1073," CC, *12*	480
42530	PC NS Heritage SD70ACe Diesel "1971," nonpowered, *12*	240
42531	Reading NS Heritage SD70ACe Diesel "1067," CC, *13*	480
42532	Reading NS Heritage SD70ACe Diesel, nonpowered, *13*	240
42533	Savannah & Atlanta NS Heritage SD70ACe Diesel "1065," CC, *13*	480
42534	Savannah & Atlanta NS Heritage SD70ACe Diesel, nonpowered, *13*	240
42535	Virginian NS Heritage SD70ACe Diesel "1069," CC, *13*	480
42536	Virginian NS Heritage SD70ACe Diesel "1910," nonpowered, *13*	240
42537	Wabash NS Heritage SD70ACe Diesel "1070," CC, *13*	480
42538	Wabash NS Heritage SD70ACe Diesel "1880," nonpowered, *13*	240
42542	Central of Georgia NS Heritage ES44AC Diesel "8101," CC, *13–16*	515
42543	Central of Georgia NS Heritage ES44AC Diesel "1833," nonpowered, *13–16*	270
42544	Conrail NS Heritage ES44AC Diesel "8098," CC, *13–16*	515
42545	Conrail NS Heritage ES44AC Diesel "1976," nonpowered, *13*	270
42546	Interstate NS Heritage ES44AC Diesel "8105," CC, *13–16*	515
42547	Interstate NS Heritage ES44AC Diesel "1896," nonpowered, *13*	270
42548	LV NS Heritage ES44AC Diesel "8104," CC, *13*	515
42549	LV NS Heritage ES44AC Diesel "1847," nonpowered, *13*	270
42550	Nickel Plate Road NS Heritage ES44AC Diesel "8100" CC, *13–16*	515
42551	Nickel Plate Road NS Heritage ES44AC Diesel "1881," nonpowered, *13*	270
42552	N&W NS Heritage ES44AC Diesel "8103," CC, *13–16*	515
42553	N&W NS Heritage ES44AC Diesel "1838," nonpowered, *13*	270
42554	PRR NS Heritage ES44AC Diesel "8102," CC, *13–16*	515
42555	PRR NS Heritage ES44AC Diesel "1846," nonpowered, *13*	270
42556	Southern NS Heritage ES44AC Diesel "8099," CC, *13*	515
42557	Southern NS Heritage ES44AC Diesel "1894," nonpowered, *13*	270
42558	Norfolk Southern NS Heritage ES44AC Diesel "8114," CC, *13–15*	515
42559	Norfolk Southern NS Heritage ES44AC Diesel "1982," nonpowered, *13*	270
42560	Monongahela NS Heritage ES44AC Diesel "8025," CC, *13*	515
42561	Monongahela NS Heritage ES44AC Diesel "1901," nonpowered, *13*	270

42562	NKP 2-8-4 Berkshire Locomotive "765," *15–16*	350____
42563	Bethlehem Steel 0-6-0 Dockside Steam Switcher "71," *13–16*	95____
42564	Reading 0-6-0 Dockside Steam Switcher "1242," *13–16*	95____
42565	C&O 0-6-0 Dockside Steam Switcher "65," *13*	95____
42566	AFL 0-6-0 Dockside Steam Switcher "269," *13–16*	95____
42567	Christmas 0-6-0 Dockside Steam Locomotive "2013," *13–14*	98____
42569	C&O 2-8-4 Berkshire Locomotive "2687," *15–16*	350____
42570	D&H Alco PA A-A Diesel Set "18-19," CC, *14*	650____
42573	SP Alco PA A-A Diesel Set "94-95," CC, *14*	650____
42580	BNSF ES44AC Diesel "6438," CC, *13*	515____
42581	BNSF ES44AC Diesel "6423," CC, *14*	515____
42582	CP ES44AC Diesel "8744," CC, *14*	515____
42583	CP ES44AC Diesel "8730," CC, *14*	515____
42584	CSX ES44AC Diesel "924," CC, *14*	515____
42585	CSX ES44AC Diesel "937," CC, *14*	515____
42586	KCS ES44AC Diesel "4692," CC, *14*	515____
42587	KCS ES44AC Diesel "4696," CC, *14*	515____
42588	UP ES44AC Diesel "7523," CC, *14*	515____
42589	UP ES44AC Diesel "7494," CC, *14*	515____
42597	CP Baldwin Diesel Switcher "7070," *14–16*	283____
42598	UP Baldwin Diesel Switcher "1206," *14–16*	283____
42599	Youngstown Steel Diesel Switcher "805," *15–16*	290____
47900	D&H Streamlined Coach 2-pack, *15–16*	160____
47903	D&H Streamlined Diner/Vista Dome 2-pack, *15–16*	160____
47906	D&H Streamlined Full Vista/Combo 2-pack, *15–16*	160____
47909	D&H Streamlined Baggage/Observation 2-pack, *15–16*	160____
47912	SP Streamlined Coach 2-pack, *15–16*	160____
47915	SP Streamlined Diner/Vista Dome 2-pack, *15–16*	160____
47918	SP Streamlined Combo/Observation 2-pack, *15–16*	160____
47921	Pere Marquette 2-8-4 Berkshire Locomotive "1225," *15–16*	350____
47922	Erie 2-8-4 Berkshire Locomotive "3360," *15–16*	350____
47923	Southern 2-8-4 Berkshire Locomotive "2716," *15–16*	350____
47940	FasTrack R20 Command/Remote Switch, right-hand, *15–16*	110____
47941	FasTrack R20 Command/Remote Switch, left-hand, *15–16*	110____
47941	UP B-W Caboose "24591," *16*	75____
47942	MKT UP Heritage SD70ACe Diesel "1988," CC, *16*	600____
47943	WP UP Heritage SD70ACe Diesel "1983," CC, *16*	600____
47944	UP SD70ACe Diesel "8444," CC, *16*	600____
47945	EMD Demonstrator SD70ACe Diesel "2012," CC, *16*	600____
47946	BNSF SD70ACe Diesel "9358," CC, *16*	600____
47947	KCS SD70ACe Diesel "4054," CC, *16*	600____
47948	NS SD70ACe Diesel "1030," CC, *16*	600____
47949	CSX UP SD70ACe Diesel "4817," CC, *16*	600____
47950	MILW 4-8-4 Northern Locomotive "265," *16*	500____
47951	UP 4-8-4 Northern Locomotive "808," *16*	500____
47952	Frisco 4-8-4 Northern Locomotive "4501," *16*	500____
47953	NYC 4-8-4 Northern Locomotive "6015," *16*	500____
47958	Pennsylvania Docksider Freight Set, *16*	320____
47959	Shell Tank Car, *16*	65____
47960	UP Boxcar "196881," *16*	65____
47961	NYC Boxcar "168245," *16*	65____
47963	PRR 2-bay Covered Hopper, *16*	60____

		Mint
____47964	NS Gondola with containers, *16*	65
____47965	NH Log Dump Car, *16*	80
____47966	NATX 3-D Tank Car, *16*	65
____47967	CSX Waffle-sided Boxcar "136156," *16*	65
____47968	C&NW Stock Car "14300," *16*	65
____47970	NYC B-W Caboose "20300," *16*	75
____47972	B&M Cupola Caboose "C-48," *16*	65
____47973	Nickel Plate Road Cupola Caboose "775," *16*	65
____47974	Christmas Boxcar, *16*	65
____47980	Suburban Station, *16*	80
____47981	AT&SF Extended Vision Caboose "999702," *16*	65
____47982	Chessie Extended Vision Caboose "3181," *16*	65
____48000	Southern Pacific GP9 Diesel "8000," *87*	190
____48001	Illinois Central Gulf GP20 Diesel "8001," *87*	195
____48002	SP GP9 Diesel Dummy Unit "8002," *88*	135
____48003	Santa Fe GP20 Diesel Dummy Unit "8553," *88*	122
____48004	Chessie System GP20 Diesel Dummy Unit "8460," *88*	160
____48005	Pennsylvania GP9 Diesel "8005," *89*	167
____48007	Burlington Northern GP20 Diesel "8007," *90*	304
____48008	New Haven EP-5 Electric Locomotive "8008," *91*	200
____48009	American Flyer GM GP7 Diesel "8009," *91*	173
____48010	MILW EP-5 Electric Locomotive "8010," *92*	209
____48013	Conrail GP7 Diesel "5600," *95*	230
____48014	Northern Pacific GP9 Diesel "8014," *95*	190
____48016	"Merry Christmas" GP20 Diesel "1225," *95*	227
____48017	Nickel Plate Road GP9 Diesel Set, *97*	289
____48019	SP GP20 Diesel "4060," *98*	175
____48020	Milwaukee Road GP9 Diesel "304," *98*	220
____48023	Santa Fe Merger GP9 Diesel "2927," *99*	362
____48033	Rock Island GP9 Diesel "1272," *02*	250
____48034	Seaboard Baldwin Switcher "1413," *03*	198
____48035	Santa Fe Baldwin Switcher "2257," *03*	205
____48036	NYC 2-8-2 Light Mikado Locomotive "1849," *04*	593
____48038	GN EP-5 Electric Locomotive "5011," *04–05*	205
____48039	Baltimore & Ohio 0-6-0 Dockside Switcher, *05*	93
____48040	Santa Fe 0-6-0 Dockside Switcher, *05*	100
____48041	UP Light Mikado Locomotive "2549," RailSounds, *05*	510
____48042	Southern Light Mikado Locomotive "4501," RailSounds, *05*	448
____48043	NYC Baldwin Switcher "8100," *04*	213
____48044	Southern Baldwin Switcher, *04*	200
____48047	UP 4-8-4 Northern Locomotive "800," RailSounds, *06*	395
____48048	DM&IR SD9 Diesel, *05*	220
____48049	Southern Pacific SD9 Diesel, *05*	220
____48051	Burlington SD9 Diesel "373," *06*	202
____48052	Erie 4-6-2 Pacific Locomotive "2934," TMCC, *06*	555
____48053	Pennsylvania 2-8-2 Mikado "9628," CC, *06*	473
____48054	UP 4-8-4 Northern Locomotive "809," *06*	488
____48055	Bethlehem Steel 0-6-0 Dockside Switcher, *06*	100
____48056	NYC 0-6-0 Dockside Switcher, *06*	96
____48058	Chessie System SD9 Diesel, *06*	235
____48059	North Pole Central Switcher "25," *06*	100
____48060	C&O 2-8-2 Mikado Locomotive "1068," RailSounds, *07–09*	525
____48061	B&O 4-6-2 Pacific Locomotive "5213," RailSounds, *07–09*	475
____48062	PRR Dockside Switcher, *07–09*	103

Mint

48063	UP Dockside Switcher, *07–09*	113____
48064	MILW 4-8-4 Northern Locomotive "261," RailSounds, *07–09*	382____
48065	American Flyer SD9 Diesel "1956," *07*	388____
48066	UP SD9 Diesel, *07*	288____
48067	C&NW Baldwin Switcher "1044," *07*	265____
48070	UP 4-8-8-4 Big Boy Locomotive "4014," CC, *08–09*	682____
48071	CN GP9 Diesel "4232," *08*	275____
48072	ACL 4-6-2 Pacific Locomotive "1523," CC, *08*	650____
48075	NH EP-5 Electric Locomotive "378," *08–09*	234____
48078	Commemorative Handcar and Shed, *09*	93____
48081	WP 2-8-2 Mikado Locomotive "319," CC, *10*	700____
48082	UP Challenger Steam Locomotive "3985," CC, *11*	1000____
48084	UP Greyhound Challenger Locomotive "3977," CC, *11*	1000____
48085	Denver & Rio Grande Western 4-6-6-4 Challenger, *10*	1000____
48087	Commemorative Dockside Switcher "1958," *11–13*	110____
48088	Christmas GP9 Diesel, *11–12*	300____
48089	Clinchfield Challenger Steam Locomotive "675," CC, *11*	1000____
48090	NP Challenger Steam Locomotive "5121," CC, *11*	1000____
48091	WP Challenger Steam Locomotive "402," CC, *11*	1000____
48092	GN Challenger Steam Locomotive "4000," CC, *11*	1000____
48094	Spokane Portland & Seattle Steam Locomotive, *11*	1000____
48096	AF Christmas Handcar with shed, *12*	120____
48097	Clear 0-6-0 Dockside Steam Switcher "1967," *12*	110____
48100/01	Wabash Alco PA1 AA Set, *88*	245____
48102/03	C&O Alco PA1 AA Set, *89*	334____
48106/07	UP Alco PA1 AA Set, *90*	477____
48112/13	MP Alco PA1 AA Set, *91*	452____
48114/15/16	NP Alco PA1 ABA Set, *92*	420____
48117	NP Alco PA1 Diesel B Unit "8117," RailSounds, *92*	105____
48118	MP Alco PA1 Diesel B Unit "8118," RailSounds, *92 u*	110____
48119	UP Alco PA1 Diesel B Unit "8119," RailSounds, *92 u*	130____
48120/21	WP Alco PA1 Diesel AA Set, *93*	225____
48122	WP Alco PA1 Diesel B Unit, RailSounds, *93*	123____
48123	SP Alco PA1 Diesel B Unit "8123," RailSounds, *93*	140____
48126/27	Silver Flash Alco Diesel PA1 AB Set, *95*	522____
48128	Silver Flash Alco PA1 Diesel B Unit "480," *95*	105____
48129	Silver Flash Alco PA1 Diesel Dummy A Unit "479," *96*	115____
48130	SF Alco PA1 and PB-1 Diesel Set, *97*	266____
48135	NYC Alco PA Diesel B Unit "4302," *03*	145____
48136	Santa Fe Alco PB Diesel B Unit, *04*	145____
48139	Pennsylvania Alco PB Diesel B Unit, RailSounds, *05*	135____
48141	WM Baldwin Switcher "132," *06*	230____
48142	Erie-Lackawanna U33C Diesel "3320," CC, *09*	370____
48144	PRR Baldwin Switcher "5618," *08*	245____
48146	SP U33C Diesel "8773," CC, *09*	370____
48147	ATSF Alco PA Diesel AA Set, *09*	370____
48155	D&RGW Alco PA Diesel AA Set, *10*	370____
48158	Burlington Northern U33C Diesel, *10*	440____
48159	Great Northern U33C Diesel, *10*	440____
48161	Northern Pacific U33C Diesel, *10*	440____
48162	Texas Special Alco PA Diesel AA Set, *11, 13–14*	470____
48165	M&StL Baldwin Diesel Switcher, *12–16*	290____
48166	UP "Building America" SD70ACe Diesel "8348," *12–14*	480____
48167	UP "Building America" SD70ACe Diesel, nonpowered, *12–13*	245____

		Mint
48168	UP "Building America" SD70ACe Diesel "8461," CC, *12–13*	
____		480
____ **48169**	KCS SD70ACe Diesel "4042," CC, *12–13*	480
____ **48170**	NS SD70ACe Diesel "1011," CC, *12–13*	480
____ **48171**	BNSF SD70ACe Diesel "9344," CC, *12*	480
____ **48172**	CSX SD70ACe Diesel "4847," CC, *12–13*	480
____ **48173**	KCS SD70ACe Diesel "4022," gray, CC, *12*	480
____ **48174**	SP UP Heritage SD70ACe Diesel "1865," CC, *12–14*	480
48175	D&RGW UP Heritage SD70ACe Diesel "1870," CC, *12–14*	
____		480
48176	C&NW UP Heritage SD70ACe Diesel "1859," CC, *12–13*	
____		480
____ **48177**	MP UP Heritage SD70ACe Diesel "1851," CC, *12–13*	480
____ **48178**	AT&SF 2-8-8-2 Steam Locomotive "1795," CC, *12–13*	1000
____ **48179**	PRR 2-8-8-2 Steam Locomotive "374," CC, *12–13*	1000
____ **48180**	N&W 2-8-8-2 Steam Locomotive "2009," CC, *12–13*	1000
____ **48181**	UP 2-8-8-2 Steam Locomotive "3672," CC, *12–13*	1000
____ **48182**	Virginian 2-8-8-2 Steam Locomotive "741," CC, *12–13*	1000
____ **48185**	AT&SF U33C Diesel Locomotive "8522," CC, *12*	480
____ **48186**	AT&SF U33C Diesel Locomotive "8509," CC, *12*	480
____ **48187**	D&H U33C Diesel Locomotive "755," CC, *12*	480
____ **48188**	D&H U33C Diesel Locomotive "752," CC, *12*	480
____ **48189**	IC U33C Diesel Locomotive "5054," CC, *12*	480
____ **48190**	IC U33C Diesel Locomotive "5052," CC, *12*	480
____ **48191**	MILW U33C Diesel Locomotive "5702," CC, *12*	480
____ **48192**	MILW U33C Diesel Locomotive "8002," CC, *12*	480
____ **48193**	PC U33C Diesel Locomotive "6552," CC, *12*	480
____ **48194**	PC U33C Diesel Locomotive "6541," CC, *12*	480
____ **48195**	Christmas U33C Diesel "1225," CC, *12*	480
____ **48197**	Santa Fe 2-8-8-2 Steam Locomotive "1797," CC, *13*	1000
____ **48198**	N&W 2-8-8-2 Steam Locomotive "2020," CC, *13*	1000
____ **48200**	ATSF Boxcar (TCA), *97*	113
____ **48203**	NYC Reefer (TTOS), *97*	45
____ **48204**	D&RGW Boxcar (TCA), *97*	70
____ **48205**	Pacific Fruit Express Reefer (NASG), *97*	52
____ **48208**	New England Hopper (TCA), *98*	55
____ **48209**	Cotton Belt Boxcar (TTOS), *98*	105
____ **48210**	New England Hopper (TCA), *98*	83
____ **48211**	Magnolia Tank Car (NASG), *98*	58
____ **48212**	SP Tank Car (TTOS), *99*	70
____ **48213**	L&N Boxcar (TCA), *99 u*	129
____ **48214**	GN Caboose (NASG), *99 u*	55
____ **48215**	Monsanto Hopper, *99 u*	91
____ **48217**	SP Gondola (TTOS), *00*	110
____ **48218**	SP Crane Car (TTOS), *00*	110
____ **48219**	"Ship It on the Frisco" Boxcar (TCA), *01 u*	75
____ **48220**	Deep Rock Tank Car (NASG), *00 u*	115
____ **48221**	Norfolk Southern 2-bay Hopper (TCA), *01*	105
____ **48222**	British Columbia Tank Car (TTOS), *00*	70
____ **48223**	Toy Train Museum 1-D Tank Car (TCA), *01 u*	80
____ **48224**	Gulf Tank Car (NASG), *01*	80
____ **48225**	Salt Lake Route Boxcar (TTOS), *02 u*	102
____ **48226**	Toy Train Museum Flatcar with wheel load (TCA), *02 u*	109
____ **48227**	D&S Hopper (TTOS), *02 u*	60
____ **48228**	Cook Paint Tank Car (NASG), *02 u*	117
____ **48229**	D&RGW Tank Car (TTOS), *03*	78
____ **48230**	Toy Train Museum Gondola with pipe load (TCA), *03 u*	60

LIONEL PRODUCTION 1979-2017

Mint

48231	Linde Boxcar (TTOS), *03*	110____
48232	NH Flatcar with N.E. Transport trailer (NETCA), *03*	110____
48233	UP 1-D Tanker (NASG), *03*	91____
48234	Toy Train Museum Boxcar (TCA), *04*	55____
48235	Forest Service/Smokey Bear Tank Car (TTOS), *04*	112____
48236	BNSF Icicle Reefer (TTOS), *04*	98____
48237	Poland Spring Boxcar (NETCA), *04*	110____
48238	GE Cable Reel Car (NASG), *04*	125____
48239	Gilbert's Milk Tank Car (TTOS), *05*	95____
48240	Toy Train Museum Combination Car (TCA), *05*	73____
48241	Las Vegas & Tonopah Boxcar (TTOS), *05*	70____
48242	Fisk Tire Boxcar (NETCA), *05*	110____
48243	GE Twin Searchlight Car (NASG), *05*	90____
48244	Ward Kimball Boxcar (TTOS Cal-Stewart), *05*	72____
48245	A.C. Gilbert Coach (TTOS), *06*	85____
48246	SP Flatcar with trailers (TTOS), *06*	92____
48247	Toy Train Museum Idler Caboose (TCA), *06*	68____
48248	Indian Motocycle Boxcar (NETCA), *06*	250____
48249	Yule Marble Flatcar (TCA), *07*	106____
48250	GE Crane Car (NASG), *06*	87____
48253	Coors Reefer (TCA), *07*	91____
48254	Toy Train Museum Crane Car, *07*	90____
48255	PRR 2-bay Hopper with coal load (TTOS), *07*	79____
48256	Forest Service/Smokey Bear Boxcar (TTOS), *08*	83____
48257	Oilzum Tanker 2-car Set (NETCA), *08*	100____
48260	Sacramento Northern Reefer (SVAFC), *07*	112____
48261	UP Generator Car (St. Louis S Gaugers), *07*	107____
48261X	C&NW Safety and Generator Car (St. Louis S Gaugers), *11*	90____
48262	Union Tank Car (TTOS), *07*	103____
48263	Cape Cod Potato Chip Boxcar (NETCA), *07*	103____
48264	GE Boom Car (NASG), *07*	81____
48265	Life Savers Tank Car (TTOS Cal-Stewart), *07*	86____
48267	Rutland Boxcar (TCA), *08*	80____
48268	Rutland Boxcar (TCA), *08*	80____
48269	ATSF Grand Canyon Reefer (TCA), *09*	85____
48270	GE Baldwin Diesel Switcher, *08*	345____
48271	Hoover Dam Power Co. Flatcar (TCA), *09*	50____
48272	Forest Service/Smokey Bear Flatcar with airplane (TTOS), *08*	127____
48273	Northwestern Reefer (TTOS), *09*	60____
48274	Western Pacific Stock Car (TTOS), *09*	85____
48275	Life Savers Wild Cherry Tank Car (TTOS Cal-Stewart), *08*	93____
48276	Bay State Beer Reefer (NETCA), *09*	73____
48281	GN Boxcar (Southeastern Michigan S Gaugers), *10*	75____
48284	Elgin, Joliet & Eastern Gondola with coil covers (NASG), *09*	70____
48285	Karo Tank Car (Southern California S Gaugers), *10*	125____
48286	Carling Black Label Beer Reefer #1 (TCA), *10*	80____
48287	Carling Black Label Beer Reefer #2 (TCA), *10*	80____
48288	Life Savers Pep-O-Mint Tank Car (TTOS Cal-Stewart), *09*	60____
48290	Life Savers Butter Rum Tank Car (TTOS Cal-Stewart), *10*	75____
48291	Jenney 3-D Tank Car (NASG), *10*	85____
48292	Sacramento Canning Tank Car (TCA), *11*	90____
48293	Charleston & West Carolina Boxcar (TTOS), *11*	95____

Mint

			Mint
____ 48294	Dixie Honey 1-D Tank Car (NASG), *11*		80
____ 48295	Flatcar with Howard Johnson trailers (NETCA), *11*		75
48296 ____	Life Savers Wint O Green Tank Car (TTOS Cal-Stewart), *12*		90
____ 48297	NS Flatcar with jet engines (TCA), *12*		70
____ 48298	Spreckels Sugar Hopper (TCA Rocky Mountain), *12*		65
____ 48299	Spreckels Sugar Hopper (TCA Rocky Mountain), *13*		80
____ 48300	Southern Pacific Overnight Boxcar, *87*		41
____ 48301	D&RGW Boxcar, *87*		37
____ 48302	Canadian Pacific Boxcar, *87*		42
____ 48303	Chessie System Boxcar, *87*		42
____ 48304	Burlington Northern Boxcar, *87*		44
____ 48305	Wabash Boxcar, *88*		31
____ 48306	Seaboard Coast Line Boxcar, *88*		36
____ 48307	Western Pacific Boxcar, *88*		37
____ 48308	Maine Central Boxcar "8308," *90*		67
____ 48309	Christmas Boxcar "8309," *90 u*		206
____ 48310	MKT Boxcar "8310," *91*		39
____ 48311	Christmas Boxcar "8311," *91 u*		53
____ 48312	Missouri Pacific Boxcar "8312," *92*		45
____ 48313	BAR State of Maine Boxcar "8313," *92*		52
____ 48314	Christmas Boxcar "8314," *92 u*		68
____ 48316	Bangor & Aroostook Reefer "29425," *93*		34
____ 48317	Rath Packing Reefer "29426," *93*		33
____ 48318	A.C. Gilbert Boxcar "8318," *93*		42
____ 48319	Christmas Boxcar "8319," *93*		45
____ 48320	NKP Boxcar, *94*		34
____ 48321	Christmas Boxcar "8321," *94*		37
____ 48322	New Haven Boxcar, *95*		47
____ 48323	Christmas Boxcar, *95*		47
____ 48324	AF 50th Anniversary Boxcar "1946-1996," *96*		53
____ 48325	Holiday Boxcar, *96*		38
____ 48326	B&O Boxcar (TCA), *96*		67
____ 48327	AF Christmas Boxcar "900," *97*		44
____ 48328	GN Boxcar "900-197," *97*		32
____ 48329	ATSF Boxcar "900-297," map graphic, *97*		28
____ 48330	PRR Boxcar "900-397," *97*		30
____ 48332	MKT Boxcar "937," *98*		43
____ 48333	Bangor & Aroostook Boxcar "982," *98*		39
____ 48334	Seaboard Boxcar "942," *98*		25
____ 48335	Christmas Gondola, *98*		50
____ 48340	American Flyer Christmas Car, *00*		70
____ 48341	American Flyer Christmas Car, *99*		93
____ 48342	American Flyer Christmas Boxcar, *01*		49
____ 48343	Great Northern Boxcar, *01*		50
____ 48346	Christmas Boxcar, *02*		55
____ 48347	C&O Boxcar "2701," *02*		48
____ 48348	NP Boxcar "31226," *02*		57
____ 48349	Goofy Boxcar, *03*		30
____ 48351	Donald Duck Boxcar, *04–05*		24
____ 48352	Pennsylvania Boxcar "47133," *03*		50
____ 48353	American Flyer Christmas Boxcar, *03–04*		45
____ 48354	Southern Pacific Boxcar, *04*		50
____ 48355	American Flyer Christmas Boxcar, *05*		45
____ 48356	Pluto Boxcar, *05*		32
____ 48357	Winnie the Pooh Boxcar, *04–05*		23
____ 48358	Santa Fe Boxcar "272197," *05*		43

Mint

48359	Holiday Boxcar, *05*	48____
48362	Burlington Boxcar "63114," *06*	55____
48363	Holiday Boxcar, *06*	55____
48364	Gilbert AF 60th Anniversary Boxcar, *06*	62____
48365	Western Maryland Boxcar, *06*	125____
48366	Jersey Central Boxcar "20958," *07*	43____
48367	CP Rail Stock Car "277315," *07*	55____
48368	American Flyer Holiday Boxcar, *07*	48____
48370	UPS Centennial Boxcar "1937," *07*	39____
48372	CN Boxcar "36298," *08*	60____
48373	UP Stock Car "48155D," *08*	60____
48374	American Flyer Holiday Boxcar, *08*	60____
48375	American Flyer Stock Car with reindeer, *08*	52____
48376	American Flyer Holiday Boxcar, *09*	70____
48378	IC Boxcar "400664," *09*	70____
48379	GN Stock Car, *09*	70____
48380	American Flyer Circus Stock Car "3636," *09–10*	48____
48381	1953 Catalog Art Boxcar, *09*	50____
48383	U.S. Mail Post Office Boxcar "8383," *09–11*	70____
48384	American Flyer Holiday Boxcar, *10*	55____
48385	American Flyer 1959 Catalog Art Boxcar, *10*	55____
48386	NYC Pacemaker Stock Car "23243," *10*	70____
48387	Airco Boxcar "4838," *10*	70____
48388	WP Boxcar "1955," *10*	70____
48389	Angela Trotta Thomas "Flyer Fantasy" Boxcar, *10*	55____
48390	American Flyer 1955 Catalog Art Boxcar, *11*	70____
48391	Timken Boxcar, *11*	70____
48393	Keystone Camera Boxcar, *11*	70____
48394	Holiday Boxcar, *11*	70____
48395	NP "Pig Palace" Stock Car, *11–13*	70____
48396	Coca-Cola Christmas Boxcar, *11–14*	55____
48397	Halloween Boxcar, *11–13*	70____
48399	Ringling Bros. Boxcar, *11*	70____
48400	SP 3-D Tank Car, *87*	34____
48402	Penn Salt 1-D Tank Car "24319," *92*	63____
48403	British Columbia 1-D Tank Car "8403," *93*	87____
48404	U.S. Army 1-D Tank Car, *94*	44____
48405	Shell 1-D Tank Car "8681," *95*	54____
48406	Celanese Chemicals Tank Car, *96*	62____
48407	Gilbert Chemicals Tank Car, *96*	47____
48408	Sunoco 1-D Tank Car "625," *97*	33____
48410	Tank Train 1-D Tank Car "44587," *99*	75____
48411	Gilbert Chemicals Tank Car "48411," *02*	67____
48412	Alaska 3-D Tank Car, *02*	50____
48413	Diamond Chemicals Tank Car "19418," *03*	42____
48414	Nestle Nesquik 1-D Tank Car "48414," *04*	48____
48415	Hooker Chemicals 3-D Tank Car "48515," *04*	47____
48416	Campbell's Soup 1-D Tank Car, *04*	46____
48417	Pillsbury 1-D Tank Car, *05*	49____
48418	Protex 3-D Tank Car "PDAX 1054," *05*	45____
48419	Jack Frost 1-D Tank Car "107," *06*	55____
48420	Union Pacific 3-D Tank Car, *06*	45____
48421	Philadelphia Quartz 1-D Tank Car "806," *07*	55____
48422	Simonin's 3-D Tank Car "9565," *07*	43____
48424	American Flyer Candy Cane 1-D Tank Car, *08*	60____
48425	NYC 3-D Tank Car, *08*	60____

	48426	American Flyer Commemorative Freight Car 3-pack, *08–09*	165
	48428	DM&IR 1-D Tank Car "817," *09*	70
	48430	Comet 1-D Tank Car, *09*	70
	48431	Sunoco 1-D Tank Car, *09–10*	58
	48433	Coca-Cola 1-D Tank Car, *10–11*	70
	48434	American Flyer Smoke Fluid 1-D Tank Car, *12–13*	70
	48435	Hershey's 1-D Tank Car, *11*	70
	48437	Gilbert Chemicals 3-D Tank Car, *11*	70
	48438	Cities Service 3-D Tank Car, *12–13, 15*	60
	48440	Track Cleaning Fluid 3-D Tank Car, *13–16*	60
	48442	AFL Air Service 1-D Tank Car, *13–16*	60
	48443	Union Starch 1-D Tank Car, *15–16*	60
	48459	Chessie GP20 Diesel, *07*	258
	48470	Jersey Central Boxcar (NASG), *88 u*	165
	48471	MKT 1-D Tank Car "120089" (NASG), *89 u*	243
	48472	Pennzoil 3-D Tank Car "390" (NASG), *90 u*	160
	48473	Central of Georgia Boxcar (TCA), *90 u*	68
	48474	C&NW Reefer "70165" (TCA), *91 u*	197
	48475	American Flyer Lines Smoking Caboose, *11*	80
	48475	Boraxo Covered Hopper "591" (NASG), *91 u*	70
	48476	NYC Reefer "491" (NASG), *91 u*	70
	48477	Ralston Purina Boxcar "11492" (TCA), *92 u*	92
	48478	Burlington Boxcar "792" (NASG), *92 u*	93
	48479	NKP Flatcar "20602" with Ertl trailer (NASG), *92 u*	127
	48480	Susquehanna Boxcar "993" (NASG), *93 u*	91
	48481	REA Reefer "893" (NASG), *93 u*	67
	48482	Great Northern Boxcar "3993" (TCA), *93 u*	92
	48483	A.C. Gilbert Society "Boys Club" Boxcar, *93 u*	65
	48484	A.C. Gilbert Society "Boys at the Gate" Boxcar, *93 u*	80
	48485	Northern Pacific Boxcar "1094" (NASG), *94 u*	72
	48486	NYNH&H Boxcar "1194" (NASG), *94 u*	51
	48487	Yorkrail Boxcar "1994" (TCA), *94 u*	93
	48489	Pennsylvania Dutch Boxcar "91653" (TCA), *97 u*	286
	48490	Western Pacific Boxcar "101645" (TTOS), *95 u*	70
	48491	BN Flatcar "1995" with trailers (TCA), *95 u*	100
	48492	Northern Pacific Boxcar "1261" (TCA), *95 u*	74
	48493	SP TTUX Flatcar Set with trailers (NASG), *95 u*	75
	48494	LV Covered Grain Hopper "1295" (NASG), *95 u*	60
	48495	Monsanto 1-D Tank Car, white (St. Louis S Gaugers), *95 u*	174
	48496	Monsanto 1-D Tank Car, orange (St. Louis S Gaugers), *95 u*	1018
	48497	MKT 3-D Tank Car "117018" (TCA), *95 u*	105
	48498	Western Pacific Boxcar "31337" (TTOS), *96 u*	105
	48500	SP Gondola with canisters, *87*	25
	48501	Southern Pacific Flatcar with trailers, *87*	41
	48502	Wabash Flatcar with trailers, *88*	46
	48503	Wabash Gondola with canisters, *88*	22
	48505	IC Gulf Bulkhead Flatcar "8505," *90*	37
	48507/08	U.S. Army Flatcars with 2 tanks, *95*	61
	48509	AF Flatcar with 2 farm tractors, *95*	45
	48510	Nickel Plate Road Gondola with canisters, *95*	34
	48511	TTUX Triple Crown Flatcars with trailers, *96*	73
	48513	CSX Flatcar with generator, *96*	28
	48514	Intermodal TTUX Set with 2 cars and 2 trailers, *97*	53
	48515	New Haven Flatcar, *97*	50

Mint

48516	SP Searchlight Car "627," *97*	47___
48524	Borden's Flatcar, *01*	45___
48525	Burlington Gondola, *01*	39___
48526	Reading Gondola "38708" with pipes, *02*	40___
48527	Santa Fe Flatcar "90019" with jet rocket, *02*	46___
48528	Conrail Flatcar with wheel loader, *02*	53___
48529	NYC Flatcar with wheel load, *02*	48___
48531	Chessie Depressed Center Flatcar with cable reel, *03*	59___
48532	SP Flatcar "513183" with trailers, *03*	48___
48533	PFE Flatcar with trailers, *04–05*	42___
48534	NYC Depressed Center Flatcar with cable reel, *04*	55___
48535	GN Bulkhead Flatcar "48535," *04–05*	46___
48536	Southern Flatcar with wheel load, *04*	65___
48537	Nestle Nesquik Flatcar with milk containers, *04–05*	44___
48538	Hood's Flatcar with milk containers, *04–05*	46___
48539	REA Flatcar "TLCX2" with trailers, *05*	50___
48540	B&O Flatcar "8652" with girder, *05*	49___
48541	D&H Gondola "13903" with pipe load, *05*	45___
48542	UPS Flatcar with trailer, *05*	45___
48543	Supplee Flatcar with milk containers, *06*	55___
48544	WM Flatcar "2632" with girder, *06*	55___
48545	DM&IR Gondola "4290" with pipe load, *06*	55___
48546	Alaska Depressed Center Flatcar with cable reel, *06*	59___
48547	Chessie System Gondola, *06*	100___
48548	PRR Flatcar "480078" with trailers, *07*	35___
48549	UP Gondola with canisters, *07*	38___
48550	GN Depressed Center Service Car, *07*	44___
48553	AF Christmas Gondola with candy canes, *07*	55___
48554	Bethlehem Steel Gondola with coil covers, *08*	50___
48555	Reading Flatcar "9314" with wheel load, *08*	60___
48559	Christmas Gondola with presents, *09*	36___
48560	BNSF Flatcar with jet engine, *09–11*	53___
48561	CNJ Flatcar with boat, *10*	70___
48563	Reindeer Express Agency Flatcar with trailers, *10*	70___
48565	Commemorative Flatcar with piggyback trailers, *11*	70___
48566	Gondola with Christmas trees, *11*	70___
48568	Ringling Bros. Flatcar with piggyback trailers, *11*	70___
48569	Buttermilk Bay Creamery Flatcar with milk containers, *11*	70___
48570	PRR Gondola with coil covers, *12–13*	70___
48571	Flatcar with Santa's sleigh, *12–13*	70___
48572	Naughty or Nice Gondola, coil covers, *13–14*	70___
48576	AFL Gilbert Dairy Flatcar with milk containers, *13–16*	60___
48577	Flatcar with Santa's sleigh, *13–14*	70___
48579	AFL Depressed Center Flatcar with cable reel, *14–15*	50___
48580	U.S. Navy Flatcar with Jeeps, *14–15*	70___
48600	Southern Pacific Hopper, *87*	31___
48601	Union Pacific Covered Hopper, *87*	30___
48602	Erie Covered Hopper, *87*	29___
48603	Wabash Hopper with coal load, *88*	26___
48604	Milwaukee Road Covered Hopper, *88*	31___
48605	Burlington Northern Covered Hopper, *88*	41___
48609	D&H Covered Hopper "8609," *93*	37___
48610	NKP Covered Hopper, *94*	31___
48611	Cargill Covered Grain Hopper, *95*	37___
48612	ADM 3-bay Covered Hopper, *97*	42___
48613	B&LE Hopper 4-pack, *98*	229___

			Mint
____	**48614**	B&LE Hopper, *98*	77
____	**48619**	Union Pacific Hopper, *01*	40
____	**48620**	B&O Hopper "435350," *02*	50
____	**48621**	CN Covered Hopper, *02*	41
____	**48622**	Burlington Hopper "170616," *03*	32
____	**48623**	"Naughty & Nice" Hopper 2-pack, *04–05*	88
____	**48627**	Southern Hopper with ballast load, *04*	55
____	**48628**	DM&IR Hopper, *05*	51
____	**48629**	CP Hopper, *06*	55
____	**48630**	Milwaukee Road 3-bay Hopper, *07*	38
____	**48631**	NYC 2-bay Hopper, *07*	30
____	**48632**	Santa's Candy Shop 2-bay Hopper, *09–10*	70
____	**48633**	UP 2-bay Hopper "82173," *09–10*	55
____	**48635**	Hershey's Special Dark 2-Bay Hopper, *12*	70
____	**48636**	WP 3-Bay Hopper, *12*	70
____	**48637**	Santa Fe Midnight Chief 2-Bay Hopper, *13–16*	60
____	**48638**	North Pole Express Hopper, *12, 15–16*	70
____	**48639**	CN Scale Cylindrical Hopper "370708," *12, 15–16*	80
____	**48640**	BN Scale Cylindrical Hopper "458856," *12, 15–16*	80
____	**48641**	MP UP Heritage Scale Cylindrical Hopper "27421," *12, 15–16*	80
____	**48642**	Saskatchewan Scale Cylindrical Hopper "397015," *12*	80
____	**48643**	SP Scale Cylindrical Hopper "491020," *12, 15–16*	80
____	**48644**	D&RGW UP Heritage Scale Cylindrical Hopper, *12*	80
____	**48645**	C&NW UP Heritage Scale Cylindrical Hopper, *12, 15–16*	80
____	**48646**	UP "Building America" Scale Cylindrical Hopper, *12, 15–16*	80
____	**48647**	AFL Artificial Coal 3-Bay Hopper, *13–16*	60
____	**48648**	Alberta Cylindrical Hopper "396161," *12, 15–16*	80
____	**48649**	PRR Cylindrical Hopper "260411," *12, 15–16*	80
____	**48650**	Govt. of Canada Cylindrical Hopper "607002," *12, 15–16*	80
____	**48651**	NS Cylindrical Hopper "81022," *12, 15–16*	80
____	**48652**	CNJ NS Heritage Cylindrical Hopper "68110," *12, 15–16*	80
____	**48653**	DL&W NS Heritage Cylindrical Hopper "11254," *12, 15–16*	80
____	**48654**	Erie NS Heritage Cylindrical Hopper "91068," *12, 15–16*	80
____	**48655**	Illinois Terminal NS Heritage Cylindrical Hopper "107296," *12, 16*	80
____	**48656**	NYC NS Heritage Cylindrical Hopper "18292," *12*	80
____	**48657**	PC NS Heritage Cylindrical Hopper "32428," *12, 15–16*	80
____	**48658**	Reading NS Heritage Cylindrical Hopper, *13*	80
____	**48659**	Savannah & Atlanta NS Heritage Cylindrical Hopper "19065," *13–16*	80
____	**48660**	Virginian NS Heritage Cylindrical Hopper, *13–16*	80
____	**48661**	Wabash NS Heritage Cylindrical Hopper, *13–16*	80
____	**48662**	AFL Scenery Gravel 3-Bay Hopper, *13–16*	60
____	**48664**	Christmas Cylindrical Hopper, *13*	80
____	**48665**	Central of Georgia NS Heritage Cylindrical Hopper, *13–16*	80
____	**48666**	Conrail NS Heritage Cylindrical Hopper, *13*	80
____	**48667**	Interstate NS Heritage Cylindrical Hopper "13488," *13–16*	80
____	**48668**	LV NS Heritage Cylindrical Hopper, *13–16*	80

48669	Nickel Plate Road NS Heritage Cylindrical Hopper, *13–16*	80____
48670	N&W NS Heritage Cylindrical Hopper, *13–16*	80____
48671	PRR NS Heritage Cylindrical Hopper, *13*	80____
48672	Southern NS Heritage Cylindrical Hopper, *13–16*	80____
48673	Norfolk Southern NS Heritage Cylindrical Hopper, *13, 16*	80____
48674	Monongahela NS Heritage Cylindrical Hopper, *13–16*	80____
48700	SP Bay Window Caboose, *87*	35____
48701	Illinois Central Gulf Bay Window Caboose, *87*	40____
48702	Wabash Square Window Caboose, *88*	42____
48703	Union Pacific Square Window Caboose, *88*	36____
48705	Pennsylvania Square Window Caboose, *89*	47____
48706	BN Square Window Caboose "8706," *90*	98____
48707	NH Square Window Caboose "8707," *91*	41____
48710	Conrail Bay Window Caboose "21503," *95*	46____
48711	Northern Pacific Bay Window Caboose "8711," *95*	43____
48712	"Happy New Year" Bay Window Caboose "0101," *95*	48____
48713	Nickel Plate Road Caboose, *97*	44____
48714	SP Square Window Caboose "990," *97*	45____
48715	Milwaukee Road Caboose, *97*	53____
48718	C&NW Caboose, *98*	48____
48721	Santa Fe Caboose "999628," *99*	70____
48722	Rock Island Bay Window Caboose "17778," *02*	55____
48723	Santa Fe Boom Car "206982," *03*	39____
48724	Seaboard Square Window Caboose "49658," *03*	54____
48725	NYC Caboose "17560," *03–04*	48____
48726	NYC Boom Car "48726," *04–05*	42____
48727	UP Bay Window Caboose "24554," *05*	71____
48728	Southern Bay Window Caboose "X545," *05*	48____
48729	Southern Boom Car, *04*	50____
48730	DM&IR Extended Vision Caboose "C-227," *05*	55____
48731	SP Bay Window Caboose "1338," *05*	55____
48732	UP Boom Car, *05*	55____
48733	Erie Caboose "C107," *06*	53____
48734	PRR Caboose "477810," *08*	60____
48735	Burlington Extended Vision Caboose "13853," *06*	55____
48736	WM Caboose "1864," *06*	48____
48738	Chessie System Caboose, *06*	45____
48739	American Flyer Christmas Caboose, *06*	55____
48740	M.O.W. Boom Car "916," *07*	75____
48741	C&NW Extended Vision Caboose "13653," *07*	55____
48742	American Flyer Caboose, *07*	55____
48743	C&O Caboose "90877," *07*	55____
48746	ACL Caboose "0400," *08*	60____
48747	CN Extended Vision Caboose "79644," *08*	52____
48750	Erie-Lack. Extended Vision Caboose, *09*	60____
48751	Cotton Belt Bay Window Caboose, *09*	70____
48752	BN Extended View Caboose, *11*	70____
48754	WP Bay Window Caboose, *10–11*	70____
48755	NP Extended View Caboose, *11*	70____
48756	Conrail Extended View Caboose, *11*	70____
48757	GN Extended View Caboose, *11*	70____
48759	Clear Smoking Caboose "997," *12*	80____
48800	Wabash Reefer, *88*	36____
48801	Union Pacific Reefer, *88*	29____
48802	Pennsylvania Reefer, *88*	37____

____48805	National Dairy Despatch Insulated Boxcar "8805," *90*	43
____48806	REA Reefer "8806," *94*	32
____48807	NKP Reefer "8807," *94*	35
____48808	PFE Reefer "30000," *03*	49
____48809	NP Reefer "139," *04*	36
____48814	Fruit Growers Express Reefer "40703," *06*	52
____48815	Needham Reefer "60500," *07–08*	55
____48823	Hershey's Reefer, *10*	70
____48824	Pacific Fruit Express Reefer "47760," *11*	70
____48825	Holiday Boxcar, *12–13*	70
____48826	American Flyer 1956 Catalog Art Boxcar, *12*	60
____48827	M&StL Boxcar, *12–13*	57
____48828	Mr. Goodbar Reefer, *12–14*	70
____48829	Pabst Beer Reefer, *12*	70
____48830	Schlitz Beer Reefer, *12*	70
48831	Angela Trotta Thomas "Circus Comes to Town" Boxcar,	
____	*12–13*	70
____48832	American Flyer 1951 Catalog Art Boxcar, *13–14*	50
____48833	Christmas Boxcar, *13*	50
____48835	Boy Scouts of America Cub Scout Boxcar, *13–14*	55
____48836	Boy Scouts of America Eagle Scout Boxcar, *13–14*	55
____48838	Penguin Seafood Reefer, *13–14*	50
____48839	Smoke Cartridge Transport Boxcar, *13–14, 16*	60
____48844	Christmas Mint Car, *13*	60
____48845	Fort Knox Mint Car, *13–16*	70
____48846	Gilbert Mines Mint Car, *13*	60
____48847	New York Federal Reserve Mint Car, *13–16*	70
____48848	San Francisco Federal Reserve Mint Car, *13–16*	70
____48851	AFL Stock Car, *14–16*	60
____48852	AT&SF Grand Canyon Line Boxcar, *14–16*	60
____48854	Boston Federal Reserve Mint Car, *14–16*	70
____48855	AFL Waffle-sided Boxcar, *14–16*	50
____48856	NH Waffle-sided Boxcar, *14–16*	50
____48857	C&NW Waffle-sided Boxcar, *14–16*	50
____48858	BNSF 57' Mechanical Reefer "798879," *14*	80
____48859	UP 57' Mechanical Reefer "455995," *14*	80
____48860	PFE 57' Mechanical Reefer "458455," *14*	80
____48861	GN 57' Mechanical Reefer "8870," *14*	80
____48862	Govt. of Canada Cylindrical Hopper "106010," *14–16*	80
____48863	CN Cylindrical Hopper "369290," *14–16*	80
____48864	Santa Fe Cylindrical Hopper "300022," *14–15*	80
____48865	Frisco Cylindrical Hopper "81028," *14–16*	80
____48866	GN Cylindrical Hopper "71600," *14–16*	80
____48867	U.S. Army Unloading Boxcar, *15–16*	80
____48868	NP 57' Mechanical Reefer "794," *14–16*	80
____48870	GN Boxcar, Steam RailSounds, *14–16*	170
____48871	Erie Boxcar, Steam RailSounds, *14–16*	170
____48874	Christmas Boxcar, *14*	50
____48875	North Pole Gondola with cocoa containers, *14*	50
____48876	Reading 2-bay Hopper "81001," *15–16*	60
____48877	U.S. Army Missile Launch Flatcar, *15–16*	70
____48878	U.S. Army Flatcar with Rockets, *15–16*	60
____48879	NH Gondola with pipes, *15–16*	65
____48880	AFL Commemorative Work Caboose, *15–16*	65
____48882	Christmas Boxcar, *15*	65
____48900	C&O Combination Car, *89*	49
____48901	C&O Coach, *89*	63

Mint

48902	C&O Vista Dome Car, *89*	58____
48903	C&O Observation Car, *89*	49____
48904	UP Combination Car "8904," *90*	54____
48905	UP Coach "8905," *90*	90____
48906	UP Vista Dome Car "8906," *90*	73____
48907	UP Observation Car "8907," *90*	47____
48908	UP Coach "8908," *90 u*	113____
48909	UP Vista Dome Car "8909," *90 u*	118____
48910	Missouri Pacific Combination Car "8910," *91*	50____
48911	Missouri Pacific Vista Dome Car "8911," *91*	78____
48912	Missouri Pacific Coach "8912," *91*	78____
48913	Missouri Pacific Observation Car "8913," *91*	69____
48914	Missouri Pacific Coach "8914," *91*	94____
48915	Missouri Pacific Vista Dome Car "8915," *91*	75____
48920	Northern Pacific Combination Car "8920," *92*	55____
48921	Northern Pacific Coach "8921," *92*	67____
48922	Northern Pacific Vista Dome Car "8922," *92*	67____
48923	Northern Pacific Observation Car "8923," *92*	50____
48924	Northern Pacific Vista Dome Car "8924," *92*	67____
48925	Northern Pacific Coach "8925," *92*	72____
48926	WP California Zephyr Combination Car "801," *93*	37____
48927	WP California Zephyr Vista Dome Car "814," *93*	40____
48928	WP California Zephyr Vista Dome Car "815," *93*	40____
48929	WP California Zephyr Vista Dome Car "813," *93*	54____
48930	WP California Zephyr Vista Dome Car "811," *93*	60____
48931	WP California Zephyr Observation Car "882," *93*	37____
48932	WP California Zephyr Dining Car "842," *93*	43____
48933	Missouri Pacific Dining Car "8933," *94*	90____
48934	Northern Pacific Dining Car "8934," *94*	90____
48935	New Haven Combination Car, *95*	57____
48936	New Haven Vista Dome Car, *95*	55____
48937	New Haven Observation Car, *95*	57____
48938	Silver Flash Combination Car "960," *95*	75____
48939	Silver Flash Coach "961," *95*	67____
48940	Silver Flash Observation Car "963," *95*	79____
48941	Union Pacific Vista Dome Dining Car "8941," *95*	97____
48942	Vista Dome Car "962," *96*	140____
48943	New Haven Vista Dome Dining Car, *96*	65____
48944	ATSF Super Chief Passenger Car 4-pack, *97*	260____
48961	NYC Streamliner Passenger Car 2-pack, *02*	160____
48964	NYC Baggage Car "9149," *03*	50____
48965	B&O Passenger Car 2-pack, *03*	157____
48968	Santa Fe Passenger Car 2-pack, *04–05*	85____
48975	Pennsylvania Passenger Car 2-pack, *05*	130____
48976	Pennsylvania Baggage Car, *05*	75____
48977	Pennsylvania Dining Car, *05*	75____
48978	UP Heavyweight Passenger Car 4-pack, *06*	334____
48983	UP Heavyweight Passenger Car 2-pack, *06*	148____
48990	NYC Heavyweight Passenger Car 4-pack, *07*	265____
48991	NYC Heavyweight Passenger Car 2-pack, *07*	140____
48992	PRR Heavyweight Passenger Car 4-pack, *07*	265____
48993	Pennsylvania Heavyweight Passenger Car 2-Pack, *07*	140____
48994	Blue Comet Heavyweight Passenger Car 2-pack, *07*	140____
49001	NYC Searchlight Car "9001," *90*	48____
49002	B&M Flatcar with logs, *83*	83____
49003	Union Pacific Searchlight Car "9003," *91*	43____
49006	MILW Animated Square Window Caboose, *92*	47____

____49009	AFL Flatcar with derrick, *96*	32
____49010	"Stable of Champions" Horse Car, *96*	32
____49011	UP Moe & Joe Animated Flatcar "15100," *03*	65
____49012	Santa Fe Crane Car "199707," *03*	68
____49013	PRR Depressed Center Searchlight Car, *04–05*	80
____49014	NYC Crane Car "X-15," *04–05*	63
____49015	Westside Lumber Moe & Joe Animated Flatcar, *04–05*	63
____49016	Santa Fe Walking Brakeman Boxcar, *04–05*	65
____49017	GN Animated Caboose "X84," *04–05*	62
____49019	Southern Crane Car, *04*	65
____49021	UP Crane Car "JPX-251," *05*	70
____49022	M.O.W. Searchlight Car, *05*	69
____49023	NYC Walking Brakeman Car "174226," *05*	68
____49024	Pennsylvania Coal Dump Car "494979," *05*	73
____49025	American Flyer Dump Car with presents, *05*	75
____49026	American Flyer Operating Tie Car, *06*	58
____49027	Pennsylvania Log Dump Car, *06*	80
____49028	American Flyer Candy Cane Dump Car, *06*	78
____49029	Santa Fe Animated Caboose, *06*	70
____49031	GN Walking Brakeman Car, *06*	60
____49032	Bethlehem Steel Depressed Center Searchlight Car, *06*	65
____49033	NYC Coal Dump Car, *06*	74
____49035	Southern Operating Coal Dump Car, *06*	65
____49037	M.O.W. Crane Car "900," *07*	85
____49038	D&RGW Walking Brakeman Car "69676," *07*	85
____49039	Santa Fe Log Dump Car, *07–08*	85
____49040	Chessie System Animated Caboose "3507," *07*	85
____49041	C&O Tie Car, *07*	50
____49042	Erie Coal Dump Car "05473," *07*	85
____49045	American Flyer 915 Unloading Car, *08*	74
____49046	American Flyer Santa Animated Caboose, *08*	73
____49047	CP Rail Coal Dump Car "5522," *09*	90
____49048	NYC Operating Boxcar "75509," *09*	68
____49049	AF Commemorative Unloading Car, *10*	85
____49050	Ringling Bros. Flatcar with Moe and Joe clowns, *11*	80
____49054	GN Operating Log Dump Car, *10*	80
____49055	Wabash Coal Dump Car, *10*	90
____49056	NP Coal Dump Car, *11*	90
____49057	WP Log Dump Car, *11*	85
____49060	Ringling Bros. Searchlight Car, *11*	80
____49061	Christmas Music Reefer, *12–13*	80
____49062	Route of the Reindeer Animated Caboose, *12–14*	85
____49063	Zombie Walking Brakeman Car, *13, 15–16*	80
____49064	NH Boxcar, Diesel RailSounds, *13–16*	170
____49065	UP Boxcar, Diesel RailSounds, *13–16*	170
____49078	Polar Express Elf Handcar, *14–16*	100
____49081	70-Ton Truck with rotating bearing caps, pair, *14*	25
____49082	C&O Coal Dump Car, *14–16*	79
____49083	Santa Fe Depressed Center Searchlight Car, *14–16*	80
____49084	PRR Gas Unloading Car, *14–16*	80
____49085	FasTrack Activator Rail, *14–16*	20
____49086	Telephone Poles, *15–16*	30
____49088	SP Crane Car "7072," *15*	90
____49089	SP Boom Car "7073," *15*	65
____49600	Union Pacific Pony Express Set, *90*	570
____49601	Missouri Pacific Eagle Set, *91*	618
____49602	Northern Pacific North Coast Limited Set, *92*	699

Mint

49604	Western Pacific California Zephyr Set, *93*	448___
49605	New Haven Passenger Car Set, *95*	193___
49606	Silver Flash Passenger Car Set, *95*	658___
49608	Domino Sugar Covered Hopper, *92*	57___
49611	NYC Alco PA Diesel Passenger Set, *02*	610___
49612	B&O Passenger Car 4-pack, *03*	770___
49613	Southern Baldwin Switcher Work Train Set, *04*	413___
49614	Pennsylvania Alco PA Diesel Passenger Set, *05*	575___
49615	Chessie System SD9 Diesel Freight Set, *06*	424___
49616	Alton Limited Passenger Set, CC, *06*	740___
49617	Blue Comet Steam Passenger Set, *07*	763___
49618	NYC Dockside Switcher Freight Set, *07*	275___
49621	American Flyer Christmas Steam Train, *09*	350___
49622	Freedom Train Passenger Set, *08*	548___
49624	American Flyer 959 Defender Freight Set, *10*	600___
49625	Bakelite Plastics Freight Car 2-pack, *10*	135___
49626	Ringling Bros. GP9 Diesel Circus Train Set, *11*	550___
49627	Southern Crescent Limited Passenger Train Set, *11*	900___
49632	Polar Express Berkshire Steam Passenger Set, *14–16*	400___
49634	SP Dockside Switcher Steam Freight Set, *13–14*	270___
49805	American Flyer 23780 Gabe the Lamplighter, *01*	114___
49806	American Flyer 23796 Sawmill, *01*	75___
49807	American Flyer 752 Seaboard Coaler, *01*	145___
49808	American Flyer 594 Animated Track Gang Set, *06*	88___
49809	American Flyer 772 Water Tower, *02*	53___
49810	American Flyer 787 Log Loader, *04–05*	110___
49811	American Flyer 773 Oil Derrick, *04–05*	53___
49812	American Flyer 755 Talking Station, *04–05*	88___
49813	American Flyer 789 Baggage Smasher, *04–05*	74___
49814	American Flyer 774 Floodlight Tower, *04–05*	58___
49815	American Flyer 741 Handcar and Shed, *04–05*	82___
49818	American Flyer 23830 Piggyback Unloader and Flatcar, *04–05*	62___
49819	American Flyer 583A Electromagnetic Crane, *04–05*	148___
49820	American Flyer 758 Sam the Semaphore Man, *07–09*	95___
49824	American Flyer 770 Loading Platform and Car, *05*	125___
49825	American Flyer 571 Truss Bridge, *07–09*	27___
49827	54" Curved Track, *07–11*	3___
49828	10" Straight Track, *07–11*	3___
49829	36" Straight Track, *07–11*	9___
49830	Fiber Insulator Pins, *07–14*	2___
49831	Steel Pins, *07–18*	3___
49832	American Flyer 582 Blinking Signal, *07–08*	55___
49833	American Flyer 587 Block Signal, *07–08*	55___
49835	American Flyer 588 Semaphore Block Signal, *07–09*	55___
49838	American Flyer 792 Railroad Terminal, *08*	79___
49839	American Flyer 793 Union Station, *08–10*	53___
49843	Suburban Station, *09–10*	70___
49844	Christmas Animated Billboard, *10–13*	40___
49845	Truss Bridge, *10–15*	23___
49846	American Flyer 773 Sunoco Oil Derrick, *10*	73___
49847	American Flyer 774 Floodlight Tower, *10–12, 15-16*	100___
49848	American Flyer Lines Girder Bridge, *10*	21___
49849	Lackawanna Girder Bridge, *10*	18___
49850	D&RGW Girder Bridge, *10–11*	21___
49851	Gilbert Oil Storage Tank, *11*	76___
49852	FasTrack 10" Straight Track, *12–16*	6___

____ **49853**	FasTrack R20 Curved Track, *12–16*	7
____ **49854**	FasTrack 10" Terminal Track, *12–16*	9
____ **49855**	Illuminated Station Platform, *10*	35
____ **49856**	FasTrack R20 Switch, right hand, *12–14*	100
____ **49857**	FasTrack R20 Switch, left hand, *12–14*	100
____ **49858**	FasTrack Transition Track, *12–16*	10
____ **49859**	FasTrack R27 Wide-Radius Curved Track, *13–16*	9
____ **49860**	Sunoco Oil Storage Tank with light, *12*	77
____ **49861**	Classic Billboard Set, *12*	13
____ **49862**	FasTrack 30" Straight Track, *13–16*	16
____ **49863**	FasTrack 45-Degree Crossover, *13–16*	26
____ **49864**	FasTrack 90-Degree Crossover, *13–16*	26
49865	FasTrack Grade Crossing with Gates & Flashers, *13–14*	
____		160
49866	FasTrack Straight Track with Illuminated Bumper, *13–16*	
____		33
____ **49867**	FasTrack 5" Half Straight Track, *13–16*	6
____ **49868**	FasTrack R20 Manual Switch, left hand, *13–16*	50
____ **49869**	FasTrack R20 Manual Switch, right hand, *13–16*	50
____ **49870**	FasTrack R20 Manual Switch, left hand, CC, *13–14*	120
____ **49871**	FasTrack R20 Manual Switch, right hand, CC, *13–14*	120
____ **49872**	Telephone Poles, *13–16*	40
49875	American Flyer Replacement Wheel and Axle Packs, *13–16*	
____		20
____ **49876**	Water Tower with shed, *13–16*	90
____ **49877**	Elevated Gilbert Oil Tank, *13–16*	80
____ **49878**	FasTrack R20 Half Curve, *13–16*	6
____ **49882**	Polar Express Girder Bridge, *14–16*	22
____ **49883**	FasTrack R27 Manual Switch, left-hand, *15–16*	69
____ **49884**	FasTrack R27 Manual Switch, right-hand, *15–16*	69
____ **49885**	FasTrack R27 Remote Switch, left-hand, *15–16*	150
____ **49886**	FasTrack R27 Remote Switch, right-hand, *15–16*	150
____ **49889**	FasTrack Figure-8 Add-On Track Pack, *14–16*	85
49890	FasTrack Inner Passing Loop Add-On Track Pack, *14–16*	
____		127
____ **49891**	FasTrack 10" Grade Crossing, *14*	20
____ **49892**	FasTrack R27 Half Curve, *14–16*	8
____ **49893**	FasTrack Earthen Bumper, 2 pieces, *14–16*	13
____ **49895**	FasTrack Uncoupling Section, *14–16*	43
____ **49896**	FlyerChief Terminal Track, *15–16*	9
____ **49922**	Freedom Train Heavyweight Passenger Car 2-pack, *08*	150
____ **49923**	Alton Limited Heavyweight Passenger Car 2-pack, *08*	150
____ **49927**	UP Streamlined Baggage Car "8944," *09*	75
____ **49928**	MP Streamlined Baggage Car "8933," *09*	75
____ **49929**	American Freedom Display Car "3510," *09*	73
____ **49930**	ATSF Streamliner Passenger Car 3-pack, *09*	200
____ **49934**	C&O Streamliner Baggage Car "48190," *10*	80
____ **49935**	NP Streamliner Baggage Car "8929," *10*	80
____ **49936**	D&RGW Streamliner Passenger Car 3-pack, *10*	250
____ **49940**	ATSF Streamliner Full Vista Dome Car, *10*	80
____ **49941**	UP Streamliner Full Vista Dome Car, *10*	83
____ **49942**	NYC Streamliner Full Vista Dome Car, *10*	80
____ **49943**	D&RGW Streamliner Full Vista Dome Car, *11–14*	80
____ **49944**	Erie Streamliner Baggage Car, *11–15*	80
____ **49945**	D&RGW Streamliner Baggage Car "754," *10*	80
____ **49946**	SP Daylight Streamliner Baggage Car, *11–13*	80
____ **49947**	SP Daylight Streamliner Full Vista Dome Car, *11–13*	80

Mint

49948	Erie Streamliner Full Vista Dome Car, *11–15*	80____
49949	Texas Special Streamliner Passenger Car 3-Pack, *11–13*	250____
49950	Texas Special Streamlined Combination Car, *12–13*	80____
49951	Texas Special Streamlined Vista Dome Car, *12–13*	80____
49952	Texas Special Streamlined Observation Car, *12–13*	80____
49956	Texas Special Streamlined Full Vista Dome Car, *12–14*	80____
49957	Texas Special Streamlined Baggage Car, *12–14*	80____
49958	AT&SF Streamlined Full Vista Dome Car, *12–14*	80____
49959	PRR Streamlined Vista Dome Car, *12–15*	80____
49960	North Pole Express Streamliner 3-Pack, *12–14*	250____
49972	Polar Express Abandoned Toy Car, *14–16*	70____
49973	Polar Express Baggage Car, *14–16*	70____
49977	American Flyer Work Crew People Pack, *14–16*	27____
49978	AF Classic Catalogs Billboard Set, *15–16*	13____
49979	Winter Station, *14–16*	80____
49990	FasTrack Outer Passing Loop Add-On Track Pack, *14–16*	155____
49991	FasTrack Siding Track Add-On Track Pack, *14–16*	100____
52009	WP Stock Car (SVAFC), *09*	120____
52094	Ann Arbor Covered Grain Hopper "1496" (NASG), *96 u*	55____
52095	Mobil 1-D Tank Car "1596" (NASG), *96 u*	85____

Retail

100	40' Boxcar	43
102	B&O 40' Boxcar	43
103	Cotton Belt 40' Boxcar	43
105	D&RGW 40' Boxcar	43
108	GN 40' Boxcar	46
112	Soo Line 40' Boxcar	43
113	NYC 40' Boxcar	43
114	PRR 40' Boxcar	43
115	ATSF 40' Boxcar	43
116	Seaboard 40' Boxcar	43
116C	Seaboard "Silver Comet" 40' Boxcar	43
116L	Seaboard "Robert E. Lee" 40' Boxcar	43
117	SP 40' Boxcar	43
118	UP 40' Boxcar	43
119	C&O 40' Boxcar	43
119B	C&O 40' Boxcar	43
121	NYC Pacemaker 40' Boxcar	46
122	Rutland 40' Boxcar	46
123	PRR Merchandise Service 40' Boxcar	49
125	P&LE 40' Boxcar	44
126	NP 40' Boxcar	44
128	NH 40' Boxcar	43
129	GN 40' Boxcar	43
130	GM&O 40' Boxcar	43
131	N&W 40' Boxcar	43
132	CP 40' Boxcar	43
133	M&StL 40' Boxcar	43
134	Erie-Lackawanna 40' Boxcar	43
135	SP 40' Boxcar	44
136	Susquehanna 40' Boxcar	49
137	C&NW 40' Boxcar	43
138	Conrail 40' Boxcar	43
139	Southern 40' Boxcar	43
140	MP 40' Boxcar	43
141	NYC 40' Boxcar	44
142	Rock Island 40' Boxcar	43
143	Virginian 40' Boxcar	43
144	SP 40' Boxcar, silver	44
145	CNJ 40' Boxcar	43
146	Wabash 40' Boxcar	43
147	Central of Georgia 40' Boxcar	48
148	B&M 40' Boxcar	48

		Retail	
149	Soo Line 40' Boxcar	43	____
150	D&RGW 40' Boxcar	46	____
151	B&O Sentinel 40' Boxcar	43	____
152	MKT 40' Boxcar	43	____
153	Texas & Pacific 40' Boxcar	43	____
175	Illinois Central Gulf 40' Boxcar	49	____
176	Reading 40' Boxcar	49	____
177	Akron, Canton & Youngstown 40' Boxcar	43	____
178	BN 40' Boxcar	43	____
179	Burlington 40' Boxcar	46	____
180G	NP 40' Boxcar, green	46	____
180R	NP 40' Boxcar, red	46	____
200	2-bay Rib-sided Hopper	30	____
201	C&O 2-bay Rib-sided Hopper	30	____
202	WM 2-bay Rib-sided Hopper	30	____
204	Erie 2-bay Rib-sided Hopper	30	____
205	N&W 2-bay Rib-sided Hopper	30	____
206	NYC 2-bay Rib-sided Hopper	30	____
207	PRR 2-bay Rib-sided Hopper	30	____
208	Peabody 2-bay Rib-sided Hopper	30	____
209	Southern 2-bay Rib-sided Hopper	30	____
210	UP 2-bay Rib-sided Hopper	30	____
211	SP 2-bay Rib-sided Hopper	30	____
212	D&RGW 2-bay Rib-sided Hopper	30	____
213	Virginian 2-bay Rib-sided Hopper	30	____
214	Reading 2-bay Rib-sided Hopper	30	____
215	CB&Q 2-bay Rib-sided Hopper	30	____
216	LV 2-bay Rib-sided Hopper	30	____
217	Interstate 2-bay Rib-sided Hopper	30	____
218	BN 2-bay Rib-sided Hopper	30	____
223	Burlington Express 40' Plug Door Boxcar	31	____
250	2-bay Offset-sided Hopper	30	____
251	ATSF 2-bay Offset-sided Hopper	30	____
252	CP 2-bay Offset-sided Hopper	30	____
253	GN 2-bay Offset-sided Hopper	30	____
254	NP 2-bay Offset-sided Hopper	30	____
255	IC 2-bay Offset-sided Hopper	30	____
256	NYC 2-bay Offset-sided Hopper	30	____
257	L&N 2-bay Offset-sided Hopper	30	____
258	MILW 2-bay Offset-sided Hopper	30	____
259	UP 2-bay Offset-sided Hopper	30	____
260	Frisco 2-bay Offset-sided Hopper	30	____
261	LNE 2-bay Offset-sided Hopper	30	____
262	D&H 2-bay Offset-sided Hopper	30	____
263	NKP 2-bay Offset-sided Hopper	30	____
264	MP 2-bay Offset-sided Hopper	30	____

_____ 265	Conrail 2-bay Offset-sided Hopper	30
_____ 266	C&NW 2-bay Offset-sided Hopper	30
_____ 267	Monon 2-bay Offset-sided Hopper	30
_____ 268	B&O 2-bay Offset-sided Hopper	30
_____ 352	CP 2-bay Offset-sided Hopper	30
_____ 355	IC 2-bay Offset-sided Hopper	30
_____ 359	UP 2-bay Offset-sided Hopper	30
_____ 361	LNE 2-bay Offset-sided Hopper	30
_____ 364	MP 2-bay Offset-sided Hopper	30
_____ 366	C&NW 2-bay Offset-sided Hopper	30
_____ 368	B&O 2-bay Offset-sided Hopper	30
_____ 420	BN Gondola	30
_____ 500	Tank Car	48
_____ 501	Corn Products Tank Car	48
_____ 502	GATX Tank Car	48
_____ 503	Cargill Tank Car	48
_____ 504	J.M. Huber Tank Car	48
_____ 505	Englehard Tank Car	48
_____ 506	Georgia Kao Tank Car	48
_____ 507	New Jersey Zinc Tank Car	48
_____ 508	BASF Wyandotte Tank Car	48
_____ 509	American Maize Tank Car	48
_____ 510	B.F. Goodrich Tank Car	48
_____ 511	Elcor Chemical Tank Car	48
_____ 512	Domino Sugar Tank Car	48
_____ 513B	American Models Tank Car	48
_____ 513G	American Models Tank Car, green	48
_____ 514	Aeron Tank Car	48
_____ 515	DuPont Tank Car	48
_____ 517	Sinclair Diesel Tank Car	48
_____ 518	Sinclair Gas Tank Car	48
_____ 519	Texaco Tank Car	48
_____ 520	Sunoco Tank Car	48
_____ 521	Dow Tank Car	48
_____ 772	Automatic Water Tower	80
_____ 774	Floodlight Tower	80
_____ 1100	40' Boxcar	31
_____ 1100	WFE 40' Boxcar, Premium Series	32
_____ 1102	B&O 40' Boxcar	31
_____ 1103	Cotton Belt 40' Boxcar	31
_____ 1105	BN/WFE 40' Boxcar	33
_____ 1105	D&RGW 40' Boxcar	31
_____ 1108	GN 40' Boxcar, Classic Series	35
_____ 1112	Soo Line 40' Boxcar	25
_____ 1113	NYC 40' Boxcar	31
_____ 1114	PRR 40' Boxcar	31

Retail

		Retail	
1115	ATSF 40' Boxcar	31	____
1116	Seaboard 40' Boxcar	31	____
1117	SP 40' Boxcar	31	____
1118	UP 40' Boxcar	31	____
1119	C&O 40' Boxcar	31	____
1121	NYC 40' Boxcar, Classic Series	35	____
1122	Rutland 40' Boxcar, Classic Series	35	____
1125	P&LE 40' Boxcar, Premium Series	32	____
1126	NP 40' Boxcar, Premium Series	32	____
1128	NH 40' Boxcar	31	____
1129	GN 40' Boxcar	31	____
1130	GM&O 40' Boxcar	31	____
1131	N&W 40' Boxcar	31	____
1132	CP 40' Boxcar	31	____
1133	M&StL 40' Boxcar	31	____
1133	NYC 40' Boxcar	31	____
1134	Erie-Lackawanna 40' Boxcar	31	____
1135	SP 40' Boxcar, Premium Series	32	____
1136	Susquehanna 40' Boxcar, Classic Series	35	____
1137	C&NW 40' Boxcar	31	____
1138	Conrail 40' Boxcar	31	____
1500	50' Rib-sided Boxcar	40	____
1501	Railbox 50' Rib-sided Boxcar	40	____
1502	Evergreen 50' Rib-sided Boxcar	40	____
1503	MEC 50' Rib-sided Boxcar	40	____
1504	C&NW 50' Rib-sided Boxcar	40	____
1505	UP 50' Rib-sided Boxcar	42	____
1506	Conrail 50' Rib-sided Boxcar	40	____
1507	BN 50' Rib-sided Boxcar	40	____
1508	Tropicana 50' Rib-sided Boxcar	40	____
1509	D&RGW 50' Rib-sided Boxcar	40	____
1510	Rail Link 50' Rib-sided Boxcar	40	____
1511	CSX Link 50' Rib-sided Boxcar	41	____
1512	Soo Line 50' Rib-sided Boxcar	40	____
1513	Miller 50' Rib-sided Boxcar	40	____
1514	PRR 50' Rib-sided Boxcar	43	____
1515	NYC 50' Rib-sided Boxcar	40	____
1516	Amtrak 50' Rib-sided Boxcar	42	____
1516P3	Amtrak 50' Rib-sided Boxcar, Phase III	45	____
1517	NS 50' Rib-sided Boxcar	41	____
1518B	Rock Island 50' Rib-sided Boxcar, blue	40	____
1518W	Rock Island 50' Rib-sided Boxcar, white	40	____
2002	RI City of Chicago Observation (TCA)	55	____
2003	RI City of Los Angeles Pullman Coach (TCA)	55	____
2004	RI Redman/Fraley Pullman Combine (TCA)	55	____
2200	40' Plug Door Boxcar	42	____

____ 2202	PFE 40' Boxcar, Premium Series	43
____ 2203	ART 40' Boxcar, Premium Series	43
____ 2204	FGE 40' Boxcar, Premium Series	43
____ 2206	Dubuque 40' Boxcar, Premium Series	43
____ 2207	WP 40' Plug Door Boxcar	40
____ 2208	CN 40' Plug Door Boxcar	40
____ 2209	DT&I 40' Boxcar, Premium Series	43
____ 2210	ATSF 40' Boxcar, Premium Series	43
____ 2211	PRR 40' Plug Door Boxcar	40
____ 2212	Soo Line 40' Plug Door Boxcar	40
____ 2213	Milwaukee Road 40' Plug Door Boxcar	40
____ 2215	NYC 40' Boxcar, Premium Series	43
____ 2216	BN 40' Boxcar, Premium Series	43
____ 2217	GN 40' Plug Door Boxcar	45
____ 2218	CP 40' Plug Door Boxcar	45
____ 2219	Pacific Great Eastern 40' Plug Door Boxcar	42
____ 2220	B&A 40' Boxcar, Classic Series	42
____ 2221	NP 40' Boxcar, Classic Series	42
____ 2222	Miller 40' Plug Door Boxcar	39
____ 2223	Burlington 40' Plug Door Boxcar, Classic Series	45
____ 2224	CP 40' Plug Door Boxcar, Classic Series	45
____ 2225	Frisco 40' Plug Door Boxcar, Classic Series	45
____ 2226	ADM 40' Plug Door Boxcar	39
____ 2227	State of Maine 40' Plug Door Boxcar	42
____ 2228	Reading 40' Plug Door Boxcar	43
____ 2229	Milwaukee Road 40' Plug Door Boxcar	43
____ 3200	2-bay Rib-sided Hopper	40
____ 3201	C&O 2-bay Rib-sided Hopper	40
____ 3202	WM 2-bay Rib-sided Hopper	40
____ 3203	B&O 2-bay Rib-sided Hopper	40
____ 3204	Erie 2-bay Rib-sided Hopper	40
____ 3205	N&W 2-bay Rib-sided Hopper	40
____ 3206	NYC 2-bay Rib-sided Hopper	40
____ 3206R	NYC 2-bay Rib-sided Hopper, red	40
____ 3207	PRR 2-bay Rib-sided Hopper	40
____ 3208	Peabody 2-bay Rib-sided Hopper	40
____ 3209	Southern 2-bay Rib-sided Hopper	40
____ 3211	SP 2-bay Rib-sided Hopper	40
____ 3213	Virginia 2-bay Rib-sided Hopper	40
____ 3214	Reading 2-bay Rib-sided Hopper	40
____ 3215	CB&Q 2-bay Rib-sided Hopper	40
____ 3216	LV 2-bay Rib-sided Hopper	40
____ 3217	Interstate RR 2-bay Rib-sided Hopper	40
____ 3218	Burlington 2-bay Rib-sided Hopper	40
____ 3218	D&RGW 2-bay Rib-sided Hopper	40
____ 3219	NH 2-bay Rib-sided Hopper	40

3220	Texas & Pacific 2-bay Offset-sided Hopper	40 ____
3250	2-bay Offset-sided Hopper	40 ____
3251	ATSF 2-bay Offset-sided Hopper	40 ____
3252	CP 2-bay Offset-sided Hopper	40 ____
3253	GN 2-bay Offset-sided Hopper	40 ____
3254	NP 2-bay Offset-sided Hopper	40 ____
3255	IC 2-bay Offset-sided Hopper	40 ____
3256	NYC 2-bay Offset-sided Hopper	40 ____
3257	L&N 2-bay Offset-sided Hopper	40 ____
3258	MILW 2-bay Offset-sided Hopper	40 ____
3259	UP 2-bay Offset-sided Hopper	40 ____
3260	Frisco 2-bay Offset-sided Hopper	40 ____
3261	LNE 2-bay Offset-sided Hopper	40 ____
3262	D&H 2-bay Offset-sided Hopper	40 ____
3263	NKP 2-bay Offset-sided Hopper	40 ____
3264	MP 2-bay Offset-sided Hopper	40 ____
3265	Conrail 2-bay Offset-sided Hopper	40 ____
3266	C&NW 2-bay Offset-sided Hopper	40 ____
3267	Monon 2-bay Offset-sided Hopper	40 ____
3268	B&O 2-bay Offset-sided Hopper	40 ____
3269	ACL 2-bay Offset-sided Hopper	40 ____
3270	GM&O 2-bay Offset-sided Hopper	40 ____
3271	Reading 2-bay Offset-sided Hopper	40 ____
3272	Southern 2-bay Offset-sided Hopper	40 ____
3273	Reading Blue Coal 2-bay Offset-sided Hopper	40 ____
3274	Rock Island 2-bay Offset-sided Hopper	40 ____
3275	CNJ 2-bay Offset-sided Hopper	40 ____
3276	C&O 2-bay Offset-sided Hopper	40 ____
3300	PS-2 CD 3-bay Hopper	50 ____
3301	ADM PS-2 CD 3-bay Hopper	50 ____
3302	BN PS-2 CD 3-bay Hopper	50 ____
3303	Cargill PS-2 CD 3-bay Hopper	50 ____
3304	C&NW PS-2 CD 3-bay Hopper	50 ____
3305	Conrail PS-2 CD 3-bay Hopper	50 ____
3306	GN PS-2 CD 3-bay Hopper	50 ____
3307	IC PS-2 CD 3-bay Hopper	50 ____
3308	PRR PS-2 CD 3-bay Hopper	50 ____
3309	Pillsbury PS-2 CD 3-bay Hopper	50 ____
3310	D&RGW PS-2 CD 3-bay Hopper	50 ____
3311	The Rock PS-2 CD 3-bay Hopper	50 ____
3312	ATSF PS-2 CD 3-bay Hopper	50 ____
3313	UP PS-2 CD 3-bay Hopper	50 ____
3351	Santa Fe 3-bay Offset-sided Hopper	43 ____
3352	Burlington 3-bay Offset-sided Hopper	43 ____
3353	B&M 3-bay Offset-sided Hopper	43 ____
3354	B&LE 3-bay Offset-sided Hopper	43 ____

____ 3357	C&NW 3-bay Offset-sided Hopper	43
____ 3358	C&O 3-bay Offset-sided Hopper	43
____ 3359	CN 3-bay Offset-sided Hopper	43
____ 3360	CP 3-bay Offset-sided Hopper	43
____ 3362	Erie 3-bay Offset-sided Hopper	43
____ 3364	GTW 3-bay Offset-sided Hopper	43
____ 3365	IC 3-bay Offset-sided Hopper, orange	43
____ 3366	IC 3-bay Offset-sided Hopper	43
____ 3367	MP 3-bay Offset-sided Hopper	43
____ 3368	B&O 3-bay Offset-sided Hopper	43
____ 3369	NYC 3-bay Offset-sided Hopper	43
____ 3370	NKP 3-bay Offset-sided Hopper	43
____ 3371	P&LE 3-bay Offset-sided Hopper	43
____ 3372	Peabody 3-bay Offset-sided Hopper	43
____ 3373	Reading Blue Coal 3-bay Offset-sided Hopper	43
____ 3375	Rock Island 3-bay Offset-sided Hopper	43
____ 3377	Southern 3-bay Offset-sided Hopper	43
____ 3378	SP 3-bay Offset-sided Hopper	43
____ 3379	UP 3-bay Offset-sided Hopper	43
____ 3400	4-bay Offset-sided Hopper	40
____ 3401	B&O 4-bay Offset-sided Hopper	40
____ 3402	C&O 4-bay Offset-sided Hopper	40
____ 3403	IC 4-bay Offset-sided Hopper	40
____ 3404	NH 4-bay Offset-sided Hopper	40
____ 3405	MP 4-bay Offset-sided Hopper	40
____ 3406	Peabody Coal 4-bay Offset-sided Hopper	40
____ 3407	Rock Island 4-bay Offset-sided Hopper	40
____ 3408	ATSF 4-bay Offset-sided Hopper	40
____ 3409	WM 4-bay Offset-sided Hopper	40
____ 3410	NYC 4-bay Offset-sided Hopper	40
____ 3411	NP 4-bay Offset-sided Hopper	40
____ 3412	MKT 4-bay Offset-sided Hopper	40
____ 3414	Reading Blue Coal 4-bay Offset-sided Hopper	40
____ 3415	B&M 4-bay Offset-sided Hopper	40
____ 3451	BN 4-bay Rib-sided Hopper	40
____ 3452	CB&Q 4-bay Rib-sided Hopper	40
____ 3453	C&NW 4-bay Rib-sided Hopper	40
____ 3454	Conrail 4-bay Rib-sided Hopper	40
____ 3455	CSX 4-bay Rib-sided Hopper	40
____ 3456	D&RGW 4-bay Rib-sided Hopper	40
____ 3457	GN 4-bay Rib-sided Hopper	40
____ 3458B	GN 4-bay Rib-sided Hopper	40
____ 3458C	PRR 4-bay Rib-sided Hopper, brown	40
____ 3458R	PRR 4-bay Rib-sided Hopper	40
____ 3459	UP 4-bay Rib-sided Hopper	40
____ 3460	SP 4-bay Rib-sided Hopper	40

		Retail	
3461	Virginian 4-bay Rib-sided Hopper	40	____
3463	LV 4-bay Rib-sided Hopper	40	____
4400	Gondola	40	____
4401	Frisco Gondola	40	____
4402	Wabash Gondola	40	____
4403	Southern Gondola	40	____
4404	PRR Gondola	40	____
4405	GN Gondola	40	____
4406	LV Gondola	40	____
4407	B&O Gondola	40	____
4408	C&O Gondola	40	____
4409	Milwaukee Road Gondola	40	____
4410	SP Gondola	40	____
4411	WM Gondola	40	____
4412	Soo Line Gondola	40	____
4413	Lackawanna Gondola	40	____
4414	IC Gondola	40	____
4415	NYC Gondola	40	____
4416	NKP Gondola	40	____
4417	N&W Gondola	40	____
4418	UP Gondola	40	____
4419	ATSF Gondola	40	____
4420	BN Gondola	40	____
4421	CP Gondola	40	____
4422	NP Gondola	40	____
4423	D&H Gondola	40	____
4424	Reading Gondola	40	____
4425	D&RGW Gondola	40	____
4426	C&NW Gondola	40	____
4427	Conrail Gondola	40	____
4428	MP Gondola	40	____
4429	CB&Q Gondola	40	____
4430	NH Gondola	40	____
4430B	NH Gondola, black	40	____
4431	P&LE Gondola	40	____
4432	Rock Island Gondola	40	____
4433	NS Gondola, black	40	____
4433R	NS Gondola, red	40	____
4434	Virginian Gondola	40	____
4435	IC Gondola	40	____
4436G	MKT Gondola, green	40	____
4436R	MKT Gondola, red	40	____
4437	Texas& Pacific Gondola	40	____
4599	Chevron Tank Car (TCA)	90	____
6000	USRA 46' Flatcar	44	____
6001	B&O USRA 46' Flatcar	44	____

_____	6002	Burlington USRA 46' Flatcar	44
_____	6003	BN USRA 46' Flatcar	44
_____	6004	Conrail USRA 46' Flatcar	44
_____	6005	C&NW USRA 46' Flatcar	44
_____	6006	C&O USRA 46' Flatcar	44
_____	6007	CSX USRA 46' Flatcar	44
_____	6008	CP USRA 46' Flatcar	44
_____	6009	D&RGW USRA 46' Flatcar	44
_____	6010	GN USRA 46' Flatcar	44
_____	6011	IC USRA 46' Flatcar	44
_____	6012	NH USRA 46' Flatcar	44
_____	6013	NYC USRA 46' Flatcar	44
_____	6014	NP USRA 46' Flatcar	44
_____	6015	N&W USRA 46' Flatcar	44
_____	6016	MP USRA 46' Flatcar	44
_____	6017	PRR USRA 46' Flatcar	44
_____	6018	ATSF USRA 46' Flatcar	44
_____	6019	Southern USRA 46' Flatcar	44
_____	6020	SP USRA 46' Flatcar	44
_____	6021	UP USRA 46' Flatcar	44
_____	6022	Frisco USRA 46' Flatcar	44
_____	6023	Milwaukee Road USRA 46' Flatcar	44
_____	6024	Rock Island USRA 46' Flatcar	44
_____	6025	B&M USRA 46' Flatcar	44
_____	6026	MKT USRA 46' Flatcar	44
_____	6027	Texas & Pacific USRA 46' Flatcar	44
_____	7500	Wood-sided Caboose	55
_____	7501	ATSF Wood-sided Caboose	55
_____	7502	ACL Wood-sided Caboose	55
_____	7503	B&O Wood-sided Caboose	55
_____	7504	CP Wood-sided Caboose	55
_____	7505	CB&Q Wood-sided Caboose	55
_____	7506	C&O Wood-sided Caboose	55
_____	7507	C&NW Wood-sided Caboose	55
_____	7508	D&RGW Wood-sided Caboose	55
_____	7509	Erie Wood-sided Caboose	55
_____	7510	Frisco Wood-sided Caboose	55
_____	7511	GN Wood-sided Caboose	55
_____	7512	GM&O Wood-sided Caboose	55
_____	7513	IC Wood-sided Caboose	55
_____	7514	Lackawanna Wood-sided Caboose	55
_____	7515	Milwaukee Road Wood-sided Caboose	55
_____	7516	MP Wood-sided Caboose	55
_____	7517	NH Wood-sided Caboose	55
_____	7518	NYC Wood-sided Caboose	55
_____	7519	N&W Wood-sided Caboose	55

Retail

7520	NP Wood-sided Caboose	55 ____
7521	PRR Wood-sided Caboose	55 ____
7522	Rock Island Wood-sided Caboose	55 ____
7523	Southern Wood-sided Caboose	55 ____
7524	SP Wood-sided Caboose	55 ____
7525	UP Wood-sided Caboose	55 ____
7526	Rio Grande 4-stripe Wood-sided Caboose	55 ____
7527	NYC Pacemaker Wood-sided Caboose	55 ____
7528	Pere Marquette Wood-sided Caboose	55 ____
7529	LV Wood-sided Caboose	55 ____
7530	Cotton Belt Wood-sided Caboose	55 ____
7531	WM Wood-sided Caboose	55 ____
7532	MKT Wood-sided Caboose	55 ____
7533	Texas & Pacific Wood-sided Caboose	55 ____
7700	Bay Window Caboose	45 ____
7701	Chessie Bay Window Caboose	45 ____
7702	Erie Bay Window Caboose	45 ____
7703	Erie-Lackawanna Bay Window Caboose, red	45 ____
7704	Conrail Bay Window Caboose	45 ____
7705	C&NW Bay Window Caboose	45 ____
7706	Southern Bay Window Caboose	45 ____
7707	NYC Bay Window Caboose	45 ____
7708	PRR Bay Window Caboose	45 ____
7709	Norfolk & Western Bay Window Caboose	45 ____
7710	ATSF Bay Window Caboose	45 ____
7711	SP Bay Window Caboose	45 ____
7712	GN Bay Window Caboose	45 ____
7713	NP Bay Window Caboose	45 ____
7714	UP Bay Window Caboose	45 ____
7715	NH Bay Window Caboose	45 ____
7716	CP Bay Window Caboose	45 ____
7717	Virginian Bay Window Caboose, Premium	50 ____
7718	Erie-Lack. Bay Window Caboose, Premium	50 ____
7719	BN Bay Window Caboose	45 ____
7720	Burlington Bay Window Caboose,Premium	50 ____
7721	Milwaukee Road Bay Window Caboose	45 ____
7722	Frisco Bay Window Caboose, Premium	50 ____
7723	MP Bay Window Caboose	45 ____
7724	CSX Bay Window Caboose	45 ____
7725	NYC Bay Window Caboose	45 ____
7726	SP Bay Window Caboose	45 ____
7728	Virginian Bay Window Caboose	45 ____
7729	CNJ Bay Window Caboose	45 ____
7730	Wabash Bay Window Caboose	45 ____
7731	WP Bay Window Caboose	45 ____

___	**46000-UndecAC**	USRA 4-6-2 Pacific Locomotive, full sound	426
___	**46000-UndecHR**	USRA 4-6-2 Pacific, hi-rail	380
___	**46000-UndecL**	USRA 4-6-2 Pacific, limited sound	400
___	**46000-UndecS**	USRA 4-6-2 Pacific, scale	380
___	**46000-ATSFAC**	ATSF 4-6-2 Pacific Locomotive, full sound	426
___	**46000-ATSFHR**	ATSF 4-6-2 Pacific, hi-rail	380
___	**46000-ATSFL**	ATSF 4-6-2 Pacific, limited sound	400
___	**46000-ATSFS**	ATSF 4-6-2 Pacific, scale	380
___	**46000-CBQAC**	CB&Q 4-6-2 Pacific Locomotive, full sound	426
___	**46000-CBQHR**	CB&Q 4-6-2 Pacific Locomotive, hi-rail	380
___	**46000-CBQL**	CB&Q 4-6-2 Pacific, limited sound	400
___	**46000-CBQS**	CB&Q 4-6-2 Pacific, scale	380
___	**46000-GNAC**	GN 4-6-2 Pacific Locomotive, full sound	426
___	**46000-GNHR**	GN 4-6-2 Pacific, hi-rail	380
___	**46000-GNL**	GN 4-6-2 Pacific, limited sound	400
___	**46000-GNS**	GN 4-6-2 Pacific, scale	380
___	**46000-KATYAC**	MKT 4-6-2 Pacific Locomotive, full sound	426
___	**46000-KATYHR**	MKT 4-6-2 Pacific, hi-rail	380
___	**46000-KATYL**	MKT 4-6-2 Pacific, limited sound	400
___	**46000-KATYS**	MKT 4-6-2 Pacific, scale	380
___	**46000-NHAC**	NH 4-6-2 Pacific Locomotive, full sound	426
___	**46000-NHHR**	NH 4-6-2 Pacific, hi-rail	380
___	**46000-NHL**	NH 4-6-2 Pacific, limited sound	400
___	**46000-NHS**	NH 4-6-2 Pacific, scale	380
___	**46000-NYCAC**	NYC 4-6-2 Pacific Locomotive, full sound	426
___	**46000-NYCHR**	NYC 4-6-2 Pacific, hi-rail	380
___	**46000-NYCL**	NYC 4-6-2 Pacific, limited sound	400
___	**46000-NYCS**	NYC 4-6-2 Pacific, scale	380
___	**46000-PMAC**	Pere Marquette 4-6-2 Pacific Locomotive, full sound	426
___	**46000-PMHR**	Pere Marquette 4-6-2 Pacific, hi-rail	380
___	**46000-PML**	Pere Marquette 4-6-2 Pacific, limited sound	400
___	**46000-PMS**	Pere Marquette 4-6-2 Pacific, scale	380
___	**46000-PRRAC**	PRR 4-6-2 Pacific Locomotive, full sound	426
___	**46000-PRRHR**	PRR 4-6-2 Pacific, hi-rail	380
___	**46000-PRRL**	PRR 4-6-2 Pacific, limited sound	400
___	**46000-PRRS**	PRR 4-6-2 Pacific, scale	380
___	**46000-SPAC**	SP 4-6-2 Pacific Locomotive, full sound	426
___	**46000-SPHR**	SP 4-6-2 Pacific, hi-rail	380
___	**46000-SPL**	SP 4-6-2 Pacific, limited sound	400
___	**46000-SPS**	SP 4-6-2 Pacific, scale	380
___	**46000-UPAC**	UP 4-6-2 Pacific Locomotive, full sound	426
___	**46000-UPHR**	UP 4-6-2 Pacific, hi-rail	380
___	**46000-UPL**	UP 4-6-2 Pacific, limited sound	400
___	**46000-UPS**	UP 4-6-2 Pacific, scale	380
___	**46001**	B&O USRA 4-6-2 Locomotive	350

46003AC	MILW 4-6-2 Pacific Locomotive, full sound	426 ____
46003HR	MILW 4-6-2 Pacific, hi-rail	380 ____
46003L	MILW 4-6-2 Pacific, limited sound	400 ____
46003S	MILW 4-6-2 Pacific, scale	380 ____
46006AC	Southern 4-6-2 Pacific Locomotive, full sound	426 ____
46006HR	Southern 4-6-2 Pacific, hi-rail	380 ____
46006L	Southern 4-6-2 Pacific, limited sound	400 ____
46006S	Southern 4-6-2 Pacific, scale	380 ____
46007AC	Rock Island 4-6-2 Pacific Locomotive, full sound	426 ____
46007HR	Rock Island 4-6-2 Pacific, hi-rail	380 ____
46007L	Rock Island 4-6-2 Pacific, limited sound	400 ____
46007S	Rock Island 4-6-2 Pacific, scale	380 ____
46200AC	LV 4-6-2 Pacific Locomotive, full sound	426 ____
46200HR	LV 4-6-2 Pacific, hi-rail	380 ____
46200L	LV 4-6-2 Pacific, limited sound	400 ____
46200S	LV 4-6-2 Pacific, scale	380 ____
46500	USRA 4-6-2 Locomotive	620 ____
46500AC	4-6-2 Pacific Steam Passenger Set	700 ____
46500HR	4-6-2 Pacific Steam Passenger Set, hi-rail	620 ____
46500S	4-6-2 Pacific Steam Passenger Set, scale	620 ____
46501	B&O USRA 4-6-2 Locomotive	620 ____
46502	Southern USRA 4-6-2 Locomotive	620 ____
46502AC	Southern 4-6-2 Pacific Steam Passenger Set	700 ____
46502HR	Southern 4-6-2 Pacific Steam Passenger Set, hi-rail	620 ____
46502S	Southern 4-6-2 Pacific Steam Passenger Set, scale	620 ____
46503AC	MILW 4-6-2 Pacific Steam Passenger Set	660 ____
46503HR	MILW 4-6-2 Pacific Steam Passenger Set, hi-rail	600 ____
46503S	MILW 4-6-2 Pacific Steam Passenger Set, scale	600 ____
46504AC	NH 4-6-2 Pacific Steam Passenger Set	700 ____
46504HR	NH 4-6-2 Pacific Steam Passenger Set, hi-rail	620 ____
46504S	NH 4-6-2 Pacific Steam Passenger Set, scale	620 ____
48400	4-8-4 Northern Locomotive	500 ____
48400-6	4-8-4 Northern Locomotive, coal tender	500 ____
48401	Santa Fe 4-8-4 Northern Locomotive	500 ____
48402	Rock Island 4-8-4 Northern Locomotive	500 ____
48403	LV 4-8-4 Northern Locomotive	500 ____
48404	CB&Q 4-8-4 Northern Locomotive	500 ____
48405	WM 4-8-4 Northern Locomotive	500 ____
48406	Cotton Belt 4-8-4 Northern Locomotive	500 ____
48407	SP 4-8-4 Northern Locomotive	500 ____
48408	C&O 4-8-4 Northern Locomotive	500 ____
48409	Lackawanna 4-8-4 Northern Locomotive	500 ____
48410	MILW 4-8-4 Northern Locomotive	500 ____

			Retail
____	**95247**	CB&Q USRA 46' Flatcar with Burlington trailer (S Fest)	90
____	**547798**	C&NW 4-bay Hopper (TCA)	85
____	**BD8RPO**	Budd Railway Post Office Car	60
____	**BD8200**	Budd Coach, silver	90
____	**BD8200C**	Budd Coach, chrome	90
____	**BD8201**	B&O Budd Coach	90
____	**BD8202**	Southern Budd Coach	90
____	**BD8203**	UP Budd Coach	90
____	**BD8204**	New Haven Budd Coach	90
____	**BD8205**	NYC Budd Coach	90
____	**BD8206**	ATSF Budd Coach	90
____	**BD8209**	PRR Budd Coach	90
____	**BD8214**	ACL Budd Coach	90
____	**BD8215**	Burlington Budd Coach	90
____	**BD8216**	Rock Island Budd Coach	90
____	**BD8217**	IC Budd Coach	90
____	**BD8218**	Central of Georgia Budd Coach	90
____	**BD8223**	MP Colorado Eagle Budd Coach	90
____	**BD8224**	SP Budd Coach	90
____	**BD8225**	Texas Special Budd Coach	90
____	**BDBS00**	Budd 4-Car Set, silver	340
____	**BDBS00C**	Budd 4-Car Set, chrome	340
____	**BDBS01**	B&O Budd 4-Car Set	340
____	**BDBS02**	Southern Budd 4-Car Set	340
____	**BDBS03**	UP Budd 4-Car Set	340
____	**BDBS04**	New Haven Budd 4-Car Set	340
____	**BDBS05**	NYC 4-Car Budd Set	340
____	**BDBS06**	ATSF Budd 4-Car Set	340
____	**BDBS09**	PRR Budd 4-Car Set	340
____	**BDBS14**	ACL Budd 4-Car Set	340
____	**BDBS15**	Burlington Budd 4-Car Set	340
____	**BDBS16**	Rock Island Budd 4-Car Set	340
____	**BDBS17**	IC Budd 4-Car Set	340
____	**BDBS18**	Central of Georgia Budd 4-Car Set	340
____	**BDBS23**	MP Colorado Eagle Budd 4-Car Set	340
____	**BDBS24**	SP Budd 4-Car Set	340
____	**BSSC1**	Conrail Trailer Hauler Freight Set	300
____	**BSSC4**	SP Trailer Hauler Freight Set	300
____	**CB208S**	Ground Throw	5
____	**DXF211AB**	B&O FA Diesel AB Set, sound	370
____	**DXF211ABA**	B&O FA Diesel ABA Set, sound	500
____	**DXF211ABPW**	B&O FA Diesel AB Set, powered B Unit	370
____	**DXF214AB**	RI FA Diesel AB Set, sound	370
____	**DXF214ABA**	RI FA Diesel ABA Set, sound	500
____	**DXF214ABPW**	RI FA Diesel AB Set, powered B Unit	370

Retail

DXF710AB	ACL FP7 Diesel AB Set, sound	370 ____
DXF710ABA	ACL FP7 Diesel AB Set, sound	500 ____
DXF710ABPW	ACL FP7 Diesel AB Set, powered B Unit	370 ____
DXF711AB	B&O FP7 Diesel AB Set, sound	370 ____
DXF711ABA	B&O FP7 Diesel ABA Set, sound	500 ____
DXF711ABPW	B&O FP7 Diesel AB Set, powered B Unit	370 ____
DXF712AB	C&O FP7 Diesel AB Set, sound	370 ____
DXF712ABA	C&O FP7 Diesel ABA Set, sound	500 ____
DXF712ABPW	C&O FP7 Diesel AB Set, powered B Unit	370 ____
DXF713AB	D&RGW FP7 Diesel AB Set, sound	370 ____
DXF713ABA	D&RGW FP7 Diesel ABA Set, sound	500 ____
DXF713ABPW	D&RGW FP7 Diesel AB Set, powered B Unit	370 ____
DXF714AB	RI FP7 Diesel AB Set, sound	370 ____
DXF714ABA	RI FP7 Diesel ABA Set, sound	500 ____
DXF714ABPW	RI FP7 Diesel AB Set, powered B Unit	370 ____
DXF715AB	Southern FP7 Diesel AB Set, sound	500 ____
DXF715ABA	Southern FP7 Diesel ABA Set, sound	370 ____
DXFA2011	B&O FA Diesel A Unit	250 ____
DXFA2014	Rock Island FA Diesel A Unit	250 ____
DXFA211DNS	B&O FA Diesel B Unit, sound	250 ____
DXFB211PW	B&O FA Diesel B Unit, powered	250 ____
DXFB214PW	Rock Island B Unit, powered	250 ____
DXFB214SND	Rock Island B Unit, sound	250 ____
DXFB710PW	ACL FP7 Diesel B Unit, powered	250 ____
DXFB711PW	B&O FP7 Diesel B Unit, powered	250 ____
DXFB711SND	B&O FP7 Diesel B Unit, sound	250 ____
DXFB712PW	C&O FP7 Diesel B Unit, powered	250 ____
DXFB712SND	C&O FP7 Diesel B Unit, sound	250 ____
DXFB713PW	D&RGW FP7 Diesel B Unit, powered	250 ____
DXFB713SND	D&RGW FP7 Diesel B Unit, sound	250 ____
DXFB714	Rock Island FP7 Diesel A Unit	250 ____
DXFB714PW	Rock Island FP7 Diesel B unit, powered	250 ____
DXFB714SND	Rock Island FP7 Diesel B Unit, sound	250 ____
DXFB715PW	Southern FP7 Diesel B Unit, powered	250 ____
DXFB715SND	Southern FP7 Diesel B Unit, sound	250 ____
DXFP7010	ACL FP7 Diesel A Unit	250 ____
DXFP7011	B&O FP7 Diesel A Unit	250 ____
DXFP7012	C&O FP7 Diesel A Unit	250 ____
DXFP7013	D&RGW FP7 Diesel A Unit	250 ____
DXFP715	Southern FP7 Diesel A Unit	250 ____
DXFP7B710SND	ACL FP7 Diesel B Unit, sound	250 ____
E800	E8 Diesel, DC scale or hi-rail	250 ____
E800AA	E8 Diesel AA Set, DC scale or hi-rail	470 ____
E803	NYC E8 Diesel, DC scale or hi-rail	250 ____
E803AA	NYC E8 Diesel AA Set, DC scale or hi-rail	470 ____
E805	PRR E8 Diesel, DC scale or hi-rail, red	250 ____

____	**E805AA**	PRR E8 Diesel AA Set, DC scale or hi-rail, red	470
____	**E806**	PRR E8 Diesel, DC scale or hi-rail, green	250
____	**E806AA**	PRR E8 Diesel AA Set, DC scale or hi-rail, green	470
____	**E808**	UP E8 Diesel, DC scale or hi-rail	250
____	**E808AA**	UP E8 Diesel AA Set, DC scale or hi-rail	470
____	**E811**	B&O E8 Diesel, DC scale or hi-rail	250
____	**E811AA**	B&O E8 Diesel AA Set, DC scale or hi-rail	470
____	**E818**	ATSF E8 Diesel, DC scale or hi-rail	250
____	**E818AA**	ATSF E8 Diesel AA Set, DC scale or hi-rail	470
____	**E819**	Burlington E8 Diesel, DC scale or hi-rail	250
____	**E819AA**	Burlington E8 Diesel AA Set, DC scale or hi-rail	470
____	**E820**	IC E8 Diesel, DC scale or hi-rail	250
____	**E820AA**	IC E8 Diesel AA Set, DC scale or hi-rail	470
____	**E821**	Central of Georgia E8 Diesel, DC scale or hi-rail	250
____	**E821AA**	Central of Georgia E8 Diesel AA Set, DC scale or hi-rail	470
____	**E822**	Lackawanna E8 Diesel, DC scale or hi-rail	250
____	**E822AA**	Lackawanna E8 Diesel AA Set, DC scale or hi-rail	470
____	**E823**	MP E8 Diesel, DC scale or hi-rail	250
____	**E823AA**	MP E8 Diesel AA Set, DC scale or hi-rail	470
____	**E824**	SP E8 Diesel, DC scale or hi-rail	250
____	**E824AA**	SP E8 Diesel AA Set, DC scale or hi-rail	470
____	**ESE01**	Empire State Express Set	700
____	**F40PIIAC**	Amtrak F40 Diesel, phase II	210
____	**F40PIIIAC**	Amtrak F40 Diesel, phase III	210
____	**F200AB**	FA2 Diesel AB Set, sound	350
____	**F200ABA**	FA2 Diesel ABA Set, sound	500
____	**F200ABPW**	FA2 Diesel AB Set, powered	350
____	**F201AB**	CP FA2 Diesel AB Set, sound	350
____	**F201ABA**	CP FA2 Diesel ABA Set, sound	500
____	**F201ABPW**	CP FA2 Diesel AB Set, powered	350
____	**F202AB**	GN FA2 Diesel AB Set, sound	350
____	**F202ABA**	GN FA2 Diesel ABA Set, sound	500
____	**F202ABPW**	GN FA2 Diesel AB Set, powered	350
____	**F203AB**	NH FA2 Diesel AB Set, sound	350
____	**F203ABA**	NH FA2 Diesel ABA Set, sound	500
____	**F203ABPW**	NH FA2 Diesel AB Set, powered	350
____	**F204AB**	NYC FA2 Diesel AB Set, sound	350
____	**F204ABA**	NYC FA2 Diesel ABA Set, sound	500
____	**F204ABPW**	NYC FA2 Diesel AB Set, powered	350
____	**F205AB**	UP FA2 Diesel AB Set, sound	350
____	**F205ABA**	UP FA2 Diesel ABA Set, sound	500
____	**F205ABPW**	UP FA2 Diesel AB Set, powered	350
____	**F206AB**	PRR FA2 Diesel AB Set, sound	350
____	**F206ABA**	PRR FA2 Diesel ABA Set, sound	500

Retail

F206ABPW	PRR FA2 Diesel AB Set, powered	350 ____
F700AB	FP7 Diesel AB Set, sound	360 ____
F700ABA	FP7 Diesel ABA Set, sound	500 ____
F700ABPW	FP7 Diesel AB Set, powered	360 ____
F701AB	BN FP7 Diesel AB Set, sound	360 ____
F701ABA	BN FP7 Diesel ABA Set, sound	500 ____
F701ABPW	BN FP7 Diesel AB Set, powered	360 ____
F702AB	GN FP7 Diesel AB Set, sound	360 ____
F702ABA	GN FP7 Diesel ABA Set, sound	500 ____
F702ABPW	GN FP7 Diesel AB Set, powered	360 ____
F703AB	NYC FP7 Diesel AB Set, sound	360 ____
F703ABA	NYC FP7 Diesel ABA Set, sound, gray	500 ____
F703ABPW	NYC FP7 Diesel AB Set, powered, gray	360 ____
F704AB	NP FP7 Diesel AB Set, sound	360 ____
F704ABA	NP FP7 Diesel ABA Set, sound	500 ____
F704ABPW	NP FP7 Diesel AB Set, powered	360 ____
F705AB	PRR FP7 Diesel AB Set, sound	360 ____
F705ABA	PRR FP7 Diesel ABA Set, sound, red	500 ____
F705ABPW	PRR FP7 Diesel AB Set, powered, red	360 ____
F706AB	PRR FP7 Diesel AB Set, sound	360 ____
F706ABA	PRR FP7 Diesel ABA Set, sound, green	500 ____
F706ABPW	PRR FP7 Diesel AB Set, powered, green	360 ____
F707AB	SP FP7 Diesel AB Set, sound	360 ____
F707ABA	SP FP7 Diesel ABA Set, sound	500 ____
F707ABPW	SP FP7 Diesel AB Set, powered	360 ____
F708AB	UP FP7 Diesel AB Set, sound	360 ____
F708ABA	UP FP7 Diesel ABA Set, sound	500 ____
F708ABPW	UP FP7 Diesel AB Set, powered	360 ____
F709AB	NYC FP7 Diesel AB Set, sound	360 ____
F709ABA	NYC FP7 Diesel ABA Set, sound, black	500 ____
F709ABPW	NYC FP7 Diesel AB Set, powered, black	360 ____
F7B00PW	FP7 Diesel B Unit, powered	190 ____
F7B00SND	FP7 Diesel B Unit, sound	190 ____
F7B01PW	BN FP7 Diesel B Unit, powered	190 ____
F7B01SND	BN FP7 Diesel B Unit, sound	190 ____
F7B02PW	GN FP7 Diesel B Unit, powered	190 ____
F7B02SND	GN FP7 Diesel B Unit, sound	190 ____
F7B03PW	NYC FP7 Diesel B Unit, powered, gray	190 ____
F7B03SND	NYC FP7 Diesel B Unit, sound, gray	190 ____
F7B04PW	NP FP7 Diesel B Unit, powered	190 ____
F7B04SND	NP FP7 Diesel B Unit, sound	190 ____
F7B05PW	PRR FP7 Diesel B Unit, powered, red	190 ____
F7B05SND	PRR FP7 Diesel B Unit, sound, red	190 ____
F7B06PW	PRR FP7 Diesel B Unit, powered, green	190 ____
F7B06SND	PRR FP7 Diesel B Unit, sound, green	190 ____
F7B07PW	SP FP7 Diesel B Unit, powered	190 ____

	Item	Description	Retail
____	**F7B07SND**	SP FP7 Diesel B Unit, sound	190
____	**F7B08PW**	UP FP7 Diesel B Unit, powered	190
____	**F7B08SND**	UP FP7 Diesel B Unit, sound	190
____	**F7B09PW**	NYC FP7 Diesel B Unit, powered, black	190
____	**F7B09SND**	NYC FP7 Diesel B Unit, sound, black	190
____	**FA2000**	Alco FA2 Diesel	250
____	**FA2001**	CP Alco FA2 Diesel	250
____	**FA2002**	GN Alco FA2 Diesel	250
____	**FA2003**	NH Alco FA2 Diesel	250
____	**FA2004**	NYC Alco Diesel FA2	250
____	**FA2005**	UP Alco Diesel FA2	250
____	**FA2006**	PRR Alco Diesel FB2	250
____	**FB200PW**	FA2 Diesel B Unit, powered	190
____	**FB200SND**	FA2 Diesel B Unit, sound	190
____	**FB201PW**	CP FA2 Diesel B Unit, powered	190
____	**FB201SND**	CP FA2 Diesel B Unit, sound	190
____	**FB202PW**	GN FA2 Diesel B Unit, powered	190
____	**FB202SND**	GN FA2 Diesel B Unit, sound	190
____	**FB203PW**	NH FA2 Diesel B Unit, powered	190
____	**FB203SND**	NH FA2 Diesel B Unit, sound	190
____	**FB204PW**	NYC FA2 Diesel B Unit, powered	190
____	**FB204SND**	NYC FA2 Diesel B Unit, sound	190
____	**FB205PW**	UP FA2 Diesel B Unit, powered	190
____	**FB205SND**	UP FA2 Diesel B Unit, sound	190
____	**FB206PW**	PRR FA2 Diesel B Unit, powered	190
____	**FB206SND**	PRR FA2 Diesel B Unit, sound	190
____	**FB2000**	Alco FB2 Diesel	190
____	**FB2001**	CP Alco FB2 Diesel	190
____	**FB2002**	GN Alco FB2 Diesel	190
____	**FB2003**	NH Alco FB2 Diesel	190
____	**FB2004**	NYC Alco FB2 Diesel	190
____	**FB2005**	UP Alco FB2 Diesel	190
____	**FB2006**	PRR Alco FB2 Diesel	190
____	**FB7000**	FB-7 Diesel	250
____	**FB7001**	BN FB-7 Diesel	250
____	**FB7002**	GN FB-7 Diesel	250
____	**FB7003**	NYC FB-7 Diesel	250
____	**FB7004**	NP FB-7 Diesel	250
____	**FB7005**	PRR FB-7 Diesel, tuscan	250
____	**FB7006**	PRR FB-7 Diesel, green	250
____	**FB7007**	SP FB-7 Diesel	250
____	**FB7008**	UP FB-7 Diesel	250
____	**FP7000**	FP7 Diesel	250
____	**FP7001**	BN FP7 Diesel	250
____	**FP7002**	GN FP7 Diesel	250
____	**FP7003**	NYC FP7 Diesel	250

AMERICAN MODELS 1981-2017

Retail

FP7004	NP FP7 Diesel	250 ____
FP7005	PRR FP7 Diesel, tuscan	250 ____
FP7006	PRR FP7 Diesel, green	250 ____
FP7007	SP FP7 Diesel	250 ____
FP7008	UP FP7 Diesel	250 ____
GG1200	GG1 Electric Locomotive	310 ____
GG1201	PRR GG1 Electric Locomotive, green	310 ____
GG1202	PRR GG1 Electric Locomotive, tuscan	310 ____
GGCCAC	PRR Congressional GG1 Electric Locomotive, chrome	280 ____
GGCSAC	PRR Congressional GG1 Electric Locomotive, silver	280 ____
GGGIAC	PRR GG1 Electric Locomotive, green, 1-stripe	280 ____
GGGSAC	PRR GG1 Electric Locomotive, green, 5-stripe	280 ____
GGR6AC	PRR GG1 Electric Locomotive, tuscan, 5-stripe	280 ____
GGRIAC	PRR GG1 Electric Locomotive, tuscan, 1-stripe	280 ____
GP9000AC	GP9 Diesel	210 ____
GP9001AC	Conrail GP9 Diesel	210 ____
GP9002AC	Erie-Lackawanna GP9 Diesel	210 ____
GP9003AC	NH GP9 Diesel	210 ____
GP9004AC	NYC GP18 Diesel	210 ____
GP9005AC	N&W GP9 Diesel	210 ____
GP9006AC	PRR GP9 Diesel	210 ____
GP9007AC	ATSF GP9 Diesel	210 ____
GP9008AC	SP GP9 Diesel	210 ____
GP9009AC	UP GP9 Diesel	210 ____
GP9010AC	C&O GP9 Diesel	210 ____
GP35000AC	GP35 Diesel	210 ____
GP35001AC	C&O GP35 Diesel	210 ____
GP35002AC	C&NW GP35 Diesel	210 ____
GP35003AC	Conrail GP35 Diesel	210 ____
GP35004AC	Erie-Lackawanna GP35 Diesel	210 ____
GP35005AC	GN GP35 Diesel	210 ____
GP35006AC	MP GP35 Diesel	210 ____
GP35007AC	NYC GP35 Diesel	210 ____
GP35008AC	PRR GP35 Diesel	210 ____
GP35010AC	SP GP35 Diesel	210 ____
GP35011AC	UP GP35 Diesel	210 ____
GP35012AC	BN GP35 Diesel	210 ____
GP35013AC	CSX GP35 Diesel	210 ____
GP35014AC	ATSF GP35 Diesel, warbonnet	210 ____
GP35015AC	Soo Line GP35 Diesel	210 ____
GP35016AC	D&RGW GP35 Diesel	210 ____
GP35017AC	Ann Arbor GP35 Diesel	210 ____
HA8000	80' Passenger Lightweight Set	250 ____
HA8001	GN 80' Passenger Lightweight Set	250 ____

____ **HA8002**	NP 80' Passenger Lightweight Set	250
____ **HA8003**	NYC 80' Passenger Lightweight Set	250
____ **HA8004**	PRR 80' Passenger Lightweight Set	250
____ **HA8006**	UP 80' Passenger Lightweight Set	250
____ **HA8100**	Baggage-Dormitory Car	45
____ **HA8101**	NP Baggage-Dormitory Car	45
____ **HA8103**	NYC Baggage-Dormitory Car	45
____ **HA8104**	PRR Baggage-Dormitory Car	45
____ **HA8106**	UP Baggage-Dormitory Car	45
____ **HA8111**	GN Baggage-Dormitory Car	45
____ **HA8200**	60-seat Coach	45
____ **HA8201**	NP 60-seat Coach	45
____ **HA8203**	NYC 60-seat Coach	45
____ **HA8204**	PRR 60-seat Coach	45
____ **HA8206**	UP 60-seat Coach	45
____ **HA8211**	GN 60-seat Coach	45
____ **HA8300**	Vista Dome Car	45
____ **HA8301**	NP Vista Dome Car	45
____ **HA8303**	NYC Vista Dome Car	45
____ **HA8304**	PRR Vista Dome Car	45
____ **HA8306**	UP Vista Dome Car	45
____ **HA8311**	GN Vista Dome Car	45
____ **HA8400**	4-16 Duplex Sleeper Car	45
____ **HA8401**	NP 4-16 Duplex Sleeper Car	45
____ **HA8403**	NYC 4-16 Duplex Sleeper Car	45
____ **HA8404**	PRR 4-16 Duplex Sleeper Car	45
____ **HA8406**	UP 4-16 Duplex Sleeper Car	45
____ **HA8411**	GN 4-16 Duplex Sleeper Car	45
____ **HA8500**	Observation Lounge Car	45
____ **HA8501**	NP Observation Lounge Car	45
____ **HA8503**	NYC Observation Lounge Car	45
____ **HA8504**	PRR Observation Lounge Car	45
____ **HA8506**	UP Observation Lounge Car	45
____ **HA8511**	GN Observation Lounge Car	45
____ **HW8000**	72' Heavyweight Passenger Set	330
____ **HW8001**	C&NW 72' Heavyweight Passenger Set	330
____ **HW8002**	Southern Crescent 72' Heavyweight Passenger Set	330
____ **HW8003**	UP 72' Heavyweight Passenger Set	330
____ **HW8004**	NH 72' Heavyweight Passenger Set	330
____ **HW8005**	NYC 72' Heavyweight Passenger Set	330
____ **HW8006**	ATSF 72' Heavyweight Passenger Set	330
____ **HW8007**	D&RGW 72' Heavyweight Passenger Set	330
____ **HW8008**	C&NW 72' Heavyweight Passenger Set	330
____ **HW8009**	PRR 72' Heavyweight Passenger Set	290
____ **HW8010**	PRR 72' Heavyweight Passenger Set	330

		Retail	
HW8011	MILW 72' Heavyweight Passenger Set	330	____
HW8012	SP 72' Heavyweight Passenger Set	330	____
HW8013	Heavyweight Passenger Set, Pullman green, no lettering	330	____
HW8014	Heavyweight Passenger Set, Pullman green, green roof	330	____
HW8015	SP 72' Heavyweight Passenger Set, gray	330	____
HW8016	C&O 72' Heavyweight Passenger Set	330	____
HW8017	CNJ 72' Heavyweight Passenger Set	330	____
HW8018	NH 72' Heavyweight Passenger Set	330	____
HW8019	Lackawanna 72' Heavyweight Passenger Set	330	____
HW8020	MKT 72' Heavyweight Passenger Set	330	____
HW8200	Heavyweight Coach	70	____
HW8201	C&NW Heavyweight Coach	70	____
HW8202	Southern Crescent Heavyweight Coach	70	____
HW8203	UP Heavyweight Coach	70	____
HW8204	NH Heavyweight Coach	70	____
HW8205	NYC Heavyweight Coach	70	____
HW8206	ATSF Heavyweight Coach	70	____
HW8207	D&RGW Heavyweight Coach	70	____
HW8208	C&NW Heavyweight Coach	70	____
HW8209	PRR Heavyweight Coach	70	____
HW8210	PRR Pullman Heavyweight Coach	70	____
HW8211	MILW Heavyweight Coach	70	____
HW8212	SP Heavyweight Coach	70	____
HW8213	Heavyweight Pullman, black roof	70	____
HW8215	SP Heavyweight Passenger Coach, gray	70	____
HW8216	C&O Heavyweight Passenger Coach	70	____
HW8217	CNJ Heavyweight Coach	70	____
HW8218	NH Heavyweight Coach	70	____
HW8220	MKT Heavyweight Coach	70	____
HX8100	80' Pullman Heavyweight 12-1 Sleeper Car	70	____
HX8200	80' Pullman Heavyweight 10-1 Sleeper Car	70	____
HX8300	80' Pullman Heavyweight Cafe	70	____
HX8301	80' Pullman Heavyweight Cafe	70	____
HX8302	NYC 80' Pullman Heavyweight Cafe	70	____
HX8303	PRR 80' Pullman Heavyweight Cafe	70	____
HX8304	CN 80' Pullman Heavyweight Cafe	70	____
J3a	NYC J3a Class Hudson 4-6-4 Locomotive, tender	360	____
K46201	PRR K4 4-6-2 Torpedo Locomotive, DC, bronze	400	____
K46201AC	PRR K4 4-6-2 Torpedo Locomotive, AC, bronze	400	____
K46202	PRR K4 4-6-2 Torpedo Locomotive, DC, green	400	____
K46202AC	PRR K4 4-6-2 Torpedo Locomotive, AC, green	400	____
PABA400	Alco PA1 Diesel ABA Set	565	____
PABA401	PRR Alco PA1 Diesel ABA Set, freight scheme, green	565	____

	PABA402	ATSF Alco PA1 Diesel ABA Set, warbonnet, tuscan	565
____	**PABA403**	NYC Alco PA1 Diesel ABA Set	565
____	**PABA404**	NYC Alco PA2 Diesel ABA Set	565
____	**PABA405**	NYC System Alco PA1 Diesel ABA Set	565
____	**PABA406**	D&RGW Alco PA1 Diesel ABA Set	565
	PABA407	NH Alco PA1 Diesel ABA Set, McGuiness scheme	565
____	**PABA408**	UP Alco PA1 Diesel ABA Set	565
	PABA409	ATSF Alco PA1 Diesel ABA Set, warbonnet scheme	565
____	**PABA410**	ATSF Alco PA1 Diesel ABA Set, freight scheme	565
____	**PABA411**	D&H Alco PA1 Diesel ABA Set	565
____	**PABA412**	SP Daylight Alco PA1 Diesel ABA Set	585
____	**RS3000**	Alco RS3 Diesel	210
____	**RS3001**	Conrail Alco RS3 Diesel	210
____	**RS3002**	Cotton Belt Alco RS3 Diesel	210
____	**RS3003**	Erie-Lackawanna Alco RS3 Diesel	210
____	**RS3004**	GN Alco RS3 Diesel	210
____	**RS3005**	NH Alco RS3 Diesel	210
____	**RS3006**	NYC Alco RS3 Diesel	210
____	**RS3007**	PRR Alco RS3 Diesel	210
____	**RS3014**	Rock Island RS3 Diesel	210
____	**S1200**	Baldwin S12 Diesel	170
____	**S1201**	NH Baldwin S12 Diesel	170
____	**S1202**	C&NW Baldwin S12 Diesel	170
____	**S1203**	Conrail Baldwin S12 Diesel	170
____	**S1204**	Erie-Lackawanna Baldwin S12 Diesel	170
____	**S1205**	Erie-Lackawanna Baldwin S12 Diesel	170
____	**S1206**	Southern Baldwin S12 Diesel	180
____	**S1207**	NYC Baldwin S12 Diesel	170
____	**S1208**	PRR Baldwin S12 Diesel	170
____	**S1209**	ATSF Baldwin S12 Diesel	170
____	**S1210**	SP Baldwin S12 Diesel	170
____	**S1211**	UP Baldwin S12 Diesel	170
____	**S1212**	D&RGW Baldwin S12 Diesel	170
____	**S1213**	D&RGW Baldwin S12 Diesel	170
____	**S1214**	CB&Q Baldwin S12 Diesel	180
____	**S1215**	BN Baldwin S12 Diesel	170
____	**S1216**	BN Baldwin S12 Diesel	170
____	**S1217**	BN Baldwin S12 Diesel	170
____	**S1218**	BN Baldwin S12 Diesel	170
____	**S1219**	B&O Baldwin S12 Diesel	170
____	**S1220**	IC Baldwin S12 Diesel	170
____	**S1221**	IC Baldwin S12 Diesel	170
____	**S1222**	CP Baldwin S12 Diesel	170
____	**S1223**	CP Baldwin S12 Diesel	170

AMERICAN MODELS 1981-2017

Retail

S1224	SP Baldwin S12 Diesel	170 ____
SC65T	Trailer Train 5-Unit Spine Set	160 ____
SD60EMD	SD60 Diesel, long nose	250 ____
SD60EMDAA	SD60 Diesel AA Set, long nose	450 ____
SD6000	SD60 Diesel, long nose	250 ____
SD6000AA	SD60 Diesel AA Set, long nose	450 ____
SD6000Low	SD60 Diesel, low nose	250 ____
SD6000LowAA	SD60 Diesel AA Set, low nose	450 ____
SD6000M	SD60 Diesel, wide cab	250 ____
SD6000MAA	SD60 Diesel AA Set, wide cab	450 ____
SD6002	C&NW SD60 Diesel, long nose	250 ____
SD6002AA	C&NW SD60 Diesel AA Set, long nose	450 ____
SD6003M	Conrail SD60 Diesel, wide cab	250 ____
SD6003MAA	Conrail SD60 Diesel AA Set, wide cab	450 ____
SD6011	UP SD60 Diesel, long nose	250 ____
SD6011AA	UP SD60 Diesel AA Set, long nose	450 ____
SD6011M	UP SD60 Diesel, wide cab	250 ____
SD6011MAA	UP SD60 Diesel AA Set, wide cab	450 ____
SD6012	BN SD60 Diesel, long nose	250 ____
SD6012AA	BN SD60 Diesel AA Set, long nose	450 ____
SD6012M	BN SD60 Diesel, wide cab	250 ____
SD6012MAA	BN SD60 Diesel AA Set, wide cab	450 ____
SD6013	CSX SD60 Diesel, long nose	250 ____
SD6013AA	CSX SD60 Diesel AA Set, long nose	450 ____
SD6013M	CSX SD60 Diesel, wide cab	250 ____
SD6013MAA	CSX SD60 Diesel AA Set, wide cab	450 ____
SD6015	Soo Line SD60 Diesel, long nose	250 ____
SD6015AA	Soo Line SD60 Diesel AA Set, long nose	450 ____
SD6015M	Soo Line SD60 Diesel, wide cab	250 ____
SD6015MAA	Soo Line SD60 Diesel AA Set, wide cab	450 ____
SD6024	NS SD60 Diesel, long nose	250 ____
SD6024AA	NS SD60 Diesel AA Set, long nose	450 ____
SD6025M	BNSF SD60 Diesel, wide cab	250 ____
SD6025MAA	BNSF SD60 Diesel AA Set, wide cab	450 ____
SDK2053	Transformer	110 ____
SLBSP2	Amtrak Superliner Set, phase II	370 ____
SLBSP3	Amtrak Superliner Set, phase III	370 ____
T-1	UP 40' Semi Trailer	15 ____
T-2	Southern 40' Semi Trailer	15 ____
T-3	BN 40' Semi Trailer	15 ____
T-4	CSX 40' Semi Trailer	15 ____
T-5	D&RGW 40' Semi Trailer	15 ____
T-6	ATSF 40' Semi Trailer	15 ____
T-7	SP 40' Semi Trailer	15 ____
T-8	Quantum 40' Semi Trailer	15 ____
T-9	IC 40' Semi Trailer	15 ____

			Retail
____	**T-10**	CN&W 40' Semi Trailer	15
____	**T-11**	Conrail 40' Semi Trailer	15
____	**T-12**	American President Line 40' Semi Trailer	15
____	**T-13**	K-Line 40' Semi Trailer	15
____	**T-14**	Evergreen 40' Semi Trailer	15
____	**T-15**	N&W 40' Semi Trailer	15
____	**T-16**	Transamerica 40' Semi Trailer	15
____	**T-17**	MP 40' Semi Trailer	15
____	**T-18**	SP 40' Semi Trailer	15
____	**T-19**	NP 40' Semi Trailer	20
____	**T-20**	MKT 40' Semi Trailer	20
____	**T148B**	Bumper 2-pack	14
____	**T148C30**	30-degree Crossing	25
____	**T148C75**	75-degree Crossing	20
____	**T148L**	27"-radius Turnout, left hand, throw bar	35
____	**T148L-HT**	27"-radius Turnout, left hand, hand throw	40
____	**T148L-PW**	27"-radius Turnout, left hand, powered	50
____	**T148R**	27"-radius Turnout, right hand, throw bar	35
____	**T148R-HT**	27"-radius Turnout, right hand, hand throw	40
____	**T148R-PW**	27"-radius Turnout, right hand, powered	50
____	**T148UNC**	Electric Uncoupler	19
____	**T710**	Rail Joiners, 16 pieces	4
____	**T710INS**	Rail Joiners, insulated, 16 pieces	4
____	**T711**	Terminal with wire	3
____	**T14812**	12" Straight Track	4
____	**T14821**	21"-radius S-42 Track	4
____	**T14824**	24"-radius S-48 Track	5
____	**T14827**	27"-radius S-54 Track	5
____	**T14836**	3' Flex Track	11
____	**TM00AC**	FM H-24-66 Diesel	270
____	**TM00DC**	FM H-24-66 Diesel, scale or hi-rail	250
____	**TM00AAAC**	FM H-24-66 Diesel AA Set	500
____	**TM00AADC**	FM H-24-66 Diesel AA Set, scale or hi-rail	470
____	**TM01AC**	C&NW FM H-24-66 Diesel	270
____	**TM01DC**	C&NW FM H-24-66 Diesel, scale or hi-rail	250
____	**TM01AAAC**	C&NW FM H-24-66 Diesel AA Set	500
____	**TM01AADC**	C&NW FM H-24-66 Diesel AA Set, scale or hi-rail	470
____	**TM02AC**	Lackawanna FM H-24-66 Diesel	270
____	**TM02DC**	Lackawanna FM H-24-66 Diesel, scale or hi-rail	250
____	**TM02AAAC**	Lackawanna FM H-24-66 Diesel AA Set	500
____	**TM02AADC**	Lackawanna FM H-24-66 Diesel AA Set, scale or hi-rail	470
____	**TM03AC**	Pennsylvania FM H-24-66 Diesel	270
____	**TM03DC**	Pennsylvania FM H-24-66 Diesel, scale or hi-rail	250

TM03AAAC	Pennsylvania FM H-24-66 Diesel AA Set	500 ____
TM03AADC	Pennsylvania FM H-24-66 Diesel AA Set, scale or hi-rail	470 ____
TM04AC	Reading FM H-24-66 Diesel	270 ____
TM04DC	Reading FM H-24-66 Diesel, scale or hi-rail	250 ____
TM04AAAC	Reading FM H-24-66 Diesel AA Set	500 ____
TM04AADC	Reading FM H-24-66 Diesel AA Set, scale or hi-rail	470 ____
TM05AC	SP FM H-24-66 Diesel	270 ____
TM05DC	SP FM H-24-66 Diesel, scale or hi-rail	250 ____
TM05AAAC	SP FM H-24-66 Diesel AA Set	500 ____
TM05AADC	SP FM H-24-66 Diesel AA Set, scale or hi-rail	470 ____
TM06AC	Virginian FM H-24-66 Diesel	270 ____
TM06DC	Virginian FM H-24-66 Diesel, scale or hi-rail	250 ____
TM06AAAC	Virginian FM H-24-66 Diesel AA Set	500 ____
TM06AADC	Virginian FM H-24-66 Diesel AA Set, scale or hi-rail	470 ____
TM07AC	CNJ FM H-24-66 Diesel	270 ____
TM07DC	CNJ FM H-24-66 Diesel, scale or hi-rail	250 ____
TM07AAAC	CNJ FM H-24-66 Diesel AA Set	500 ____
TM07AADC	CNJ FM H-24-66 Diesel AA Set, scale or hi-rail	470 ____
TM08AC	CP FM H-24-66 Diesel	270 ____
TM08DC	CP FM H-24-66 Diesel, scale or hi-rail	250 ____
TM08AAAC	CP FM H-24-66 Diesel AA Set	500 ____
TM08AADC	CP FM H-24-66 Diesel AA Set, scale or hi-rail	470 ____
TM09AC	NH FM H-24-66 Diesel	270 ____
TM09DC	NH FM H-24-66 Diesel, scale or hi-rail	250 ____
TM09AAAC	NH FM H-24-66 Diesel AA Set	500 ____
TM09AADC	NH FM H-24-66 Diesel AA Set, scale or hi-rail	470 ____
TM10AC	Wabash FM H-24-66 Diesel	270 ____
TM10DC	Wabash FM H-24-66 Diesel, scale or hi-rail	250 ____
TM10AAAC	Wabash FM H-24-66 Diesel AA Set	500 ____
TM10AADC	Wabash FM H-24-66 Diesel AA Set, scale or hi-rail	470 ____
TMC-L	Left Hand Turnout Powering Kit	20 ____
TMC-R	Right Hand Turnout Powering Kit	20 ____
TMDAC	Demonstrator FM H-24-66 Diesel	270 ____
TMDDC	Demonstrator FM H-24-66 Diesel, scale or hi-rail	250 ____
TMDAAAC	Demonstrator FM H-24-66 Diesel AA Set	500 ____
TMDAADC	Demonstrator FM H-24-66 Diesel AA Set, scale or hi-rail	470 ____
TML	Turnout Motor Kit, left hand	14 ____
TMR	Turnout Motor Kit, right hand	14 ____
TSP	Throw Bar Spring	1 ____
TWS103	Rail Weathering Solution, 3 oz.	11 ____
U2500AC	U25B Diesel	230 ____

			Retail
____	**U2500DC**	U25B Diesel	190
____	**U2500AC-DUAL**	U25B Diesel Set	430
____	**U2500DC-DUAL**	U25B Diesel Set	370
____	**U2501AC**	Burlington U25B Diesel	230
____	**U2501DC**	Burlington U25B Diesel	190
____	**U2501AC-DUAL**	Burlington U25B Diesel Set	430
____	**U2501DC-DUAL**	Burlington U25B Diesel Set	370
____	**U2502AC**	C&O U25B Diesel	230
____	**U2502DC**	C&O U25B Diesel	190
____	**U2502AC-DUAL**	C&O U25B Diesel Set	430
____	**U2502DC-DUAL**	C&O U25B Diesel Set	370
____	**U2503AC**	Erie-Lack. U25B Diesel	230
____	**U2503DC**	Erie-Lack. U25B Diesel	190
____	**U2503AC-DUAL**	Erie-Lack. U25B Diesel Set	430
____	**U2503DC-DUAL**	Erie-Lack. U25B Diesel Set	370
____	**U2504AC**	Frisco U25B Diesel	230
____	**U2504DC**	Frisco U25B Diesel	190
____	**U2504AC-DUAL**	Frisco U25B Diesel Set	430
____	**U2504DC-DUAL**	Frisco U25B Diesel Set	370
____	**U2505AC**	GN U25B Diesel	230
____	**U2505DC**	GN U25B Diesel	190
____	**U2505AC-DUAL**	GN U25B Diesel Set	430
____	**U2505DC-DUAL**	GN U25B Diesel Set	370
____	**U2506AC**	NH U25B Diesel	230
____	**U2506DC**	NH U25B Diesel	190
____	**U2506AC-DUAL**	NH U25B Diesel Set	430
____	**U2506DC-DUAL**	NH U25B Diesel Set	370
____	**U2507AC**	RI U25B Diesel	230
____	**U2507DC**	RI U25B Diesel	190
____	**U2507AC-DUAL**	RI U25B Diesel Set	430
____	**U2507DC-DUAL**	RI U25B Diesel Set	370
____	**U2508AC**	Santa Fe U25B Diesel	230
____	**U2508DC**	Santa Fe U25B Diesel	190
____	**U2508AC-DUAL**	Santa Fe U25B Diesel Set	430
____	**U2508DC-DUAL**	Santa Fe U25B Diesel Set	370
____	**U2509AC**	SP U25B Diesel	230
____	**U2509DC**	SP U25B Diesel	190
____	**U2509AC-DUAL**	SP U25B Diesel Set	430
____	**U2509DC-DUAL**	SP U25B Diesel Set	370

Unnumbered Items

____	**Limited Run**	Wisconsin Central GP35 "728"	220

Retail

35-1001	15" Straight Track, 6-pack	40 ____
35-1002	10" Straight Track, 6-pack	35 ____
35-1003	5" Straight Track, 6-pack	30 ____
35-1004	40" Flex Track, 6-pack	60 ____
35-1005	40" Flex Track, 24-pack	220 ____
35-1006	20" Radius 30 Degree Curved Track, 6-pack	35 ____
35-1007	20" Radius 15 Degree Half Curved Track, 6-pack	30 ____
35-1008	25" Radius 30 Degree Curved Track, 6-pack	38 ____
35-1009	25" Radius 15 Degree Half Curved Track, 6-pack	33 ____
35-1010	30" Radius 30 Degree Curved Track, 6-pack	40 ____
35-1011	30" Radius 15 Degree Half Curved Track, 6-pack	35 ____
35-1012	STrax Railjoiner, 36-pack	10 ____
35-1013	STrax Railjoiner, insulated,36-pack	10 ____
35-1014	Flex Track Railjoiner, 36-pack	8 ____
35-1016	American Flyer Railjoiner Adapter, 36-pack	10 ____
35-1017	STrax Railjoiner Feeder Wire,12-pack	10 ____
35-1018	No. 3 Remote Control Switch, right hand	70 ____
35-1019	No. 3 Remote Control Switch, left hand)	70 ____
35-1020	Switch Controller with 40" harness extension	15 ____
35-1021	5" Bumper with operating warning light	22 ____
35-1022	5" Operating Uncoupler Track	25 ____
35-1023	5" Operating Accessory Track	25 ____
35-1101	AAR 70-Ton Friction Bearing Truck, hi-rail	20 ____
35-1102	AAR 70-Ton Friction Bearing Truck, scale	20 ____
35-1103	AAR Type Y Truck, hi-rail	20 ____
35-1104	AAR Type Y Truck, scale	20 ____
35-1105	Barber S2 70 Ton Roller Bearing Truck, hi-rail	20 ____
35-1106	Barber S2 70 Ton Roller Bearing Truck, scale	20 ____
35-1107	American Flyer Compatible Freight Car Coupler	5 ____
35-1108	33" Insulated Wheel 4-pack, hi-rail	13 ____
35-1109	Code 110 33" Insulated Wheel 4-pack, scale	13 ____
35-1110	Kadee Compatible Freight Car Coupler, scale	7 ____
35-90001	No. 23796 Saw Mill	120 ____
35-90002	No. 23772 Water Tower with bubbling pipe	120 ____
35-90003	No. 23769 Revolving Aircraft Beacon	120 ____
35-90004	No. 23774 Floodlight Tower	120 ____
35-90005	No. 787 Log Loader	200 ____
35-90006	Lamplighter	180 ____
35-20001-1	Jersey Central F3 Diesel A Unit "52"	380 ____

Retail

____	**35-20002-1** Jersey Central F3 Diesel A Unit "55"	380
____	**35-20003-3** Jersey Central F3 Diesel A Unit "56," nonpowered	200
____	**35-20004-1** Jersey Central F3 Diesel B Unit "D"	360
____	**35-20005-3** Jersey Central F3 Diesel B Unit "B," nonpowered	190
____	**35-20006-1** New York Central F3 Diesel A Unit "1608"	380
____	**35-20007-1** New York Central F3 Diesel A Unit "1635"	380
____	**35-20008-3** New York Central F3 Diesel A Unit "1616," nonpowered	200
____	**35-20009-1** New York Central F3 Diesel B Unit "2413"	360
____	**35-20010-3** New York Central F3 Diesel B Unit "2408," nonpowered	190
____	**35-20011-1** Pennsylvania F3 Diesel A Unit "9508"	380
____	**35-20012-1** Pennsylvania F3 Diesel A Unit "9509"	380
____	**35-20013-3** Pennsylvania F3 Diesel A Unit "9517," nonpowered	200
____	**35-20014-1** Pennsylvania F3 Diesel B Unit "9512B"	360
____	**35-20015-3** Pennsylvania F3 Diesel B Unit "9508," nonpowered	190
____	**35-20016-1** Seaboard F3 Diesel A Unit "4024"	380
____	**35-20017-1** Seaboard F3 Diesel A Unit "4027"	380
____	**35-20018-3** Seaboard F3 Diesel A Unit "4029," nonpowered	200
____	**35-20019-1** Santa Fe F3 Diesel A Unit "18"	380
____	**35-20020-1** Santa Fe F3 Diesel A Unit "19C"	380
____	**35-20021-3** Santa Fe F3 Diesel A Unit "24," nonpowered	200
____	**35-20022-1** Santa Fe F3 Diesel B Unit "18A"	360
____	**35-20023-3** Santa Fe F3 Diesel B Unit "24B," nonpowered	190
____	**35-20024-1** Union Pacific F3 Diesel A Unit "1404A"	380
____	**35-20025-1** Union Pacific F3 Diesel A Unit "1407A"	380
____	**35-20026-3** Union Pacific F3 Diesel A Unit "1441A," nonpowered	200
____	**35-20027-1** Union Pacific F3 Diesel B Unit "1471B"	360
____	**35-20028-3** Union Pacific F3 Diesel B Unit "1446B," nonpowered	190
____	**35-70001** Milwaukee Road PS2 Hopper 6-Car Set	330
____	**35-70002** Norfolk Southern PS2 Hopper 6-Car Set	330
____	**35-70003** BNSF PS2 Hopper 6-Car Set	330
____	**35-70004** Southern PS2 Hopper 6-Car Set	330
____	**35-70005** Bessemer & Lake Erie PS2 Hopper 6-Car Set	330
____	**35-70006** Detroit Toledo & Ironton PS2 Hopper 6-Car Set	330
____	**35-70007** Lehigh Valley PS2 Hopper 6-Car Set	330
____	**35-70008** Maryland Midland PS2 Hopper 6-Car Set	330
____	**35-70009** Milwaukee Road Ore Car 6-Car Set	330
____	**35-70010** Duluth Missabe & Iron Range Ore Car 6-Car Set	330
____	**35-70011** Chicago Northwestern Ore Car 6-Car Set	330

Retail

35-70012	Canadian Pacific Ore Car 6-Car Set	330	____
35-70013	SOO Line Ore Car 6-Car Set	330	____
35-70014	Canadian National Ore Car 6-Car Set	330	____
35-70015	Bessemer & Lake Erie Ore Car 6-Car Set	330	____
35-70016	Great Northern Ore Car 6-Car Set	330	____
35-74000	Baltimore & Ohio Steel Rebuilt Boxcar "466013"	55	____
35-74001	Christmas Steel Rebuilt Boxcar "2013"	60	____
35-74002	Boston & Maine Steel Rebuilt Boxcar "73022"	60	____
35-74003	Boston & Maine Steel Rebuilt Boxcar "73025"	60	____
35-74004	New Haven Steel Rebuilt Boxcar "36454"	60	____
35-74005	New Haven Steel Rebuilt Boxcar "36450"	60	____
35-74006	New York Central Steel Rebuilt Boxcar "174992"	60	____
35-74007	New York Central Steel Rebuilt Boxcar "174995"	60	____
35-74008	Norfolk & Western Steel Rebuilt Boxcar "43628"	60	____
35-74009	Norfolk & Western Steel Rebuilt Boxcar "43630"	60	____
35-74010	Western Maryland Steel Rebuilt Boxcar "29076"	60	____
35-74011	Western Maryland Steel Rebuilt Boxcar "29083"	60	____
35-74012	Santa Fe Steel Rebuilt Boxcar "145002"	60	____
35-74013	Santa Fe Steel Rebuilt Boxcar "145005"	60	____
35-74014	Union Pacific Steel Rebuilt Boxcar "181679"	60	____
35-74015	Union Pacific Steel Rebuilt Boxcar "181680"	60	____
35-75001	Milwaukee Road PS2 Hopper "99618"	60	____
35-75002	Milwaukee Road PS2 Hopper "99614"	60	____
35-75003	Norfolk Southern PS2 Hopper "233548"	60	____
35-75004	Norfolk Southern PS2 Hopper "233635"	60	____
35-75005	Maryland Midland PS2 Hopper "5152"	60	____
35-75006	Maryland Midland PS2 Hopper "5186"	60	____
35-75007	Lehigh Valley PS2 Hopper "50835"	60	____
35-75008	Lehigh Valley PS2 Hopper "50879"	60	____
35-75009	Bessemer & Lake Erie PS2 Hopper "3732"	60	____
35-75010	Bessemer & Lake Erie PS2 Hopper "3735"	60	____
35-75011	Southern PS2 Hopper "95420"	60	____
35-75012	Southern PS2 Hopper "95462"	60	____
35-75013	Detroit Toledo & Ironton PS2 Hopper "11120"	60	____
35-75014	Detroit Toledo & Ironton PS2 Hopper "11135"	60	____
35-75015	BNSF PS2 Hopper "405600"	60	____
35-75016	BNSF PS2 Hopper "405619"	60	____
35-75017	Bessemer & Lake Erie Ore Car "20090"	60	____
35-75018	Bessemer & Lake Erie Ore Car "20093"	60	____
35-75019	Canadian National Ore Car "123060"	60	____
35-75020	Canadian National Ore Car "123064"	60	____
35-75021	Canadian Pacific Ore Car "377120"	60	____

Retail

____	**35-75022**	Canadian Pacific Ore Car "377128"	60
____	**35-75023**	Chicago Northwestern Ore Car "111542"	60
____	**35-75024**	Chicago Northwestern Ore Car "111548"	60
____	**35-75025**	Duluth Missabe & Iron Range Ore Car "31050"	60
____	**35-75026**	Duluth Missabe & Iron Range Ore Car "31056"	60
____	**35-75027**	Great Northern Ore Car "89001"	60
____	**35-75028**	Great Northern Ore Car "89003"	60
____	**35-75029**	Milwaukee Road Ore Car "76712"	60
____	**35-75030**	Milwaukee Road Ore Car "76730"	60
____	**35-75031**	SOO Line Ore Car "81950"	60
____	**35-75032**	SOO Line Ore Car "81956"	60
____	**35-78001**	Fairmont Creamery 40' Wood-sided Reefer "30210"	60
____	**35-78002**	Fairmont Creamery 40' Wood-sided Reefer "30219"	60
____	**35-78003**	Fulton Market 40' Wood-sided Reefer "10400"	60
____	**35-78004**	Fulton Market 40' Wood-sided Reefer "10402"	60
____	**35-78005**	Jelke Good Luck Margarine 40' Wood-sided Reefer "10803"	60
____	**35-78006**	Jelke Good Luck Margarine 40' Wood-sided Reefer "10805"	60
____	**35-78007**	Krey's Ham & Bacon 40' Wood-sided Reefer "873"	60
____	**35-78008**	Krey's Ham & Bacon 40' Wood-sided Reefer "875"	60
____	**35-78009**	M.K. Goetz Brewery 40' Wood-sided Reefer "14310"	60
____	**35-78010**	M.K. Goetz Brewery 40' Wood-sided Reefer "14313"	60
____	**35-78011**	Pacific Fruit Express 40' Wood-sided Reefer "74780"	60
____	**35-78012**	Pacific Fruit Express 40' Wood-sided Reefer "74781"	60
____	**35-78013**	Santa Fe 40' Wood-sided Reefer "25090"	60
____	**35-78014**	Santa Fe 40' Wood-sided Reefer "25094"	60
____	**35-78015**	Senate Beer 40' Wood-sided Reefer "100"	60
____	**35-78016**	Senate Beer 40' Wood-sided Reefer "105"	60

Retail

00001	70-ton Truck, friction bearing, Code 110, pair	10 ____
00002	70-ton Truck, friction bearing, hi-rail, pair	10 ____
00003	70-ton Truck, roller bearing, Code 110, pair	10 ____
00004	70-ton Truck, roller bearing, hi-rail, pair	10 ____
00005	Freight Coupler, AF compatible, pair	3 ____
00006	B&M PS-2 2-bay Covered Hopper	50 ____
00007	NYC PS-2 2-bay Covered Hopper	50 ____
00008	PRR PS-2 2-bay Covered Hopper, scheme I	50 ____
00009	ATSF PS-2 2-bay Covered Hopper, scheme I #1	50 ____
00010	Wabash PS-2 2-bay Covered Hopper	50 ____
00011	WM PS-2 2-bay Covered Hopper	50 ____
00012	BN PS-2 2-bay Covered Hopper, scheme I	50 ____
00013	Chessie (WM) PS-2 2-bay Covered Hopper	50 ____
00014	C&NW (M&StL) PS-2 2-bay Covered Hopper, scheme I	50 ____
00015	Conrail PS-2 2-bay Covered Hopper, scheme I	50 ____
00016	Soo Line PS-2 2-bay Covered Hopper #1	50 ____
00017	SP PS-2 2-bay Covered Hopper, scheme I	50 ____
00018	CNJ PS-2 2-bay Covered Hopper, scheme I	50 ____
00019	MILW PS-2 2-bay Covered Hopper	50 ____
00020	Trona PS-2 2-bay Covered Hopper	50 ____
00021	PS-2 2-bay Covered Hopper, gray	50 ____
00022	PRR PS-2 2-bay Covered Hopper, scheme I	50 ____
00023	70-ton Truck, roller bearing, Code 110, 36" wheels, pair	7 ____
00024	33" Scale Wheel Set, Code 10, 4-pack	4 ____
00025	33" Wheel Set, hi-rail, 4-pack	4 ____
00026	PRR PS-2 2-bay Covered Hopper, scheme II	50 ____
00027	B&O PS-2 2-bay Covered Hopper	50 ____
00028	D&RGW PS-2 2-bay Covered Hopper	50 ____
00029	ATSF PS-2 2-bay Covered Hopper, scheme I #2	50 ____
00030	MEC PS-2 2-bay Covered Hopper	50 ____
00031	UP PS-2 2-bay Covered Hopper	50 ____
00032	Wisconsin Central PS-2 2-bay Covered Hopper	50 ____
00033	LV PS-2 2-bay Covered Hopper	50 ____
00034	Rock Island PS-2 2-bay Covered Hopper #1	50 ____
00035	Rock Island PS-2 2-bay Covered Hopper #2	50 ____
00036	DT&I PS-2 2-bay Covered Hopper (NASG)	50 ____
00037	CSX PS-2 2-bay Covered Hopper	50 ____
00038	C&NW PS-2 2-bay Covered Hopper, scheme I	50 ____
00039	C&NW (CGW) PS-2 2-bay Covered Hopper	50 ____
00040	BN PS-2 2-bay Covered Hopper, scheme II	50 ____
00041	DT&I PS-2 2-bay Covered Hopper #2 (NASG)	50 ____

_____ 00042	IMCO PS-2 2-bay Covered Hopper	50
_____ 00043	PS-2 2-bay Covered Hopper, roller bearing, gray	50
_____ 00044	Chessie (B&O) PS-2 2-bay Covered Hopper	50
_____ 00045	50-ton Truck, Code 110, pair	10
_____ 00046	50-ton Truck, hi-rail, pair	10
_____ 00047	50-ton Type Y Truck, Code 110, pair	10
_____ 00048	50-ton Type Y Truck, hi-rail, pair	10
_____ 00049	Stock Car, red	50
_____ 00050	UP Stock Car #1	50
_____ 00051	UP Stock Car #2	50
_____ 00052	D&RGW Stock Car	50
_____ 00053	C&NW Stock Car #1	50
_____ 00054	C&NW Stock Car #2	50
_____ 00055	ACL Stock Car	50
_____ 00056	GN Stock Car #1	50
_____ 00057	GN Stock Car #2	50
_____ 00058	PRR Stock Car #1	50
_____ 00059	PRR Stock Car #2	50
_____ 00060	ATSF Stock Car, scheme I #1	50
_____ 00061	ATSF Stock Car, scheme I #2	50
_____ 00062	NP Stock Car (Leventon Hobby)	50
_____ 00063	USRA Single-sheathed Boxcar, red	50
_____ 00064	NYC Stock Car	50
_____ 00065	WP Stock Car	50
_____ 00066	PRR USRA Single-sheathed Boxcar, scheme I #1	50
_____ 00067	PRR USRA Single-sheathed Boxcar, scheme I #2	50
_____ 00068	CB&Q (C&S) USRA Single-sheathed Boxcar	50
_____ 00069	CB&Q USRA Single-sheathed Boxcar	50
_____ 00070	MEC (PTM) USRA Single-sheathed Boxcar	50
_____ 00071	B&O USRA Single-sheathed Boxcar, scheme I	50
_____ 00072	SP USRA Single-sheathed Boxcar	50
_____ 00073	NYC USRA Single-sheathed Boxcar	50
_____ 00074	Yakima Valley USRA Single-sheathed Boxcar (NMRA)	50
_____ 00075	CP USRA Single-sheathed Boxcar	50
_____ 00076	GN PS-2 2-bay Covered Hopper	50
_____ 00077	NKP PS-2 2-bay Covered Hopper	50
_____ 00078	NYC (PL&E) PS-2 2-bay Covered Hopper	50
_____ 00079	Soo Line PS-2 2-bay Covered Hopper #2	50
_____ 00080	NYNH&H PS-2 2-bay Covered Hopper	50
_____ 00081	WP PS-2 2-bay Covered Hopper	50
_____ 00082	MKT PS-2 2-bay Covered Hopper	50
_____ 00083	BN PS-2 2-bay Covered Hopper, scheme II	50
_____ 00084	PC PS-2 2-bay Covered Hopper	50
_____ 00085	Chessie (CSXT) PS-2 2-bay Covered Hopper	50
_____ 00086	C&NW PS-2 2-bay Covered Hopper, scheme II	50

00087	Revere Sugar PS-2 2-bay Hopper (RSSVP Models)	75 ____
00088	Conrail PS-2 2-bay Covered Hopper, scheme II	50 ____
00089	GTW PS-2 2-bay Covered Hopper	50 ____
00090	Ready Mix Concrete PS-2 2-bay Covered Hopper	50 ____
00091	SP PS-2 2-bay Covered Hopper, scheme II	50 ____
00092	SW9 Diesel, black	200 ____
00093	ACL SW9 Diesel #1	200 ____
00094	ACL SW9 Diesel #2	200 ____
00097	B&O SW9 Diesel #1	200 ____
00098	B&O SW9 Diesel #2	200 ____
00099	B&M SW9 Diesel #1	200 ____
00100	B&M SW9 Diesel #2	200 ____
00101	BN SW9 Diesel #1	200 ____
00102	BN SW9 Diesel #2	200 ____
00103	CP SW9 Diesel #1	200 ____
00104	CP SW9 Diesel #2	200 ____
00105	CB&Q SW9 Diesel #1	200 ____
00106	CB&Q SW9 Diesel #2	200 ____
00107	Chessie (C&O) SW9 Diesel	200 ____
00108	Chessie (B&O) SW9 Diesel #1	200 ____
00109	C&NW SW9 Diesel #1	200 ____
00110	C&NW SW9 Diesel #2	200 ____
00111	Conrail SW9 Diesel, scheme I #1	200 ____
00112	Conrail SW9 Diesel, scheme I #2	200 ____
00113	Erie-Lackawanna SW9 Diesel #1	200 ____
00114	Erie-Lackawanna SW9 Diesel #2	200 ____
00115	NYC SW9 Diesel #1	200 ____
00116	NYC SW9 Diesel #2	200 ____
00117	PRR SW9 Diesel #1	200 ____
00118	PRR SW9 Diesel #2	200 ____
00119	ATSF SW9 Diesel #1	200 ____
00120	ATSF SW9 Diesel #2	200 ____
00121	UP SW9 Diesel, scheme I #1	200 ____
00122	UP SW9 Diesel, scheme I #2	200 ____
00123	UP Stock Car #3	50 ____
00124	40' Steel Rebuilt Boxcar, red	50 ____
00125	C&O 40' Steel Rebuilt Boxcar #1	50 ____
00126	C&NW 40' Steel Rebuilt Boxcar, scheme I	50 ____
00127	DL&W 40' Steel Rebuilt Boxcar	50 ____
00128	Frisco 40' Steel Rebuilt Boxcar, scheme I	50 ____
00129	NYC (PMKY) 40' Steel Rebuilt Boxcar #1	50 ____
00130	NYC (PMKY) 40' Steel Rebuilt Boxcar #2	50 ____
00131	PRR 40' Steel Rebuilt Boxcar, scheme I #1	50 ____
00132	PRR 40' Steel Rebuilt Boxcar, scheme I #2	50 ____
00133	ATSF "Scout" 40' Steel Rebuilt Boxcar	50 ____

_____ **00134**	ATSF "Grand Canyon" 40' Steel Rebuilt Boxcar	50
_____ **00135**	Vermont Central 40' Steel Rebuilt Boxcar	50
_____ **00136**	CN Stock Car #1	50
_____ **00137**	CB&Q Stock Car #1	50
_____ **00138**	MP Stock Car	50
_____ **00139**	MKT Stock Car	50
_____ **00140**	UP (Oregon Short Line) Stock Car, scheme I #1	40
_____ **00141**	Rutland USRA Single-sheathed Boxcar	50
_____ **00142**	Clinchfield USRA Single-sheathed Boxcar	50
_____ **00143**	Erie USRA Single-sheathed Boxcar	50
_____ **00144**	CMStP&P USRA Single-sheathed Boxcar	50
_____ **00145**	PRR USRA Single-sheathed Boxcar	50
_____ **00146**	Pacific Electric USRA Single-sheathed Boxcar	50
_____ **00147**	Wabash USRA Single-sheathed Boxcar	50
_____ **00148**	Chessie (B&O) SW9 Switcher #2	200
_____ **00149**	CN 40' Stock Car #2	50
_____ **00150**	CB&Q 40' Stock Car #2	50
_____ **00151**	MKT 40' Stock Car #2	50
_____ **00152**	UP (Oregon Short Line) 40' Stock Car, scheme I #2	40
_____ **00153**	C&O 40' Steel Rebuilt Boxcar #2	50
_____ **00154**	SLSF 40' Steel Rebuilt Boxcar, scheme I #2	50
_____ **00155**	Bulkhead Flatcar	56
_____ **00156**	BN Bulkhead Flatcar #1	56
_____ **00157**	BN Bulkhead Flatcar #2	56
_____ **00158**	CB&Q Bulkhead Flatcar #1	56
_____ **00159**	CB&Q Bulkhead Flatcar #2	56
_____ **00160**	D&RGW Bulkhead Flatcar	56
_____ **00161**	IC Bulkhead Flatcar #1	56
_____ **00162**	IC Bulkhead Flatcar #2	56
_____ **00163**	Southern Bulkhead Flatcar	56
_____ **00164**	UP Bulkhead Flatcar #1	56
_____ **00165**	UP Bulkhead Flatcar #2	56
_____ **00166**	Wabash Bulkhead Flatcar	56
_____ **00167**	Standard Flatcar, red	50
_____ **00168**	Standard Flatcar, black	50
_____ **00169**	BN Standard Flatcar	50
_____ **00170**	CB&Q Standard Flatcar	50
_____ **00171**	D&RGW Standard Flatcar	50
_____ **00172**	IC Standard Flatcar	50
_____ **00173**	Southern Standard Flatcar	50
_____ **00174**	UP Standard Flatcar, scheme I #1	50
_____ **00175**	Wabash Standard Flatcar	50
_____ **00176**	PRR Standard Flatcar #1	50
_____ **00177**	Flatcar with trailer	63
_____ **00178**	BAR Flatcar with trailer	63

S-HELPER SERVICE 1994-2012

Retail

00179	NKP Flatcar with trailer	63 ____
00180	Rock Island Flatcar with trailer	63 ____
00181	PRR Flatcar #1 with trailer	63 ____
00182	PRR Flatcar #2 with trailer	63 ____
00183	Seaboard Flatcar with trailer	63 ____
00184	UP Flatcar #1 with trailer	63 ____
00185	UP Flatcar #2 with trailer	63 ____
00186	Flatcar with trailer	63 ____
00187	C&NW Flatcar with trailer	63 ____
00188	C&NW Flatcar with trailer	63 ____
00189	NH Flatcar #1 with trailer	63 ____
00190	NH Flatcar #2 with trailer	63 ____
00191	NYC Flatcar #1 with trailer	63 ____
00192	NYC Flatcar #2 with trailer	63 ____
00193	TTX Flatcar with REA trailer, scheme I	63 ____
00194	TTX Flatcar with REA trailer, scheme II	63 ____
00195	35' Trailer, horizontal corrugations	16 ____
00196	35' Trailer, vertical ribs	16 ____
00197	B&A 35' Trailer, horizontal corrugations	16 ____
00198	NKP 35' Trailer, horizontal corrugations	16 ____
00199	Rock Island 35' Trailer, horizontal corrugations	16 ____
00200	PRR 35' Trailer, horizontal corrugations, scheme I	16 ____
00201	Seaboard 35' Trailer, horizontal corrugations	16 ____
00202	UP 35' Trailer, horizontal corrugations	16 ____
00203	C&NW 35' Trailer, vertical ribs	16 ____
00204	NYNH&H 35' Trailer, vertical ribs	16 ____
00205	NYC 35' Trailer, vertical ribs	16 ____
00206	REA 35' Trailer, vertical ribs, scheme I	16 ____
00207	REA 35' Trailer, vertical ribs, scheme II #1	16 ____
00208	B&A Standard Flatcar	50 ____
00209	C&NW Standard Flatcar	50 ____
00210	NH Standard Flatcar	50 ____
00211	NYC Standard Flatcar	50 ____
00212	NKP Standard Flatcar	50 ____
00213	PRR Standard Flatcar #1	50 ____
00214	Rock Island Standard Flatcar	50 ____
00215	Seaboard Standard Flatcar	50 ____
00216	UP Standard Flatcar, scheme II #1	50 ____
00217	Extended Vision Caboose	70 ____
00218	BN Extended Vision Caboose #1	70 ____
00219	BN Extended Vision Caboose #2	70 ____
00220	C&O Extended Vision Caboose #1	70 ____
00221	C&O Extended Vision Caboose #2	70 ____
00222	CB&Q Extended Vision Caboose, scheme I #1	70 ____
00223	CB&Q Extended Vision Caboose, scheme I #2	70 ____

_____ **00224**	Chessie (B&O) Extended Vision Caboose #1	70
_____ **00225**	Chessie (B&O) Extended Vision Caboose #2	70
_____ **00226**	C&NW Extended Vision Caboose #1	70
_____ **00227**	C&NW Extended Vision Caboose #2	70
_____ **00228**	Conrail Extended Vision Caboose #1	70
_____ **00229**	Conrail Extended Vision Caboose #2	70
_____ **00230**	D&RGW Extended Vision Caboose #1	70
_____ **00231**	D&RGW Extended Vision Caboose #2	70
_____ **00232**	GN Extended Vision Caboose #1	70
_____ **00233**	GN Extended Vision Caboose #2	70
_____ **00234**	ICG Extended Vision Caboose #1	70
_____ **00235**	ICG Extended Vision Caboose #2	70
_____ **00236**	MP Extended Vision Caboose #1	70
_____ **00237**	MP Extended Vision Caboose #2	70
_____ **00238**	NP Extended Vision Caboose #1	70
_____ **00239**	NP Extended Vision Caboose #2	70
_____ **00240**	ATSF Extended Vision Caboose, scheme I #1	70
_____ **00241**	ATSF Extended Vision Caboose, scheme I #2	70
_____ **00242**	Seaboard Extended Vision Caboose #1	70
_____ **00243**	Seaboard Extended Vision Caboose #2	70
_____ **00244**	Soo Line Extended Vision Caboose #1	70
_____ **00245**	Soo Line Extended Vision Caboose #2	70
_____ **00246**	Evans Product Load for flatcar	10
_____ **00247**	Gold Bond Product Load for flatcar, white	10
_____ **00248**	Gold Bond Product Load for flatcar, red	10
_____ **00249**	Johns Manville Product Load for flatcar	10
_____ **00250**	Masonite Product Load for flatcar	10
_____ **00251**	Plumb Creek Product Load for flatcar	10
_____ **00252**	United States Gypsum Product Load for flatcar	10
_____ **00253**	Rail Joiners, 12 pieces	5
_____ **00254**	Insulated Rail Joiners, 12 pieces	3
_____ **00255**	Rail Joiners with feeder wire, 12 pieces	8
_____ **00256**	Track Starter Set, 16 pieces	75
_____ **00257**	15" Straight Track, 6 pieces	40
_____ **00258**	10" Straight Track, 6 pieces	33
_____ **00259**	Curved Track, 20" radius, 30 degree, 6 pieces	33
_____ **00260**	BN Standard Flatcar #2	50
_____ **00261**	UP Standard Flatcar, scheme I #2	50
_____ **00262**	B&M Flatcar with trailer (NASG)	63
_____ **00263**	B&M Standard Flatcar (NASG)	50
_____ **00264**	B&M 35' Trailer, vertical ribs (NASG)	16
_____ **00265**	36" Scale Wheel Set, Code 110, 4-pack–99	4
_____ **00266**	CMStP&P Extended Vision Caboose #1	70
_____ **00267**	CMStP&P Extended Vision Caboose #2	70
_____ **00268**	MEC Extended Vision Caboose, scheme I	78

Retail

00271	3-bay Covered Hopper	50 ____
00272	ATSF PS-2 3-bay Covered Hopper #1	50 ____
00273	BN PS-2 3-bay Covered Hopper #1	50 ____
00274	Chessie (B&O) PS-2 3-bay Covered Hopper #1	50 ____
00275	CB&Q PS-2 3-bay Covered Hopper, scheme I #1	50 ____
00276	C&NW PS-2 3-bay Covered Hopper, scheme I #2	50 ____
00277	Conrail PS-2 3-bay Covered Hopper #1	50 ____
00278	GN PS-2 3-bay Covered Hopper #1	50 ____
00279	Erie-Lackawanna PS-2 3-bay Covered Hopper #1	50 ____
00280	NYC PS-2 3-bay Covered Hopper #1	50 ____
00281	UP PS-2 3-bay Covered Hopper #1	50 ____
00282	C&NW (MStL) PS-2 2-bay Covered Hopper, scheme II #1	50 ____
00283	Jack Frost PS-2 2-bay Hopper #1 (RSSVP Models)	68 ____
00284	LNE PS-2 2-bay Covered Hopper #1	50 ____
00285	MStL PS-2 2-bay Covered Hopper #2	50 ____
00286	Central Soya PS-2 2-bay Covered Hopper #1	50 ____
00287	NAHX PS-2 2-bay Covered Hopper #1	50 ____
00288	NAHX PS-2 2-bay Covered Hopper #2	50 ____
00289	Diesel Engineer and Fireman Figure Set	6 ____
00290	AC/DC Reverse Unit with DCC socket	40 ____
00291	Curved Track, 20" radius, 15 degree, 6 pieces	27 ____
00292	Curved Track, 25" radius, 30 degree, 6 pieces	38 ____
00293	Curved Track, 25" radius, 15 degree, 6 pieces	28 ____
00294	Curved Track, 30" radius, 30 degree, 6 pieces	40 ____
00295	Locomotive Coupler, AF compatible, pair	4 ____
00297	5" Straight Track, 6 pieces	25 ____
00298	No. 3 Switch, right hand, remote control	55 ____
00299	No. 3 Switch, left hand, remote control	55 ____
00300	ATSF Flatcar with trailer, scheme I	70 ____
00301	B&O Flatcar with trailer	70 ____
00302	Maine Central Bulkhead Flatcar	56 ____
00303	CP Flatcar with Speedway trailer	70 ____
00304	GN Flatcar with trailer	70 ____
00305	NH Flatcar with Yale trailer	70 ____
00306	PRR Flatcar with trailer #3	70 ____
00307	TTX Flatcar with Carolina trailer	70 ____
00308	D&RGW Flatcar with trailer	70 ____
00309	UP Standard Flatcar #2	50 ____
00310	WM Flatcar with trailer	70 ____
00311	ATSF Standard Flatcar, scheme I	50 ____
00312	B&O Standard Flatcar	50 ____
00313	Maine Central Standard Flatcar	50 ____
00314	CP Standard Flatcar	50 ____
00315	GN Standard Flatcar, scheme I #1	50 ____
00316	NYNH&H Standard Flatcar #3	50 ____

Retail

____ **00317**	PRR Standard Flatcar #3	50
____ **00318**	D&RGW Standard Flatcar	50
____ **00319**	UP Standard Flatcar, scheme II #2	50
____ **00320**	WM Standard Flatcar	50
____ **00321**	ATSF 35' Trailer, horizontal corrugations, scheme I	16
____ **00322**	B&O 35' Trailer, horizontal corrugations	16
____ **00323**	Speedway 35' Trailer, horizontal corrugations	16
____ **00324**	GN 35' Trailer "G322," horizontal corrugations	16
____ **00325**	Yale 35' Trailer, vertical ribs	16
____ **00326**	PRR 35' Trailer, vertical ribs, scheme II	16
____ **00327**	Carolina 35' Trailer, vertical ribs	16
____ **00328**	D&RGW 35' Trailer, horizontal corrugations	16
____ **00329**	UP 35' Trailer #2, horizontal corrugations (NMRA)	16
____ **00330**	WM 35' Trailer, vertical ribs	16
____ **00331**	ATSF Bulkhead Flatcar #1	56
____ **00332**	ATSF Bulkhead Flatcar #2	56
____ **00333**	GN Bulkhead Flatcar #1	56
____ **00334**	GN Bulkhead Flatcar #2	56
____ **00335**	Soo Line Bulkhead Flatcar #1	56
____ **00336**	Soo Line Bulkhead Flatcar #2	56
____ **00337**	D&H Bulkhead Flatcar	56
____ **00338**	Chessie (WM) Bulkhead Flatcar	56
____ **00339**	ATSF Standard Flatcar, scheme II	50
____ **00340**	GN Standard Flatcar, scheme I #2	50
____ **00341**	Soo Line Standard Flatcar #2	50
____ **00342**	Delaware & Hudson Standard Flatcar	50
____ **00343**	Chessie (WM) Standard Flatcar	50
____ **00344**	ATSF Set, 3 cars	100
____ **00345**	C&NW Set, 3 cars	100
____ **00346**	GN 40' Steel Rebuilt Boxcar, scheme 1 #1	50
____ **00347**	GN 40' Steel Rebuilt Boxcar, scheme I #2	50
____ **00348**	MP (IGN) "Eagle" 40' Steel Rebuilt Boxcar #1	50
____ **00349**	MP (IGN) "Eagle" 40' Steel Rebuilt Boxcar #2	50
____ **00350**	NYC Set, 3 cars	100
____ **00351**	RS&P 40' Steel Rebuilt Boxcar	50
____ **00352**	UP Set, 3 cars	100
____ **00353**	Muncie & Western Ball Lines 40' Steel Rebuilt Boxcar #1	50
____ **00354**	Truck with gear box, hi-rail wheels	10
____ **00355**	Truck with gear box, Code 110 wheels	10
____ **00356**	AC PCB/DCC Socket Harness Set, DC plug	40
____ **00357**	Locomotive Coupler, AF compatible, pair	4
____ **00358**	Caboose Conductor and Brakeman Figure Set	6
____ **00359**	Caboose Coupler, AF compatible, pair	3
____ **00362**	B&O F3 Diesel AB Set #1, phase II, sound	500
____ **00363**	B&O F3 Diesel AB Set #2, phase II, sound	500

Retail

00364	CB&Q F3 Diesel AB Set #1, phase II, sound	500 ____
00365	CB&Q F3 Diesel AB Set #2, phase II, sound	500 ____
00366	C&NW F3 Diesel AB Set #1, phase II, sound	500 ____
00367	C&NW F3 Diesel AB Set #2, phase II, sound	500 ____
00368	DL&W F3 Diesel AB Set #1, phase II, sound	500 ____
00369	DL&W F3 Diesel AB Set #2, phase II, sound	500 ____
00370	Maine Central F3 Diesel AB Set #1, phase II, sound	500 ____
00371	Maine Central F3 Diesel AB Set #2, phase II, sound	500 ____
00372	NYC F3 Diesel AB Set #1, phase II, sound	500 ____
00373	NYC F3 Diesel A&B Set #2, phase II, sound	500 ____
00374	Southern F3 Diesel AB Set #1, phase II, sound	500 ____
00375	Southern F3 Diesel AB Set #2, phase II, sound	500 ____
00376	SP F3 Diesel AB Set #1, phase II, sound	500 ____
00377	SP F3 Diesel AB Set #2, phase II, sound	500 ____
00378	UP F3 Diesel AB Set #1, phase II, sound	500 ____
00379	UP F3 Diesel AB Set #2, phase II, sound	500 ____
00380	WP F3 Diesel AB Set #1, phase II, sound	500 ____
00381	WP F3 Diesel AB Set #2, phase II, sound	500 ____
00382	F3 Diesel AB Set, phase II, sound	500 ____
00383	Caboose Truck, roller bearing, Code 110, pair	10 ____
00384	Caboose Truck, roller bearing, hi-rail, pair	10 ____
00385	NYC F3 Diesel AB Freight Set #1, phase II, sound	500 ____
00386	NYC F3 Diesel AB Freight Set #2, phase II, sound	500 ____
00387	UP Flatcar with trailer (NMRA)	63 ____
00388	Boise Cascade Wrapped Lumber Load	10 ____
00389	Finlay Premium Wrapped Lumber Load	10 ____
00390	Western Carrier Wrapped Lumber Load	10 ____
00391	Weyerhauser Wrapped Lumber Load	10 ____
00392	Pulpwood Load	13 ____
00393	AF Track Adaptor, 8 pieces	5 ____
00394	Bulb, 2.5-volt, 2 pieces	2 ____
00395	Rail Joiner, insulated, yellow, 12 pieces	3 ____
00396	ATSF PS-2 3-bay Covered Hopper #2	50 ____
00397	BN PS-2 3-bay Covered Hopper #2	50 ____
00398	Chessie (B&O) PS-2 3-bay Covered Hopper #2	50 ____
00399	CB&Q PS-2 3-bay Covered Hopper, scheme I #2	50 ____
00400	C&NW PS-2 3-bay Covered Hopper, scheme I #2	50 ____
00401	Conrail PS-2 3-bay Covered Hopper #2	50 ____
00402	GN PS-2 3-bay Covered Hopper #2	50 ____
00403	Erie-Lackawanna PS-2 3-bay Covered Hopper #2	50 ____
00404	NYC PS-2 3-bay Covered Hopper #2	50 ____
00405	UP PS-2 3-bay Covered Hopper #2	50 ____
00407	C&NW (M&StL) PS-2 2-bay Hopper, scheme II #2	50 ____
00408	LNE PS-2 2-bay Covered Hopper #2	50 ____
00409	Central Soya PS-2 2-bay Covered Hopper #2	50 ____

_____ 00410	Roscoe, Snyder & Pacific 40' Steel Rebuilt Boxcar #2	50
_____ 00411	Muncie & Western Ball Lines 40' Steel Rebuilt Boxcar #2	50
_____ 00412	CB&Q PS-2 3-bay Covered Hopper, scheme II #1	50
_____ 00413	Jack Frost PS-2 2-bay Hopper #2 (RSSVP Models)	50
_____ 00414	Cedar Heights Clay PS-2 3-bay Covered Hopper	55
_____ 00415	Ann Arbor PS-2 2-bay Covered Hopper #1 (TCA)	50
_____ 00416	Ann Arbor PS-2 2-bay Covered Hopper #2 (TCA)	50
_____ 00417	M&StL PS-2 3-bay Covered Hopper #1	50
_____ 00418	M&StL PS-2 3-bay Covered Hopper #2	50
_____ 00419	M&StL PS-2 2-bay Covered Hopper #2	50
_____ 00420	CB&Q PS-2 3-bay Covered Hopper, scheme II #2	50
_____ 00421	Conrail SW9 Diesel Set, 4 cars	300
_____ 00422	BN SW9 Diesel Set, 5 cars	370
_____ 00423	ATSF SW9 Diesel Set, 6 cars	430
_____ 00425	Glencoe Skokie Valley Single-sheathed Boxcar (NMRA)	63
_____ 00426	Chesapeake & Ohio SW9 Diesel #1	200
_____ 00427	Chesapeake & Ohio SW9 Diesel #2	200
_____ 00428	Great Northern SW9 Diesel #1	200
_____ 00429	Great Northern SW9 Diesel #2	200
_____ 00430	D&RGW SW9 Diesel #1	200
_____ 00431	D&RGW SW9 Diesel #2	200
_____ 00432	ICG SW9 Diesel #1	200
_____ 00433	ICG SW9 Diesel #2	200
_____ 00434	Northern Pacific SW9 Diesel #1	200
_____ 00435	Northern Pacific SW9 Diesel #2	200
_____ 00436	UP SW9 Diesel, scheme II #1	200
_____ 00437	UP SW9 Diesel, scheme II #2	200
_____ 00438	SW1 Diesel	200
_____ 00439	Boston & Maine SW1 Diesel #1	200
_____ 00440	Boston & Maine SW1 Diesel #2	200
_____ 00441	Chessie (B&O) SW1 Diesel #1	200
_____ 00442	Chessie (B&O) SW1 Diesel #2	200
_____ 00443	C&NW SW1 Diesel #1	200
_____ 00444	C&NW SW1 Diesel #2	200
_____ 00445	WP SW1 Diesel #1	200
_____ 00446	WP SW1 Diesel #2	200
_____ 00447	CMStP&P SW1 Diesel #1	200
_____ 00448	CMStP&P SW1 Diesel #2	200
_____ 00449	PRR SW1 Diesel #1	200
_____ 00450	PRR SW1 Diesel #2	200
_____ 00451	Seaboard SW1 Diesel	200
_____ 00452	Soo Line SW1 Diesel	200
_____ 00453	Lehigh Valley SW1 Diesel #1	200
_____ 00454	Lehigh Valley SW1 Diesel #2	200
_____ 00455	SP SW1 Diesel #1	200

S-HELPER SERVICE 1994-2012

Retail

00456	SP SW1 Diesel #2	200 ____
00457	C&O SW9 Diesel Set, 6 cars	370 ____
00458	Conrail SW9 Diesel Set, 4 cars	300 ____
00459	D&RGW SW9 Diesel Set, 6 cars	430 ____
00460	GN SW9 Diesel Set, 6 cars	430 ____
00461	ICG SW9 Diesel Set, 5 cars	370 ____
00462	NP SW9 Diesel Set, 5 cars	370 ____
00463	No. 3 Manual Switch, right hand	40 ____
00464	No. 3 Manual Switch, left hand	40 ____
00465	40" Flextrack, 6 pieces	51 ____
00466	40" Flextrack, 24 pieces	186 ____
00468	5" Straight Track with lighted bumper	22 ____
00469	Flatcar with John Deere combine	55 ____
00470	Flatcar with IH Harvestor combine	55 ____
00471	Flatcar with John Deere log skidder	50 ____
00472	Flatcar with John Deere backhoe and front-end loader	60 ____
00473	Flatcar with 2 John Deere bulldozers	60 ____
00474	PRR PS-2 2-bay Covered Hopper, scheme II #1	50 ____
00475	PRR PS-2 2-bay Covered Hopper, scheme II #2	50 ____
00476	Wooden Billboard Reefer	53 ____
00477	Wooden Billboard Reefer, yellow	53 ____
00478	Wooden Billboard Reefer, orange	53 ____
00479	ART Wooden Billboard Reefer #1	53 ____
00480	ART Wooden Billboard Reefer #2	53 ____
00481	ATSF "Grand Canyon" Wooden Billboard Reefer	53 ____
00482	ATSF "El Capitan" Wooden Billboard Reefer	53 ____
00483	Burlington Wooden Billboard Reefer #1	53 ____
00484	Burlington Wooden Billboard Reefer #2	53 ____
00485	Robin Hood Beer Wooden Billboard Reefer #1	53 ____
00486	Robin Hood Beer Wooden Billboard Reefer #2	53 ____
00487	Gerber Wooden Billboard Reefer #1	53 ____
00489	LV Wooden Billboard Reefer #1	53 ____
00490	LV Wooden Billboard Reefer #2	53 ____
00491	North Western Wooden Billboard Reefer, scheme I #1	53 ____
00492	North Western Wooden Billboard Reefer, scheme I #2	53 ____
00493	North Western Wooden Billboard Reefer, scheme II #1	53 ____
00494	North Western Wooden Billboard Reefer, scheme II #2	53 ____
00495	Merchants Despatch Wooden Billboard Reefer #1	53 ____
00496	Merchants Despatch Wooden Billboard Reefer #2	53 ____
00497	Pacific Great Eastern Wooden Billboard Reefer	74 ____
00498	PFE Wooden Billboard Reefer #1	53 ____
00499	PFE Wooden Billboard Reefer #2	53 ____
00500	Tivoli Beer Wooden Billboard Reefer #1	53 ____
00501	Tivoli Beer Wooden Billboard Reefer #2	53 ____
00502	A&P Wooden Billboard Reefer #1	53 ____

____	**00503**	A&P Wooden Billboard Reefer #2	53
____	**00504**	Old Heidelberg Beer Wooden Billboard Reefer #1	53
____	**00505**	Old Heidelberg Beer Wooden Billboard Reefer #2	53
____	**00506**	Chateau Martin Wooden Billboard Reefer #1 (NASG)	53
____	**00507**	Chateau Martin Wooden Billboard Reefer #2 (NASG)	53
____	**00508**	Chateau Martin Wooden Billboard Reefer #3 (NASG)	53
____	**00509**	CUVA PS-2 2-bay Covered Hopper #1 (CVSG)	50
____	**00510**	CUVA PS-2 2-bay Covered Hopper #2 (CVSG)	50
____	**00511**	Flatcar with John Deere excavator	50
____	**00512**	Flatcar with 3 Bobcats	55
____	**00513**	Berghoff Beer Billboard Reefer (Scenery Unlimited)	53
____	**00514**	Wilson Car Lines Billboard Reefer (Scenery Unlimited)	53
____	**00515**	Zion Figs Wooden Billboard Reefer	53
____	**00516**	Ballantine Beer Wooden Billboard Reefer #1	53
____	**00517**	Ballantine Beer Wooden Billboard Reefer #2	53
____	**00518**	Parrot Potatoes Wooden Billboard Reefer	53
____	**00519**	40' Steel Rebuilt Boxcar, S Gaugian 40th Anniversary	50
____	**00520**	B&O 40' Steel Rebuilt Boxcar #1 (Boys RR Club)	50
____	**00521**	PRR Merchandise Service Rebuilt Boxcar, scheme I	50
____	**00522**	GN 40' Steel Rebuilt Boxcar, scheme II #1	50
____	**00523**	GN 40' Steel Rebuilt Boxcar, scheme II #2	50
____	**00524**	B&O 40' Steel Rebuilt Boxcar #2 (Boys RR Club)	50
____	**00525**	IGA Wooden Billboard Reefer #1 (RSSVP Models)	53
____	**00526**	IGA Wooden Billboard Reefer #2 (RSSVP Models)	53
____	**00527**	Narragansett Billboard Reefer #1 (RSSVP Models)	53
____	**00528**	Narragansett Billboard Reefer #2 (RSSVP Models)	53
____	**00529**	Flatcar with 3 New Holland grinder mixers	55
____	**00530**	Flatcar with Terra Gator dry fertilizer spreader	55
____	**00531**	Flatcar with Terra Gator liquid fertilizer spreader	55
____	**00532**	Flatcar with 4 John Deere skid loaders	60
____	**00533**	Switch Controller with 42" wire and extension	10
____	**00534**	Switch Controller with extension wire, 3 pieces	8
____	**00535**	IC Bulkhead Flatcar with pipe load	56
____	**00536**	ICG Switcher Set, 4 cars	300
____	**00537**	Soo Switcher Set, 5 cars	370
____	**00538**	CMStP&P Switcher Set, 5 cars	370
____	**00539**	GN Switcher Set, 6 cars	400
____	**00540**	Seaboard Switcher Set, 6 cars	400
____	**00541**	CB&Q F3 Diesel Freight Set, 6 cars	430
____	**00542**	USRA Double-sheathed Boxcar	50
____	**00543**	ACL USRA Double-sheathed Boxcar	50
____	**00544**	B&M USRA Double-sheathed Boxcar	50
____	**00545**	C&NW USRA Double-sheathed Boxcar	50
____	**00546**	D&LW USRA Double-sheathed Boxcar	50
____	**00547**	GN USRA Double-sheathed Boxcar	50

S-HELPER SERVICE 1994-2012

Retail

00548	NYC USRA Double-sheathed Boxcar	50 ____
00549	Toronto, Hamilton & Buffalo Double-sheathed Boxcar #1	50 ____
00550	Union Pacific USRA Double-sheathed Boxcar	50 ____
00551	Flatcar with IH Harvestor and corn load	55 ____
00552	LocoMatic 10-button Controller	70 ____
00554	C&NW MOW Flatcar	50 ____
00555	C&NW (M&StL) MOW Flatcar	50 ____
00556	Conrail Standard Flatcar #1	50 ____
00557	Conrail Standard Flatcar #2	50 ____
00558	Grand Truck Western Standard Flatcar #1	50 ____
00559	Grand Truck Western Standard Flatcar #2	50 ____
00560	Reading Standard Flatcar #1	50 ____
00561	Reading Standard Flatcar #2	50 ____
00562	Union Pacific Standard Flatcar, scheme II #1	50 ____
00563	Union Pacific Standard Flatcar, scheme II #2	50 ____
00564	NP USRA Double-sheathed Boxcar	70 ____
00565	Bulb 12-volt, 2 pieces	2 ____
00566	PFE Wooden Billboard Reefer, scheme II #1	53 ____
00567	PFE Wooden Billboard Reefer, scheme II #2	53 ____
00568	Lackawanna Wooden Billboard Reefer #1 (NASG)	53 ____
00569	Lackawanna Wooden Billboard Reefer #2 (NASG)	53 ____
00570	Baby Ruth Wooden Billboard Reefer #1	53 ____
00571	Baby Ruth Wooden Billboard Reefer #2	56 ____
00572	Ralston Purina Wooden Billboard Reefer	53 ____
00573	BAR Wooden Billboard Reefer #1	53 ____
00574	BAR Wooden Billboard Reefer #2	53 ____
00575	MP (NOT&M) "Eagle" 40' Steel Rebuilt Boxcar #1	50 ____
00576	MP (NOT&M) "Eagle" 40' Steel Rebuilt Boxcar #2	50 ____
00577	CStP&O 40' Steel Rebuilt Boxcar #1	50 ____
00578	CStP&O 40' Steel Rebuilt Boxcar #2	50 ____
00579	CGW "C" 40' Steel Rebuilt Boxcar	50 ____
00580	CGW "SL" 40' Steel Rebuilt Boxcar	50 ____
00581	CGW "DF" 40' Steel Rebuilt Boxcar	50 ____
00582	CGW "DFb" 40' Steel Rebuilt Boxcar	50 ____
00583	Dutch Cleanser Wooden Billboard Reefer #1	53 ____
00584	Land O' Lakes Wooden Billboard Reefer #1	53 ____
00585	Land O' Lakes Billboard Reefer #2 (Scenery Unlimited)	53 ____
00586	Flatcar with 4 John Deere 430 Crawlers	60 ____
00587	Switch Stand with marker light	6 ____
00588	Coupler, F3 mount, Kadee style, pair	3 ____
00589	Flatcar with 4 New Holland skid steers	60 ____
00590	Flatcar with John Deere wheel loader	50 ____
00591	Flatcar with John Deere grader	50 ____
00592	Dutch Cleanser Wooden Billboard Reefer #2	53 ____
00593	Chessie Extended Vision Caboose #1	70 ____

		Retail
_____ **00594**	Chessie Extended Vision Caboose #2	70
_____ **00595**	Chessie Safety Special Extended Vision Caboose	70
_____ **00596**	C&NW Extended Vision Caboose #3	70
_____ **00597**	C&NW Extended Vision Caboose #4	70
_____ **00598**	MEC Extended Vision Caboose, scheme II	70
_____ **00599**	Reading Extended Vision Caboose #1	70
_____ **00600**	Reading Extended Vision Caboose #2	70
_____ **00601**	Rock Island Extended Vision Caboose #1	70
_____ **00602**	Rock Island Extended Vision Caboose #2	70
_____ **00603**	ATSF Extended Vision Caboose, scheme II #1	70
_____ **00604**	ATSF Extended Vision Caboose, scheme II #2	70
_____ **00605**	CGW "C" 40' Steel Boxcar, scheme II (State Line)	50
_____ **00606**	CGW "SL" 40' Steel Boxcar, scheme II (State Line)	50
_____ **00607**	CGW "DF" 40' Steel Boxcar, scheme II (State Line)	50
_____ **00608**	CGW "DFb" 40' Steel Boxcar, scheme II (State Line)	50
_____ **00609**	Flatcar with Caterpillar 609 Scraper	50
_____ **00610**	Kahn's Wooden Billboard Reefer #1 (Scenery Unlimited)	53
_____ **00611**	Kahn's Wooden Billboard Reefer #2 (Scenery Unlimited)	53
_____ **00612**	B&O F3 Diesel A Unit #1, phase II, sound	300
_____ **00613**	B&O F3 Diesel A Unit #2, phase II, sound	300
_____ **00614**	CB&Q F3 Diesel A Unit #1, phase II, sound	300
_____ **00615**	CB&Q F3 Diesel A Unit #2, phase II, sound	300
_____ **00616**	C&NW F3 Diesel A Unit #1, phase II, sound	300
_____ **00617**	C&NW F3 Diesel #2, phase II, sound	300
_____ **00618**	DL&W F3 Diesel A Unit #1, phase II, sound	300
_____ **00619**	DL&W F3 Diesel A Unit #2, phase II, sound	300
_____ **00620**	MEC F3 Diesel A Unit #1, phase II, sound	300
_____ **00621**	MEC F3 Diesel A Unit #2, phase II, sound	300
_____ **00622**	NYC Passenger F3 Diesel A Unit #1, phase II, sound	300
_____ **00623**	NYC Passenger F3 Diesel A Unit #2, phase II, sound	300
_____ **00624**	Southern F3 Diesel A Unit #1, phase II, sound	300
_____ **00625**	Southern F3 Diesel A Unit #2, phase II, sound	300
_____ **00626**	SP F3 Diesel A Unit #1, phase II, sound	300
_____ **00627**	SP F3 Diesel A Unit #2, phase II, sound	300
_____ **00628**	UP F3 Diesel A Unit #1, phase II, sound	300
_____ **00629**	UP F3 Diesel A Unit #2, phase II, sound	300
_____ **00630**	WP F3 Diesel A Unit #1, phase II, sound	300
_____ **00631**	WP F3 Diesel A Unit #2, phase II, sound	300
_____ **00632**	F3 Diesel A Unit, phase II, sound	300
_____ **00633**	NYC Freight F3 Diesel A Unit #1, phase II, sound	300
_____ **00634**	NYC Freight F3 Diesel A Unit #2, phase II, sound	300
_____ **00635**	B&O F3 Diesel B Unit #1, phase II, sound	290
_____ **00636**	B&O F3 Diesel B Unit #2, phase II, sound	290
_____ **00637**	CB&Q F3 Diesel B Unit #1, phase II, sound	290
_____ **00638**	CB&Q F3 Diesel B Unit #2, phase II, sound	290

00639	C&NW F3 Diesel B Unit #1, phase II, sound	290 ____
00640	C&NW F3 Diesel B Unit #2, phase II, sound	290 ____
00641	D&LW F3 Diesel B Unit #1, phase II, sound	290 ____
00642	D&LW F3 Diesel B Unit #2, phase II, sound	290 ____
00643	MEC F3 Diesel B Unit #1, phase II, sound	290 ____
00644	MEC F3 Diesel B Unit #2, phase II, sound	290 ____
00645	NYC Passenger F3 Diesel B Unit #1, phase II, sound	290 ____
00646	NYC Passenger F3 Diesel B Unit #2, phase II, sound	290 ____
00647	Southern F3 Diesel B Unit #1, phase II, sound	290 ____
00648	Southern F3 Diesel B Unit #2, phase II, sound	290 ____
00649	SP F3 Diesel B Unit #1, phase II, sound	290 ____
00650	SP F3 Diesel B Unit #2, phase II, sound	290 ____
00651	UP F3 Diesel B Unit #1, phase II, sound	290 ____
00652	UP F3 Diesel B Unit #2, phase II, sound	290 ____
00653	WP F3 Diesel B Unit #1, phase II, sound	290 ____
00654	WP F3 Diesel B Unit #2, phase II, sound	290 ____
00655	F3 Diesel B Unit, phase II, sound	290 ____
00656	NYC F3 Diesel B Unit #1, phase II, sound	290 ____
00657	NYC F3 Diesel B Unit #2, phase II, sound	290 ____
00658	Brookside Milk Wooden Billboard Reefer (Port Lines)	53 ____
00659	Saval Foods Wooden Billboard Reefer #1 (Port Lines)	53 ____
00660	Metal Rail Joiners for flex track, 36 pieces	4 ____
00661	PRR 40' Steel Rebuilt Boxcar, scheme II	50 ____
00662	GN 40' Steel Rebuilt Boxcar, scheme III #1	50 ____
00663	GN 40' Steel Rebuilt Boxcar, scheme III #2	50 ____
00664	33" Scale Caboose Wheel Set, Code 110, 4-pack	4 ____
00665	Speaker, 36mm diameter	3 ____
00666	Chessie SW1 Diesel Freight Set, 6 cars	370 ____
00667	MU Cables, pair	2 ____
00670	5" Uncoupler Track	22 ____
00671	5" Accessory Track	22 ____
00672	Flatcar with 2 Caterpillar D6R XL Bulldozers	60 ____
00673	Flatcar with Caterpillar D25D Articulated Truck	55 ____
00674	Flatcar with Caterpillar 950F Wheel Loader	50 ____
00675	Flatcar with Caterpillar 12G Grader	50 ____
00676	Flatcar with 2 Caterpillar Challenger Tractors	60 ____
00677	Flatcar with Caterpillar tractor and boom sprayer	55 ____
00678	Flatcar with Caterpillar tractor and spreader	55 ____
00679	Flatcar with Caterpillar tractor and Knight Slinger	55 ____
00680	Flatcar with 2 Caterpillar D6R Bulldozers	60 ____
00681	Flatcar with Caterpillar 611 Scraper	55 ____
00682	PFE Wooden Billboard Reefer Set, 3 cars	110 ____
00683	Burlington Wooden Billboard Reefer Set, 3 cars	110 ____
00684	North Western Wooden Billboard Reefer Set, 3 cars	110 ____
00685	FGE Wooden Billboard Reefer Set #1, 3 cars	110 ____

_____	**00686**	NP Wooden Billboard Reefer #1	53
_____	**00687**	NP Wooden Billboard Reefer #2	53
_____	**00688**	Knickerbocker Billboard Reefer #1 (Port Lines)	53
_____	**00689**	Knickerbocker Billboard Reefer #2 (Port Lines)	53
_____	**00690**	Carling Black Label Billboard Reefer #1 (Port Lines)	53
_____	**00691**	Carling Black Label Billboard Reefer #2 (Port Lines)	53
_____	**00692**	C&NW SW9 Diesel Set, 5 cars	370
_____	**00693**	C&NW Diesel F Unit Set, 6 cars	430
_____	**00694**	MEC Diesel F Unit Set, 5 cars	370
_____	**00697**	Edelweiss Beer Wooden Billboard Reefer	53
_____	**00698**	Kraft Cheese Wooden Billboard Reefer	53
_____	**00699**	CN Wooden Billboard Reefer #1	53
_____	**00700**	CN Wooden Billboard Reefer #2	53
_____	**00701**	B&M 40' Steel Rebuilt Boxcar #1 (Boys RR Club)	50
_____	**00702**	B&M 40' Steel Rebuilt Boxcar #2 (Boys RR Club)	50
_____	**00703**	ATSF 40' Steel Rebuilt Boxcar #1 (Boys RR Club)	50
_____	**00704**	ATSF 40' Steel Rebuilt Boxcar #2 (Boys RR Club)	50
_____	**00705**	D&RGW 40' Steel Boxcar #1, white (Boys RR Club)	50
_____	**00706**	D&RGW 40' Steel Boxcar #2, white (Boys RR Club)	50
_____	**00707**	D&RGW 40' Steel Boxcar #1, silver (Boys RR Club)	50
_____	**00708**	D&RGW 40' Steel Boxcar #2, silver (Boys RR Club)	50
_____	**00709**	Central of Georgia Boxcar, black #1 (Boys RR Club)	50
_____	**00710**	Central of Georgia Boxcar, maroon (Boys RR Club)	50
_____	**00711**	Central of Georgia Boxcar, black #2 (Boys RR Club)	50
_____	**00712**	Central of Georgia Boxcar, black #3 (Boys RR Club)	50
_____	**00713**	NP SW9 Diesel Freight Set, 4 cars	300
_____	**00714**	CMStP&P SW1 Diesel Freight Set, 5 cars	370
_____	**00715**	CB&Q F3 Diesel Freight Set, 6 cars	430
_____	**00716**	Santa Fe "The Scout" Wooden Billboard Reefer	53
_____	**00717**	Wooden Billboard Reefer, red	53
_____	**00720**	Saval Foods Billboard Reefer #2 (Port Lines)	53
_____	**00721**	B&O 40' Steel Rebuilt Boxcar #3 (Boys RR Club)	50
_____	**00722**	B&O 40' Steel Rebuilt Boxcar #4 (Boys RR Club)	50
_____	**00723**	Ore Car, black	40
_____	**00724**	Ore Car, red	40
_____	**00725**	DM&IR Ore Car	40
_____	**00726**	DM&IR Ore Car 5-pack Set A	180
_____	**00727**	B&LE Ore Car	40
_____	**00728**	B&LE Ore Car 5-pack Set A	180
_____	**00729**	CN Ore Car	40
_____	**00730**	CN Ore Car 5-pack	180
_____	**00731**	CP Ore Car	40
_____	**00732**	CP Ore Car 5-pack	180
_____	**00735**	GN Ore Car, scheme I	40
_____	**00736**	GN Ore Car 5-pack Set A, scheme I	180

S-HELPER SERVICE 1994-2012

Retail

00737	CMStP&P Ore Car, scheme I	40 ____
00738	CMStP&P Ore Car 5-pack Set A, scheme I	180 ____
00741	SP Ore Car	40 ____
00742	SP Ore Car 5-pack	180 ____
00743	UP Ore Car	40 ____
00744	UP Ore Car 5-pack	180 ____
00745	DCC Sound Decoder, F Unit	160 ____
00746	ATSF 40' Steel Rebuilt Boxcar	50 ____
00747	C&NW 40' Steel Rebuilt Boxcar	50 ____
00748	NYC (P&LE) 40' Steel Rebuilt Boxcar #1	50 ____
00749	UP 40' Steel Rebuilt Boxcar	50 ____
00750	ATSF USRA Single-sheathed Boxcar	50 ____
00751	C&NW USRA Single-sheathed Boxcar	50 ____
00752	NYC USRA Single-sheathed Boxcar	50 ____
00753	UP USRA Single-sheathed Boxcar	50 ____
00754	ATSF Stock Car, scheme II	50 ____
00755	C&NW Stock Car #3	50 ____
00756	NYC Stock Car	50 ____
00757	UP (OSL) Stock Car, scheme II #3	50 ____
00758	Composite Side Hopper, black	50 ____
00759	Composite Side Hopper, red	50 ____
00760	Ann Arbor Composite Side Hopper 3-pack	100 ____
00761	Ann Arbor Composite Side Hopper	50 ____
00762	ATSF Composite Side Hopper 3-pack	100 ____
00763	ATSF Composite Side Hopper	50 ____
00764	B&O Composite Side Hopper 3-pack	100 ____
00765	B&O Composite Side Hopper	50 ____
00766	C&O Composite Side Hopper 3-pack	100 ____
00767	C&O Composite Side Hopper	50 ____
00768	CB&Q Composite Side Hopper 3-pack	100 ____
00769	CB&Q Composite Side Hopper	50 ____
00770	Clinchfield Composite Side Hopper 3-pack	100 ____
00771	Clinchfield Composite Side Hopper	50 ____
00772	LV Composite Side Hopper 3-pack	100 ____
00773	LV Composite Side Hopper	50 ____
00774	L&N Composite Side Hopper 3-pack	100 ____
00775	L&N Composite Side Hopper	50 ____
00776	NKP Composite Side Hopper 3-pack	100 ____
00777	NKP Composite Side Hopper	50 ____
00778	PRR Composite Side Hopper 3-pack	100 ____
00779	PRR Composite Side Hopper #4	50 ____
00780	Virginian Composite Side Hopper 3-pack	100 ____
00781	Virginian Composite Side Hopper	50 ____
00782	Wabash Composite Side Hopper 3-pack	100 ____
00783	Wabash Composite Side Hopper	50 ____

_____ **00788**	Feeder Wire Terminal, 12 pieces	4
_____ **00796**	NKP Wooden Billboard Reefer (CVSG)	53
_____ **00797**	NKP Wooden Billboard Reefer (CVSG)	53
_____ **00798**	NYNH&H Wooden Billboard Reefer #1 (Port Lines)	53
_____ **00799**	NYNH&H Wooden Billboard Reefer #2 (Port Lines)	53
_____ **00800**	Grand Union Wooden Billboard Reefer	53
_____ **00801**	Borden's Cheese Wooden Billboard Reefer	53
_____ **00802**	Pabst Blue Ribbon Wooden Billboard Reefer	53
_____ **00803**	Mexene Chili Powder Wooden Billboard Reefer	53
_____ **00804**	Swift Wooden Billboard Reefer 3-pack	110
_____ **00805**	B&O 40' Steel Rebuilt Boxcar #5 (Boys RR Club)	50
_____ **00806**	North Stratford 40' Steel Boxcar (Bristol S Gauge)	50
_____ **00807**	North Stratford 40' Steel Boxcar (Bristol S Gauge)	50
_____ **00808**	Frisco 40' Steel Rebuilt Boxcar 3-pack	100
_____ **00809**	F7 Diesel A Unit, phase I, AC/DC LocoMatic sound	300
_____ **00810**	ATSF Passenger F7 Diesel A Unit #1, phase I	300
_____ **00811**	ATSF Passenger F7 Diesel A Unit #2, phase I	300
_____ **00812**	ATSF Freight F7 Diesel A Unit #1, phase I	300
_____ **00813**	ATSF Freight F7 Diesel A Unit #2, phase I	300
_____ **00814**	B&M F7 Diesel A Unit #1, phase I	300
_____ **00815**	B&M F7 Diesel A Unit #2, phase I	300
_____ **00816**	D&RGW F7 Diesel A Unit #1, phase I	300
_____ **00817**	D&RGW F7 Diesel A Unit #2, phase I	300
_____ **00818**	GN F7 Diesel A Unit #1, phase I	300
_____ **00819**	GN F7 Diesel A Unit #2, phase I	300
_____ **00820**	MP F7 Diesel A Unit #1, phase I	300
_____ **00821**	MP F7 Diesel A Unit #2, phase I	300
_____ **00822**	PRR F7 Diesel A Unit #1, phase I	300
_____ **00823**	PRR F7 Diesel A Unit #2, phase I	300
_____ **00824**	F7 Diesel B Unit, phase I, AC/DC LocoMatic sound	290
_____ **00825**	ATSF Passenger F7 Diesel B Unit #1, phase I	290
_____ **00826**	ATSF Passenger F7 Diesel B Unit #2, phase I	290
_____ **00827**	ATSF Freight F7 Diesel B Unit #1, phase I	290
_____ **00828**	ATSF Freight F7 Diesel B Unit #2, phase I	290
_____ **00829**	B&M F7 Diesel B Unit #1, phase I	290
_____ **00830**	B&M F7 Diesel B Unit #2, phase I	290
_____ **00831**	D&RGW F7 Diesel B Unit #1, phase I	290
_____ **00832**	D&RGW F7 Diesel B Unit #2, phase I	290
_____ **00833**	GN F7 Diesel B Unit #1, phase I	290
_____ **00834**	GN F7 Diesel B Unit #2, phase I	290
_____ **00835**	MP F7 Diesel B Unit #1, phase I	290
_____ **00836**	MP F7 Diesel B Unit #2, phase II	290
_____ **00837**	PRR F7 Diesel B Unit #1, phase I	290
_____ **00838**	PRR F7 Diesel B Unit #2, phase I	290
_____ **00839**	F7 Diesel A Unit, phase I, DCC sound	300

Retail

00840	ATSF Passenger F7 Diesel A Unit #1, phase I	300 ____
00841	ATSF Passenger F7 Diesel A Unit #2, phase I	300 ____
00842	ATSF Freight F7 Diesel A Unit #1, phase I	300 ____
00843	SF Freight F7 Diesel A Unit #2, phase I	300 ____
00844	B&M F7 Diesel A Unit #1, phase I	300 ____
00845	B&M F7 Diesel A Unit #2, phase I	300 ____
00846	D&RGW F7 Diesel A Unit #1, phase I	300 ____
00847	D&RGW F7 Diesel A Unit #2, phase I	300 ____
00848	GN F7 Diesel A Unit #1, phase I	300 ____
00849	GN F7 Diesel A Unit #2, phase I	300 ____
00850	MP F7 Diesel A Unit #1, phase I	300 ____
00851	MP F7 Diesel A Unit #2, phase I	300 ____
00852	PRR F7 Diesel A Unit #1, phase I	300 ____
00853	PRR F7 Diesel A Unit #2, phase I	300 ____
00854	F7 Diesel B Unit, phase I, DCC sound	290 ____
00855	ATSF Passenger F7 Diesel B Unit #1, phase I	290 ____
00856	ATSF Passenger F7 Diesel B Unit #2, phase I	290 ____
00857	ATSF Freight F7 Diesel B Unit #1, phase I	290 ____
00858	SF Freight F7 Diesel B Unit #2, phase I	290 ____
00859	B&M F7 Diesel B Unit #1, phase I	290 ____
00860	B&M F7 Diesel B Unit #2, phase I	290 ____
00861	D&RGW F7 Diesel B Unit #1, phase I	290 ____
00862	D&RGW F7 Diesel B Unit #2, phase I	290 ____
00863	GN F7 Diesel B Unit #1, phase I	290 ____
00864	D&RGW F7 Diesel B Unit #2, phase I	290 ____
00865	MP F7 Diesel B Unit #1, phase I	290 ____
00866	MP F7 Diesel B Unit #2, phase I	290 ____
00867	PRR F7 Diesel B Unit #1, phase I	290 ____
00868	PRR F7 Diesel B Unit #2, phase I	290 ____
00869	F7 Diesel A Unit, phase I, DC no sound	200 ____
00870	ATSF Passenger F7 Diesel A Unit #1, phase I	200 ____
00871	ATSF Passenger F7 Diesel A Unit #2, phase I	200 ____
00872	ATSF Freight F7 Diesel A Unit #1, phase I	200 ____
00873	SF Freight F7 Diesel A Unit #2, phase I	200 ____
00874	B&M F7 Diesel A Unit #1, phase I	200 ____
00875	B&M F7 Diesel A Unit #2, phase I	200 ____
00876	D&RGW F7 Diesel A Unit #1, phase I	200 ____
00877	D&RGW F7 Diesel A Unit #2, phase I	200 ____
00878	GN F7 Diesel A Unit #1, phase I	200 ____
00879	GN F7 Diesel A Unit #1, phase I	200 ____
00880	MP F7 Diesel A Unit #1, phase I	200 ____
00881	MP F7 Diesel A Unit #2, phase I	200 ____
00882	PRR F7 Diesel A Unit #1, phase I	200 ____
00883	PRR F7 Diesel A Unit #2, phase I	200 ____
00884	F7 Diesel B Unit, phase I, DC no sound	190 ____

____	00885	ATSF Passenger F7 Diesel B Unit #1, phase I	190
____	00886	ATSF Passenger F7 Diesel B Unit #2, phase I	190
____	00887	ATSF Freight F7 Diesel B Unit #1, phase I	190
____	00888	ATSF Freight F7 Diesel B Unit #2, phase I	190
____	00889	B&M F7 Diesel B Unit #1, phase I	190
____	00890	B&M F7 Diesel B Unit #2, phase I	190
____	00891	D&RGW F7 Diesel B Unit #1, phase I	190
____	00892	D&RGW F7 Diesel B Unit #2, phase I	190
____	00893	GN F7 Diesel B Unit #1, phase I	190
____	00894	GN F7 Diesel B Unit #2, phase I	190
____	00895	MP F7 Diesel B Unit #1, phase I	190
____	00896	MP F7 Diesel B Unit #2, phase I	190
____	00897	PRR F7 Diesel B Unit #1, phase I	190
____	00898	PRR F7 Diesel B Unit #2, phase I	190
____	00899	F7 Diesel ABA Set, phase I, DC LocoMatic sound	680
____	00900	ATSF Passenger F7 Diesel ABA, phase I	680
____	00901	ATSF Freight F7 Diesel ABA Set, phase I	680
____	00902	B&M F7 Diesel ABA Set, phase I	680
____	00903	D&RGW F7 Diesel ABA Set, phase I	680
____	00904	GN F7 Diesel ABA Set, phase I	680
____	00905	MP F7 Diesel ABA Set, phase I	680
____	00906	PRR F7 Diesel ABA Set, phase I	680
____	00907	F7 Diesel ABA Set, phase I, DCC sound	680
____	00908	ATSF Passenger F7 Diesel ABA Set, phase I	680
____	00909	ATSF Freight F7 Diesel ABA Set, phase I	680
____	00910	B&M F7 Diesel ABA Set, phase I	680
____	00911	D&RGW F7 Diesel ABA Set, phase I	680
____	00912	GN F7 Diesel ABA Set, phase I	680
____	00913	MP F7 Diesel ABA Set, phase I	680
____	00914	PRR F7 Diesel ABA Set, phase I	680
____	00915	F7 Diesel ABA Set, phase I, DC no sound	680
____	00916	ATSF Passenger F7 Diesel ABA Set, phase I	680
____	00917	ATSF Freight F7 Diesel ABA Set, phase I	680
____	00918	B&M F7 Diesel ABA Set, phase I	680
____	00919	D&RGW F7 Diesel ABA Set, phase I	680
____	00920	GN F7 Diesel ABA Set, phase I	680
____	00921	MP F7 Diesel ABA Set, phase I	680
____	00922	PRR F7 Diesel ABA Set, phase I	680
____	00923	Kahn's Wooden Billboard Reefer, scheme II #1	53
____	00924	Kahn's Wooden Billboard Reefer, scheme II #2	53
____	00925	Accessory Control Button	10
____	00926	5" Straight Track with unlighted bumper	15
____	00927	F7 Diesel AB Set, phase I, DC LocoMatic sound	490
____	00928	ATSF Passenger F7 Diesel AB Set #1, phase I	490
____	00929	ATSF Passenger F7 Diesel AB Set #2, phase I	490

Retail

00930	ATSF Freight F7 Diesel AB Set #1, phase I	490 ___
00931	ATSF Freight F7 Diesel AB Set #2, phase I	490 ___
00932	B&M F7 Diesel AB Set #1, phase I	490 ___
00933	B&M F7 Diesel AB Set #2, phase I	490 ___
00934	D&RGW F7 Diesel AB Set #1, phase I	490 ___
00935	D&RGW F7 Diesel AB Set #2, phase I	490 ___
00936	GN F7 Diesel AB Set #1, phase I	490 ___
00937	GN F7 Diesel AB Set #2, phase I	490 ___
00938	MP F7 Diesel AB Set #1, phase I	490 ___
00939	MP F7 Diesel AB Set #2, phase I	490 ___
00940	PRR F7 Diesel AB Set #1, phase I	490 ___
00941	PRR F7 Diesel AB Set #2, phase I	490 ___
00942	F7 Diesel AA Set, phase I, AC/DC LocoMatic sound	490 ___
00943	ATSF Passenger F7 Diesel AA Set, phase I	490 ___
00944	ATSF Freight F7 Diesel AA Set, phase I	490 ___
00945	B&M F7 Diesel AA Set, phase I	490 ___
00946	D&RGW F7 Diesel AA Set, phase I	490 ___
00947	GN F7 Diesel AA Set, phase I	490 ___
00948	MP F7 Diesel AA Set, phase I	490 ___
00949	PRR F7 Diesel AA Set, phase I	490 ___
00950	F7 Diesel ABB Set, phase I, AC/DC LocoMatic sound	680 ___
00951	ATSF Passenger F7 Diesel ABB Set, phase I	680 ___
00952	ATSF Freight F7 Diesel ABB Set, phase I	680 ___
00953	B&M F7 Diesel ABB Set, phase I	680 ___
00954	D&RGW F7 Diesel ABB Set, phase I	680 ___
00955	GN F7 Diesel ABB Set, phase I	680 ___
00956	MP F7 Diesel ABB Set, phase I	680 ___
00957	PRR F7 Diesel ABB Set, phase I	680 ___
00958	F7 Diesel ABBA Set, phase I, AC/DC LocoMatic sound	880 ___
00959	ATSF Passenger F7 Diesel ABBA Set, phase I	880 ___
00960	ATSF Freight F7 Diesel ABBA Set, phase I	880 ___
00961	B&M F7 Diesel ABBA Set, phase I	880 ___
00962	D&RGW F7 Diesel ABBA Set, phase I	880 ___
00963	GN F7 Diesel ABBA Set, phase I	880 ___
00964	MP F7 Diesel ABBA Set, phase I	880 ___
00965	PRR F7 Diesel ABBA Set, phase I	880 ___
00966	CNJ PS-2 2-bay Covered Hopper, scheme II	50 ___
00967	33" Wheel Set, AF, single insulated, 4-pack	5 ___
00968	Brachs PS-2 2-bay Hopper, scheme I #1 (RSSVP Models)	50 ___
00969	Brachs PS-2 2-bay Hopper, scheme I #2 (RSSVP Models)	50 ___
00970	Brachs PS-2 2-bay Hopper, scheme II #1 (RSSVP Models)	50 ___
00971	Brachs PS-2 2-bay Hopper, scheme II #2 (RSSVP Models)	50 ___
00972	Jack Frost PS-2 2-bay Hopper #2 (RSSVP Models)	58 ___
00973	G&W PS-2 3-bay Covered Hopper #1	50 ___
00974	G&W PS-2 3-bay Covered Hopper #2	50 ___

____	**00975**	Reading PS-2 3-bay Covered Hopper #1	50
____	**00976**	Reading PS-2 3-bay Covered Hopper #2	50
____	**00977**	Wabash PS-2 3-bay Covered Hopper #1	50
____	**00978**	Wabash PS-2 3-bay Covered Hopper #2	50
____	**00979**	33" Wheel Set, AF, double insulated, 4-pack	5
____	**00980**	Panel Side Hopper, black	50
____	**00981**	Panel Side Hopper, red	50
____	**00982**	Anderson Panel Side Hopper 3-pack Set A	100
____	**00983**	Anderson Panel Side Hopper #4	50
____	**00984**	Ann Arbor Panel Side Hopper 3-pack	100
____	**00985**	Ann Arbor Panel Side Hopper	50
____	**00986**	C&O Panel Side Hopper 3-pack	100
____	**00987**	C&O Panel Side Hopper	50
____	**00988**	SLSF Panel Side Hopper 3-pack	100
____	**00989**	SLSF Panel Side Hopper	50
____	**00990**	D&H Panel Side Hopper 3-pack	100
____	**00991**	D&H Panel Side Hopper	50
____	**00992**	NYC Panel Side Hopper Car 3-pack, scheme I	100
____	**00993**	NYC Panel Side Hopper Car, scheme I	50
____	**00994**	NYC Panel Side Hopper 3-pack, scheme II	100
____	**00995**	NYC Panel Side Hopper, scheme I	50
____	**00996**	NYNH&H Panel Side Hopper	50
____	**00997**	PRR Panel Side Hopper	50
____	**00998**	Wabash Panel Side Hopper 3-pack	100
____	**00999**	Wabash Panel Side Hopper	50
____	**01000**	PFE Wooden Billboard Reefer, scheme I #1	53
____	**01001**	PFE Wooden Billboard Reefer, scheme I #2	53
____	**01002**	ART Wooden Billboard Reefer #3	53
____	**01003**	ART Wooden Billboard Reefer #4	53
____	**01004**	CNW Wooden Billboard Reefer #1 (Chicagoland)	53
____	**01005**	CNW Wooden Billboard Reefer #2 (Chicagoland)	59
____	**01006**	Northern "Bananas" Wooden Billboard Reefer	53
____	**01007**	Schlitz Beer Wooden Billboard Reefer	53
____	**01008**	MP "Eagle" 40' Steel Rebuilt Boxcar #1	50
____	**01009**	MP "Eagle" 40' Steel Rebuilt Boxcar #2	50
____	**01010**	CN 40' Steel Rebuilt Boxcar #1	50
____	**01011**	CN 40' Steel Rebuilt Boxcar #2	50
____	**01012**	Seaboard "Orange Blossom Special" Rebuilt Boxcar	50
____	**01013**	Seaboard "Silver Meteor" 40' Steel Rebuilt Boxcar	50
____	**01014**	ATSF "Super Chief" 40' Steel Rebuilt Boxcar	50
____	**01015**	FGE Wooden Billboard Reefer #1	53
____	**01016**	FGE Wooden Billboard Reefer #2	53
____	**01017**	Century Beer Wooden Billboard Reefer	53
____	**01018**	Burlington Route 40' Steel Boxcar #1 (Boys RR Club)	53
____	**01019**	Burlington Route 40' Steel Boxcar #2 (Boys RR Club)	53

01020	State of Maine BAR 40' Steel Boxcar (Boys RR Club)	53 ___
01021	State of Maine NYNH&H 40' Steel Boxcar (Boys RR Club)	53 ___
01022	L&N "Dixie" 40' Steel Rebuilt Boxcar #1 (Boys RR Club)	53 ___
01023	L&N "Dixie" 40' Steel Rebuilt Boxcar #2 (Boys RR Club)	53 ___
01024	WP 40' Steel Rebuilt Boxcar #1 (Boys RR Club)	53 ___
01025	WP 40' Steel Rebuilt Boxcar #2 (Boys RR Club)	53 ___
01026	PRR 40' Steel Rebuilt Boxcar #1 (Boys RR Club)	53 ___
01027	PRR 40' Steel Rebuilt Boxcar #2 (Boys RR Club)	53 ___
01028	NYC 40' Steel Rebuilt Boxcar #1 (Boys RR Club)	53 ___
01029	NYC 40' Steel Rebuilt Boxcar #2 (Boys RR Club)	53 ___
01030	NYC 40' Steel Rebuilt Boxcar #3 (Boys RR Club)	53 ___
01031	40' Steel Rebuilt Boxcar (CVSG)	53 ___
01032	Tipo Wine Billboard Reefer #1 (Scenery Unlimited)	53 ___
01033	Tipo Wine Billboard Reefer #2 (Scenery Unlimited)	53 ___
01034	ATSF F7 Diesel Freight Set, 6 cars	430 ___
01036	MP F7 Diesel Freight Set, 6 cars	430 ___
01037	S-Trax Bumper, yellow, 2-pack	6 ___
01038	S-Trax Bumper, red, 2-pack	6 ___
01043	ICG SW9 Diesel Freight Set, 4 cars	300 ___
01044	D&RGW SW9 Diesel Freight Set, 5 cars	370 ___
01045	Seaboard SW1 Diesel Freight Set, 5 cars	370 ___
01046	MEC F3 Diesel Freight Set, 5 cars	400 ___
01047	D&RGW Extended Vision Caboose #3	70 ___
01048	D&RGW Extended Vision Caboose #4	70 ___
01049	GTW Panel Side Hopper 3-pack	100 ___
01050	GTW Panel Side Hopper	50 ___
01051	2-8-0 Locomotive, hi-rail wheels, AC/DC LocoMatic sound	600 ___
01052	B&O 2-8-0 Locomotive #1	600 ___
01053	B&O 2-8-0 Locomotive #2	600 ___
01054	ATSF 2-8-0 Locomotive #1	600 ___
01055	ATSF 2-8-0 Locomotive #2	600 ___
01056	C&NW 2-8-0 Locomotive #1	600 ___
01057	C&NW 2-8-0 Locomotive #2	600 ___
01058	Erie 2-8-0 Locomotive #1	600 ___
01059	Erie 2-8-0 Locomotive #2	600 ___
01060	MEC 2-8-0 Locomotive #1	600 ___
01061	MEC 2-8-0 Locomotive #2	600 ___
01062	NYC 2-8-0 Locomotive #1	600 ___
01063	NYC 2-8-0 Locomotive #2	600 ___
01064	Southern 2-8-0 Locomotive #1	600 ___
01066	UP 2-8-0 Locomotive #1	600 ___
01067	UP 2-8-0 Locomotive #2	600 ___
01068	WM 2-8-0 Locomotive #1	600 ___
01069	WM 2-8-0 Locomotive #2	600 ___
01070	Flatcar with Oliver corn picker	55 ___

_____ **01071**	2-8-0 Locomotive, hi-rail wheels, DCC sound	600
_____ **01072**	B&O 2-8-0 Locomotive #1	600
_____ **01073**	B&O 2-8-0 Locomotive #2	600
_____ **01074**	ATSF 2-8-0 Locomotive #1	600
_____ **01075**	ATSF 2-8-0 Locomotive #2	600
_____ **01076**	C&NW 2-8-0 Locomotive #1	600
_____ **01077**	C&NW 2-8-0 Locomotive #2	600
_____ **01078**	Erie 2-8-0 Locomotive #1	600
_____ **01079**	Erie 2-8-0 Locomotive #2	600
_____ **01080**	MEC 2-8-0 Locomotive #1	600
_____ **01081**	MEC 2-8-0 Locomotive #2	600
_____ **01082**	NYC 2-8-0 Locomotive #1	600
_____ **01083**	NYC 2-8-0 Locomotive #2	600
_____ **01084**	Southern 2-8-0 Locomotive #1	600
_____ **01086**	UP 2-8-0 Locomotive #1	600
_____ **01087**	UP 2-8-0 Locomotive #2	600
_____ **01088**	WM 2-8-0 Locomotive #1	600
_____ **01089**	WM 2-8-0 Locomotive #2	600
_____ **01090**	Flatcar with IH Farmall corn picker	55
_____ **01091**	2-8-0 Locomotive, hi-rail wheels, DC no sound	450
_____ **01092**	B&O 2-8-0 Locomotive #1	450
_____ **01093**	B&O 2-8-0 Locomotive #2	450
_____ **01094**	ATSF 2-8-0 Locomotive #1	450
_____ **01095**	ATSF 2-8-0 Locomotive #2	450
_____ **01096**	C&NW 2-8-0 Locomotive #1	450
_____ **01097**	C&NW 2-8-0 Locomotive #2	450
_____ **01098**	Erie 2-8-0 Locomotive #1	450
_____ **01099**	Erie 2-8-0 Locomotive #2	450
_____ **01100**	MEC 2-8-0 Locomotive #1	450
_____ **01101**	MEC 2-8-0 Locomotive #2	450
_____ **01102**	NYC 2-8-0 Locomotive #1	450
_____ **01103**	NYC 2-8-0 Locomotive #2	450
_____ **01104**	Southern 2-8-0 Locomotive #1	450
_____ **01106**	UP 2-8-0 Locomotive #1	450
_____ **01107**	UP 2-8-0 Locomotive #2	450
_____ **01108**	WM 2-8-0 Locomotive #1	450
_____ **01109**	WM 2-8-0 Locomotive #2	450
_____ **01110**	GN Offset Hopper	50
_____ **01111**	Green Bay & Western Offset Hopper 3-pack	100
_____ **01112**	Green Bay & Western Offset Hopper	50
_____ **01113**	IC Offset Hopper 3-pack	100
_____ **01114**	IC Offset Hopper	50
_____ **01115**	LNE Offset Hopper 3-pack	100
_____ **01116**	LNE Offset Hopper	50
_____ **01117**	NYC Offset Hopper 3-pack	100

S-HELPER SERVICE 1994-2012

Retail

01118	NYC Offset Hopper	50	____
01119	Peabody Offset Hopper 3-pack	100	____
01120	Peabody Offset Hopper	50	____
01121	Detroit & Mackinac Offset Hopper 3-pack	100	____
01122	S-Trax Track Planning Guide	8	____
01123	Detroit & Mackinac Offset Hopper	50	____
01124	TP&W Offset Hopper 3-pack	100	____
01125	TP&W Offset Hopper	50	____
01126	DT&I 40' Steel Rebuilt Boxcar #1	50	____
01127	DT&I 40' Steel Rebuilt Boxcar #2	50	____
01128	GN 40' Steel Rebuilt Boxcar, scheme IV #1	50	____
01129	GN 40' Steel Rebuilt Boxcar, scheme IV #2	50	____
01130	Swift Wooden Billboard Reefer, scheme I	53	____
01131	Swift Wooden Billboard Reefer, scheme II	53	____
01132	Swift Wooden Billboard Reefer, scheme III	53	____
01133	SLSF 40' Steel Rebuilt Boxcar, scheme II	50	____
01134	SLSF 40' Steel Rebuilt Boxcar, scheme III	50	____
01135	SLSF 40' Steel Rebuilt Boxcar, scheme I #2	50	____
01136	Armour Stock Express 40' Stock Car #1	50	____
01137	Armour Stock Express 40' Stock Car #2	50	____
01138	GN 40' Stock Car	73	____
01139	Nickel Plate Road 40' Stock Car #1	50	____
01140	Nickel Plate Road 40' Stock Car #2	50	____
01141	UP 40' Stock Car, scheme II #1	50	____
01142	UP 40' Stock Car, scheme II #2	50	____
01143	BN PS-2 2-bay Covered Hopper, scheme III #1	50	____
01144	BN PS-2 2-bay Covered Hopper, scheme III #2	50	____
01145	Chessie (C&O) PS-2 2-bay Covered Hopper #1	50	____
01146	Chessie (C&O) PS-2 2-bay Covered Hopper #2	50	____
01147	D&H PS-2 2-bay Covered Hopper #1	50	____
01148	D&H PS-2 2-bay Covered Hopper #2	50	____
01149	Boraxo PS-2 2-bay Covered Hopper	50	____
01150	Susquehanna 40' Steel Rebuilt Boxcar #1	50	____
01151	Susquehanna 40' Steel Rebuilt Boxcar #2	50	____
01152	PRR 40' Steel Rebuilt Boxcar, scheme II #1	50	____
01153	Offset Hopper, black	50	____
01154	Offset Hopper, red	50	____
01155	CNJ Offset Hopper 3-pack	100	____
01156	CNJ Offset Hopper	50	____
01157	DL&W Offset Hopper 3-pack	100	____
01158	DL&W Offset Hopper	50	____
01159	GN Offset Hopper 3-pack	100	____
01160	PRR 40' Steel Rebuilt Boxcar, scheme II #2	50	____
01161	GN Standard Flatcar, scheme II #1	50	____
01162	GN Standard Flatcar, scheme II #2	50	____

_____	**01163** NP Standard Flatcar #1	50
_____	**01164** NP Standard Flatcar #2	50
_____	**01165** SLSF Standard Flatcar #1	50
_____	**01166** SLSF Standard Flatcar #2	50
_____	**01167** SP Standard Flatcar, scheme I #1	50
_____	**01168** SP Standard Flatcar, scheme I #2	50
_____	**01170** Anderson Panel Side Hopper 3-pack Set B	100
_____	**01171** Anderson Panel Side Hopper Car #8	50
_____	**01172** CN Panel Side Hopper 3-pack	100
_____	**01173** CN Panel Side Hopper Car	50
_____	**01174** Rock Island Panel Side Hopper 3-pack	100
_____	**01175** Rock Island Panel Side Hopper Car	50
_____	**01176** USRA Rib Side Hopper, black	50
_____	**01177** USRA Rib Side Hopper, red	50
_____	**01178** B&O USRA Rib Side Hopper 3-pack	100
_____	**01179** B&O USRA Rib Side Hopper	50
_____	**01180** CNJ USRA Rib Side Hopper 3-pack	100
_____	**01181** CNJ USRA Rib Side Hopper	50
_____	**01182** CB&Q USRA Rib Side Hopper 3-pack	100
_____	**01183** CB&Q USRA Rib Side Hopper	50
_____	**01184** IH USRA Rib Side Hopper 3-pack	100
_____	**01185** IH USRA Rib Side Hopper	50
_____	**01186** L&N USRA Rib Side Hopper 3-pack	100
_____	**01187** L&N USRA Rib Side Hopper	50
_____	**01188** NYNH&H USRA Rib Side Hopper 3-pack	100
_____	**01189** NYNH&H USRA Rib Side Hopper	50
_____	**01190** NYC USRA Rib Side Hopper 3-pack	100
_____	**01191** NYC USRA Rib Side Hopper	50
_____	**01192** NYO&W USRA Rib Side Hopper 3-pack	100
_____	**01193** NYO&W USRA Rib Side Hopper	50
_____	**01194** PRR USRA Rib Side Hopper 3-pack	100
_____	**01195** PRR USRA Rib Side Hopper	50
_____	**01196** Reading USRA Rib Side Hopper 3-pack	100
_____	**01197** Reading USRA Rib Side Hopper	50
_____	**01198** 32" Pipe Load	13
_____	**01199** F7 DCC Sound Decoder	180
_____	**01200** F3 AC/DC LocoMatic Sound Unit	160
_____	**01201** F7 AC/DC LocoMatic Sound Unit	160
_____	**01202** N&W USRA Rib Side Hopper 3-pack	100
_____	**01203** N&W USRA Rib Side Hopper #4	50
_____	**01204** N&W USRA Rib Side Hopper #5	50
_____	**01205** Control Button, slide switch	8
_____	**01206** Peabody USRA Rib Side Hopper 3-pack	100
_____	**01207** Peabody USRA Rib Side Hopper	50
_____	**01208** Andrews Tender Truck, 33" Code 110 wheels	11

Retail

01209	Andrews Tender Truck, 33" hi-rail wheels	11 ____
01210	Flatcar with Case IH grinder mixers	60 ____
01211	Track-cleaning USRA Double-sheathed Boxcar	150 ____
01212	Track-cleaning Standard Flatcar	150 ____
01214	Custom Trax No. 6 Switch, right hand	48 ____
01215	Custom Trax No. 6 Switch, left hand	48 ____
01216	Custom Trax No. 8 Switch, right hand	50 ____
01217	Custom Trax No. 8 Switch, left hand	50 ____
01218	Flextrack, 36" roadbed	15 ____
01219	HomaBed 48' Straight	69 ____
01220	HomaBed 48' Curved	74 ____
01221	HomaBed 48' Straight/Curved	81 ____
01222	Monon Composite Side Hopper Car 3-pack	100 ____
01223	Monon Composite Side Hopper Car	50 ____
01224	LV Composite Side Hopper Car 3-pack Set B	100 ____
01225	LV Composite Side Hopper Car #8	50 ____
01226	PRR Composite Side Hopper Car 3-pack Set B	100 ____
01227	PRR Composite Side Hopper Car #8	50 ____
01228	36" Weathered Rail, Code 131, 33 pieces	70 ____
01229	CB&Q SW1 Diesel #1	200 ____
01230	CB&Q SW1 Diesel #2	200 ____
01231	CNJ SW1 Diesel #1	200 ____
01232	CNJ SW1 Diesel #2	200 ____
01233	Erie-Lackawanna SW1 Diesel #1	200 ____
01234	Erie-Lackawanna SW1 Diesel #2	200 ____
01235	GN SW1 Diesel #1	200 ____
01236	GN SW1 Diesel #2	200 ____
01237	B&M SW8 Diesel #1	200 ____
01238	B&M SW8 Diesel #2	200 ____
01239	BN SW8 Diesel #1	200 ____
01240	BN SW8 Diesel #2	200 ____
01241	C&NW SW8 Diesel #1	200 ____
01242	C&NW SW8 Diesel #2	200 ____
01243	CRI&P SW8 Diesel #1	200 ____
01244	CRI&P SW8 Diesel #2	200 ____
01245	Conrail SW9 Diesel, scheme II #1	200 ____
01246	Conrail SW9 Diesel, scheme II #2	200 ____
01247	FEC SW9 Diesel #1	200 ____
01248	FEC SW9 Diesel #2	200 ____
01249	SLSF SW9 Diesel #1	200 ____
01250	SLSF SW9 Diesel #2	200 ____
01251	Lehigh Valley SW9 Diesel #1	200 ____
01252	Lehigh Valley SW9 Diesel #2	200 ____
01253	ATSF NW2 Diesel #1	200 ____
01254	ATSF NW2 Diesel #2	200 ____

_____ **01255**	Chessie (C&O) NW2 Diesel #1	200
_____ **01256**	Chessie (C&O) NW2 Diesel #2	200
_____ **01259**	PRR NW2 Diesel, scheme I	200
_____ **01260**	PRR NW2 Diesel, scheme II	200
_____ **01261**	NW2 Diesel	200
_____ **01262**	SLSF Extended Vision Caboose #1	70
_____ **01263**	SLSF Extended Vision Caboose #2	70
_____ **01264**	CB&Q Extended Vision Caboose, scheme II #1	70
_____ **01265**	CB&Q Extended Vision Caboose, scheme II #2	70
_____ **01266**	D&RGW Extended Vision Caboose #5	70
_____ **01267**	D&RGW Extended Vision Caboose #6	70
_____ **01268**	GN Extended Vision Caboose #3	70
_____ **01269**	GN Extended Vision Caboose #4	70
_____ **01270**	MEC Extended Vision Caboose, scheme III	78
_____ **01271**	Silver Edge Beer Wooden Billboard Reefer	53
_____ **01272**	Columbia Soups Wooden Billboard Reefer	53
_____ **01273**	Niblets Corn Wooden Billboard Reefer	53
_____ **01274**	Monarch Foods Wooden Billboard Reefer	53
_____ **01275**	Wilson Milk Wooden Billboard Reefer #1 (Port Lines)	53
_____ **01276**	Wilson Milk Wooden Billboard Reefer #2 (Port Lines)	53
_____ **01277**	URTX MILW Wooden Billboard Reefer #1	53
_____ **01278**	URTX MILW Wooden Billboard Reefer #2	53
_____ **01279**	WFE GN Wooden Billboard Reefer #1	53
_____ **01280**	WFE GN Wooden Billboard Reefer #2	53
_____ **01281**	CNJ USRA Single-sheathed Boxcar #1	50
_____ **01282**	CNJ USRA Single-sheathed Boxcar #2	50
_____ **01283**	CMStP&P USRA Single-sheathed Boxcar #1	50
_____ **01284**	CMStP&P USRA Single-sheathed Boxcar #2	50
_____ **01285**	MKT USRA Single-sheathed Boxcar #1	50
_____ **01286**	MKT USRA Single-sheathed Boxcar #2	50
_____ **01287**	Wellsville, Addison & Galeton Single-sheathed Boxcar	50
_____ **01288**	CB&Q F3 Diesel ABA Set, phase II, DC no sound	590
_____ **01290**	BN Ore Car 5-pack	180
_____ **01291**	BN Ore Car	40
_____ **01292**	GN Ore Car 5-pack, scheme II	180
_____ **01293**	GN Ore Car, scheme II	40
_____ **01294**	DM&IR Ore Car 5-pack	180
_____ **01295**	Coupler, Kadee style, 2 pair	6
_____ **01296**	CNJ Composite Side Hopper 3-pack, scheme II (Hoquat)	100
_____ **01297**	CNJ Composite Side Hopper, scheme II (Hoquat)	50
_____ **01298**	DL&W Composite Side Hopper 3-pack, scheme II (Hoquat)	100
_____ **01299**	DL&W Composite Side Hopper, scheme II (Hoquat)	50
_____ **01300**	Public Service Composite Side Hopper 3-pack (Hoquat)	100
_____ **01301**	Public Service Composite Side Hopper (Hoquat)	50
_____ **01302**	AC/DC LocoMatic Sound Switcher Board	150

S-HELPER SERVICE 1994-2012

01303	Conrail SW9 Diesel Freight Set, 4 cars	300 ____
01304	C&NW F3 Diesel Freight Set, 4 cars	330 ____
01305	Chessie (C&O) NW2 Diesel Freight Set, 5 cars	370 ____
01306	D&RGW F7 Diesel Freight Set, 6 cars	430 ____
01307	CB&Q SW1 Diesel Freight Set, 6 cars	400 ____
01308	GN F7 Diesel Freight Set, 6 cars	430 ____
01310	Freight Coupler, short shank, AF compatible, pair	3 ____
01333	CMStP&P Wooden Billboard Reefer #1 (Badgerland)	53 ____
01363	CMStP&P Wooden Billboard Reefer #2 (Badgerland)	53 ____
01393	CMStP&P Wooden Billboard Reefer #3 (Badgerland)	53 ____
01402	DM&IR Ore Car 5-pack Set B	180 ____
01403	CMStP&P Wooden Billboard Reefer #4 (Badgerland)	53 ____
01413	CMStP&P Wooden Billboard Reefer #5 (Badgerland)	53 ____
01422	GN Ore Car 5-pack Set B, scheme I	180 ____
01423	Control Button, passing siding	8 ____
01432	CMStP&P Ore Car 5-pack Set B	180 ____
01433	Ore Car Sampler 10-pack	360 ____
01442	Flatcar with 4 Farmall tractors	60 ____
01443	D&RGW 40' Steel Rebuilt Boxcar (Boys RR Club)	50 ____
01452	D&RGW 40' Steel Rebuilt Boxcar (Boys RR Club)	50 ____
01453	Central of Georgia 40' Steel Boxcar (Boys RR Club)	50 ____
01501	MEC SW9 Diesel	200 ____
01502	MEC SW9 Diesel, holiday	200 ____
01503	MEC SW9 Diesel, AC/DC LocoMatic sound	290 ____
01504	MEC SW9 Diesel, holiday, AC/DC LocoMatic sound	290 ____
01505	MEC SW9 Diesel, DCC sound	290 ____
01506	MEC SW9 Diesel, holiday, DCC sound	290 ____
01507	MEC Locomotive and Caboose, holiday	270 ____
01508	MEC Locomotive and Caboose, holiday, AC/DC sound	360 ____
01509	MEC Locomotive and Caboose, holiday, DCC sound	360 ____
01510	Hood Milk Wooden Billboard Reefer #1 (Port Lines)	53 ____
01511	Hood Milk Wooden Billboard Reefer #2 (Port Lines)	53 ____
01512	Merchants Biscuit Wooden Billboard Reefer	53 ____
01513	E&A Opler Wooden Billboard Reefer	53 ____
01514	Carnation Milk Wooden Billboard Reefer	53 ____
01515	Great Falls Beer Wooden Billboard Reefer	53 ____
01516	Curve Beer Wooden Billboard Reefer #1 (NASG)	53 ____
01517	Curve Beer Wooden Billboard Reefer #2 (NASG)	53 ____
01518	B&M SW8 Diesel #1, AC/DC LocoMatic sound	290 ____
01519	B&M SW8 Diesel #2, AC/DC LocoMatic sound	290 ____
01520	BN SW8 Diesel #1, AC/DC LocoMatic sound	290 ____
01521	BN SW8 Diesel #2, AC/DC LocoMatic sound	290 ____
01522	C&NW SW8 Diesel #1, AC/DC LocoMatic sound	290 ____
01523	C&NW SW8 Diesel #2, AC/DC LocoMatic sound	290 ____
01524	CRI&P SW8 Diesel #1, AC/DC LocoMatic sound	290 ____

____	**01525**	CRI&P SW8 Diesel #2, AC/DC LocoMatic sound	290
____	**01526**	Conrail SW9 Diesel, scheme II #1, AC/DC LocoMatic sound	290
____	**01527**	FEC SW9 Diesel #1, AC/DC LocoMatic sound	290
____	**01528**	FEC SW9 Diesel #2, AC/DC LocoMatic sound	290
____	**01529**	SLSF SW9 Diesel #1, AC/DC LocoMatic sound	290
____	**01530**	SLSF SW9 Diesel #2, AC/DC LocoMatic sound	290
____	**01531**	Lehigh Valley SW9 Diesel #1, AC/DC LocoMatic sound	290
____	**01532**	Lehigh Valley SW9 Diesel #2, AC/DC LocoMatic sound	290
____	**01535**	Chessie (C&O) NW2 Diesel #1, AC/DC LocoMatic sound	290
____	**01536**	Chessie (C&O) NW2 Diesel #2, AC/DC LocoMatic sound	290
____	**01539**	PRR NW2 Diesel, scheme I, AC/DC LocoMatic sound	290
____	**01540**	PRR NW2 Diesel, scheme II, AC/DC LocoMatic sound	290
____	**01541**	NW2 Diesel, AC/DC LocoMatic sound	290
____	**01550**	Conrail Quality SW9 Diesel #1, DCC sound	290
____	**01551**	Florida East Coast SW9 Diesel #1, DCC sound	290
____	**01552**	Florida East Coast SW9 Diesel #2, DCC sound	290
____	**01553**	SLSF SW9 Diesel #1, DCC sound	290
____	**01554**	SLSF SW9 Diesel #2, DCC sound	290
____	**01555**	Lehigh Valley SW9 Diesel #1, DCC sound	290
____	**01556**	Lehigh Valley SW9 Diesel #2, DCC sound	290
____	**01557**	ATSF NW2 Diesel #1, DCC sound	290
____	**01558**	ATSF NW2 Diesel #2, DCC sound	290
____	**01559**	Chessie NW2 Diesel #1, DCC sound	290
____	**01560**	Chessie NW2 Diesel #2, DCC sound	290
____	**01563**	PRR NW2 Diesel, scheme I, DCC sound	290
____	**01564**	PRR NW2 Diesel, scheme II, DCC sound	290
____	**01565**	NW2 Diesel, DCC sound, DCC sound	290
____	**01566**	ATSF USRA Double-sheathed Boxcar, scheme I	50
____	**01568**	Duluth, South Shore & Atlantic Double-sheathed Boxcar	50
____	**01569**	Ivory USRA Double-sheathed Boxcar #1 (Miami Valley)	50
____	**01570**	Ivory USRA Double-sheathed Boxcar #2 (Miami Valley)	50
____	**01571**	NWP USRA Double-sheathed Boxcar #1	50
____	**01572**	D&RGW 40' Steel Rebuilt Boxcar #1 (Boys RR Club)	50
____	**01573**	D&RGW 40' Steel Rebuilt Boxcar #2 (Boys RR Club)	50
____	**01574**	D&RGW 40' Steel Rebuilt Boxcar #3 (Boys RR Club)	50
____	**01575**	Central of Georgia 40' Steel Boxcar #1 (Boys RR Club)	50
____	**01576**	Central of Georgia 40' Steel Boxcar #2 (Boys RR Club)	50
____	**01577**	Central of Georgia 40' Steel Boxcar #3 (Boys RR Club)	50
____	**01578**	Ann Arbor 40' Steel Rebuilt Boxcar	50
____	**01579**	Lancaster & Chester 40' Steel Rebuilt Boxcar #1	50
____	**01580**	Lancaster & Chester 40' Steel Rebuilt Boxcar #2	50
____	**01581**	Soo Line 40' Steel Rebuilt Boxcar #1	50
____	**01582**	Soo Line 40' Steel Rebuilt Boxcar #2	50
____	**01583**	B&O 2-8-0 Locomotive #3, hi-rail wheels, AC/DC sound	600
____	**01584**	B&O 2-8-0 Locomotive #3, hi-rail wheels, DCC sound	600

01585	B&O 2-8-0 Locomotive #3, hi-rail wheels	450 ____
01586	B&O 2-8-0 Locomotive #3, Code 110 wheels, AC/DC sound	600 ____
01587	B&O 2-8-0 Locomotive #3, Code 110 wheels, DCC sound	600 ____
01588	B&O 2-8-0 Locomotive #3, Code 110 wheels	450 ____
01589	Christmas Figure and Wreath Set	15 ____
01590	Santa and Mrs. Claus Figure Set	9 ____
01591	Matawan Junction Track Layout	430 ____
01592	Maybrook Bridge Line Track Layout	416 ____
01593	Tacoma Transfer Track Layout	410 ____
01594	Norwalk Crossing Track Layout	340 ____
01595	Macoon Yard Track Layout	630 ____
01596	Utica Terminal Track Layout	840 ____
01597	Decatur Exchange Track Layout	600 ____
01598	Gome & Dapgetid Track Layout	760 ____
01599	S-Helper Service Track Layout	620 ____
01601	B&M Double-sheathed Boxcar, scheme II #1 (Hoquat)	53 ____
01602	B&M Double-sheathed Boxcar, scheme II #2 (Hoquat)	53 ____
01603	DL&W Double-sheathed Boxcar, scheme II #1 (Hoquat)	53 ____
01604	DL&W Double-sheathed Boxcar, scheme II #2 (Hoquat)	53 ____
01605	Erie Wooden Billboard Reefer #1 (Hoquat)	53 ____
01606	Erie Wooden Billboard Reefer #2 (Hoquat)	53 ____
01607	NWX Wooden Billboard Reefer #6 (Hoquat)	53 ____
01608	NWX Wooden Billboard Reefer #7 (Hoquat)	53 ____
01609	PFE (WP) Wooden Billboard Reefer #1	53 ____
01610	PFE (WP) Wooden Billboard Reefer #2	53 ____
01611	SFRD "Super Chief" Wooden Billboard Reefer	53 ____
01612	Speaker/Switcher	40 ____
01613	NdeM 40' Steel Rebuilt Boxcar #1 (Mainstreeter)	50 ____
01614	NdeM 40' Steel Rebuilt Boxcar #2 (Mainstreeter)	50 ____
01615	Conrail SW9 Diesel Freight Set, 4 cars	300 ____
01616	SLSF SW9 Diesel Freight Set, 4 cars	300 ____
01617	Chessie (C&O) NW2 Diesel Freight Set, 5 cars	375 ____
01618	GN SW1 Diesel Freight Set, 5 cars	370 ____
01619	ATSF F7 Diesel Freight Set, 6 cars	430 ____
01620	Conrail SW9 Diesel Freight Set, 4 cars, sound	390 ____
01621	SLSF SW9 Diesel Freight Set, 4 cars, sound	390 ____
01622	Chessie (C&O) NW2 Diesel Freight Set, 5 cars, sound	460 ____
01623	NWP USRA Double-sheathed Boxcar, scheme I #2	50 ____
01624	Ann Arbor 40' Steel Rebuilt Boxcar #2	50 ____
01625	Domino Sugar PS-2 3-bay Covered Hopper	50 ____
01626	Jack Frost PS-2 3-bay Covered Hopper	50 ____
01627	B&O PS-2 3-bay Covered Hopper #1	50 ____
01628	B&O PS-2 3-bay Covered Hopper #2	50 ____

		Retail
_____ **01629**	C&NW PS-2 3-bay Covered Hopper, scheme II #1	50
_____ **01630**	C&NW PS-2 3-bay Covered Hopper, scheme II #2	50
_____ **01631**	SP PS-2 3-bay Covered Hopper #1	50
_____ **01632**	SP PS-2 3-bay Covered Hopper #2	50
_____ **01633**	AC/DC LocoMatic Sound Unit	180
_____ **01634**	DCC Socket Set for Switchers #2	25
_____ **01636**	MTC Brookside Wooden Billboard Reefer #3 (Port Lines)	53
_____ **01637**	Sunrise Onions Wooden Billboard Reefer	53
_____ **01638**	OTOE Food Products Wooden Billboard Reefer	53
_____ **01639**	PFE Wooden Billboard Reefer, scheme III #1	53
_____ **01640**	PFE Wooden Billboard Reefer, scheme III #2	53
_____ **01641**	PFE Wooden Billboard Reefer, scheme III #3	53
_____ **01642**	Heileman's Old Style Lager Wooden Billboard Reefer	53
_____ **01643**	Domino Sugar Double-sheathed Boxcar #1 (Port Lines)	50
_____ **01644**	Domino Sugar Double-sheathed Boxcar #2 (Port Lines)	50
_____ **01645**	MEC Offset Hopper	50
_____ **01646**	C&O USRA Rib Side Hopper #1	50
_____ **01647**	C&O USRA Rib Side Hopper #2	50
_____ **01648**	C&O USRA Rib Side Hopper #3	50
_____ **01649**	C&O USRA Rib Side Hopper #4	50
_____ **01650**	Waddell Coal USRA Rib Side Hopper #1	53
_____ **01651**	Waddell Coal USRA Rib Side Hopper #2	53
_____ **01652**	Waddell Coal USRA Rib Side Hopper #3	53
_____ **01653**	Waddell Coal USRA Rib Side Hopper #4	53
_____ **01654**	PRR Composite Side Hopper, scheme II #1	50
_____ **01655**	PRR Composite Side Hopper, scheme II #2	50
_____ **01656**	PRR Composite Side Hopper, scheme II #3	50
_____ **01657**	PRR Composite Side Hopper, scheme II #4	50
_____ **01658**	Spiral Hill USRA Rib Side Hopper #1 (Lehigh Valley)	50
_____ **01659**	Spiral Hill USRA Rib Side Hopper #2 (Lehigh Valley)	50
_____ **01660**	MKT 40' Steel Rebuilt Boxcar (TCA)	50
_____ **01661**	Smoke Unit Funnels, 3 pieces	3
_____ **01664**	Spiral Hill USRA Rib Side Hopper #3 (Lehigh Valley)	50
_____ **01666**	Flatcar with 2 Humvees	60
_____ **01667**	Flatcar with 2 Humvee ambulances	60
_____ **01668**	ATSF F7 Diesel Freight Set, 6 cars, sound	490
_____ **01669**	Locomotive Figure Set	6
_____ **01670**	Tender Coupler, AF compatible, pair	3
_____ **01671**	Speaker, 1-watt, 8-ohm	9
_____ **01672**	Tender LED Light Set, golden white, pair	6
_____ **01673**	Smoke Unit, pair	10
_____ **01674**	Infrared Sensor, pair	10
_____ **01675**	1.6mm Wrench	4
_____ **01676**	Motor with flywheel, pair	15
_____ **01677**	Flatcar with Bradley Fighting Vehicle	63

01678	Headlight LED Accessory, golden white, pair	10 ____
01679	Headlight Top LED Accessory, golden white, pair	10 ____
01680	Coal Load with snow	6 ____
01681	Mine Run Coal Load	6 ____
01682	Classification Lights, brass, pair	5 ____
01683	C&NW Stock Car #1 (Hoquat)	50 ____
01684	C&NW Stock Car #2 (Hoquat)	50 ____
01685	Grand Trunk Western Stock Car #1 (Hoquat)	50 ____
01686	Grand Trunk Western Stock Car #2 (Hoquat)	50 ____
01687	N&W Stock Car #1	50 ____
01688	N&W Stock Car #2	50 ____
01689	SLSF Stock Car #1	50 ____
01690	SLSF Stock Car #2	50 ____
01691	Santa Fe "Chief" Wooden Billboard Reefer (Hoquat)	53 ____
01692	Berkshire Wooden Billboard Reefer (Hoquat)	53 ____
01693	Peerless Beer Wooden Billboard Reefer	53 ____
01694	Skyland Eggs Wooden Billboard Reefer	53 ____
01695	Priebe Wooden Billboard Reefer	53 ____
01696	Central of Georgia 40' Steel Boxcar, red (Boys RR Club)	50 ____
01697	Central of Georgia 40' Steel Boxcar, black (Boys RR Club)	50 ____
01698	Central of Georgia 40' Steel Boxcar, maroon (Boys RR Club)	50 ____
01699	Central of Georgia 40' Steel Boxcar, blue (Boys RR Club)	50 ____
01700	MEC 2-8-0 Locomotive #1, Code 110 wheels	450 ____
01701	MEC 2-8-0 Locomotive #2, Code 110 wheels	450 ____
01702	NYC 2-8-0 Locomotive #1, Code 110 wheels	450 ____
01703	NYC 2-8-0 Locomotive #2, Code 110 wheels	450 ____
01704	Southern 2-8-0 Locomotive, Code 110 wheels	450 ____
01706	UP 2-8-0 Locomotive #1, Code 110 wheels	450 ____
01707	UP 2-8-0 Locomotive #2, Code 110 wheels	450 ____
01708	WM 2-8-0 Locomotive #1, Code 110 wheels	450 ____
01709	WM 2-8-0 Locomotive #2, Code 110 wheels	450 ____
01710	B&O 40' Steel Rebuilt Boxcar, blue roof (Boys RR Club)	50 ____
01711	B&O 40' Steel Rebuilt Boxcar, silver roof (Boys RR Club)	50 ____
01712	B&O 40' Steel Rebuilt Boxcar, blue roof (Boys RR Club)	50 ____
01713	B&O 40' Steel Rebuilt Boxcar, silver roof (Boys RR Club)	50 ____
01714	Great American Circus Steel Boxcar (Scenery Unlimited)	50 ____
01715	Great American Circus Steel Boxcar (Scenery Unlimited)	50 ____
01716	Great American Circus Steel Boxcar (Scenery Unlimited)	50 ____
01717	Great American Circus Stock Car (Scenery Unlimited)	50 ____
01718	Great American Circus Stock Car (Scenery Unlimited)	50 ____
01719	Great American Circus Stock Car (Scenery Unlimited)	50 ____
01720	MNS 40' Steel Rebuilt Boxcar #1 (Pines & Prairies)	50 ____
01721	MNS 40' Steel Rebuilt Boxcar #2 (Pines & Prairies)	50 ____
01722	Great American Circus Flatcar (Scenery Unlimited)	50 ____

		Retail
____ **01723**	Great American Circus Flatcar (Scenery Unlimited)	50
____ **01724**	Great American Circus Flatcar (Scenery Unlimited)	50
____ **01725**	Great American Circus Flatcar (Scenery Unlimited)	50
____ **01726**	Great American Circus Flatcar (Scenery Unlimited)	50
____ **01727**	Great American Circus Flatcar (Scenery Unlimited)	50
____ **01728**	BN Christmas Bulkhead Flatcar #3 with presents	56
____ **01729**	GM&O Bulkhead Flatcar #1 with pipe load	56
____ **01730**	GM&O Bulkhead Flatcar #2 with pipe load	56
____ **01731**	BAAFC Wooden Billboard Reefer (NASG)	53
____ **01732**	BAAFC Wooden Billboard Reefer (NASG)	53
____ **01734**	40" Unweathered Rail, Code 131, 33 pieces	70
____ **01735**	33" Scale Wheel Set/Pickup, Code 110, 4-pack	5
____ **01736**	CB&Q (FWD) NW2 Diesel	200
____ **01737**	CB&Q NW2 Diesel	200
____ **01738**	CB&Q (FWD) NW2 Diesel, AC/DC LocoMatic sound	290
____ **01739**	CB&Q NW2 Diesel, AC/DC LocoMatic sound	290
____ **01740**	CB&Q (FWD) NW2 Diesel, DCC sound	290
____ **01741**	CB&Q NW2 Diesel, DCC sound	290
____ **01742**	ICG PS-2 2-bay Covered Hopper #1	50
____ **01743**	ICG PS-2 2-bay Covered Hopper #2	50
____ **01744**	SP PS-2 2-bay Covered Hopper, scheme III #1	50
____ **01745**	SP PS-2 2-bay Covered Hopper, scheme III #2	50
____ **01746**	Lancaster & Chester PS-2 2-bay Covered Hopper #1	50
____ **01747**	Lancaster & Chester PS-2 2-bay Covered Hopper #2	50
____ **01748**	Maryland Midland PS-2 2-bay Covered Hopper (NASG)	50
____ **01749**	Maryland Midland PS-2 2-bay Covered Hopper (NASG)	50
____ **01750**	Kerr-McGee PS-2 2-bay Covered Hopper	50
____ **01751**	2-8-0 Locomotive, AC/DC LocoMatic sound	600
____ **01752**	B&O 2-8-0 Locomotive #1	600
____ **01753**	B&O 2-8-0 Locomotive #2	600
____ **01754**	ATSF 2-8-0 Locomotive #1	600
____ **01755**	ATSF 2-8-0 Locomotive #2	600
____ **01756**	C&NW 2-8-0 Locomotive #1	600
____ **01757**	C&NW 2-8-0 Locomotive #2	600
____ **01758**	Erie 2-8-0 Locomotive #1	600
____ **01759**	Erie 2-8-0 Locomotive #2	600
____ **01760**	MEC 2-8-0 Locomotive #1	600
____ **01761**	MEC 2-8-0 Locomotive #2	600
____ **01762**	NYC 2-8-0 Locomotive #1	600
____ **01763**	NYC 2-8-0 Locomotive #2	600
____ **01764**	Southern 2-8-0 Locomotive #1	600
____ **01766**	UP 2-8-0 Locomotive #1	600
____ **01767**	UP 2-8-0 Locomotive #2	600
____ **01768**	WM 2-8-0 Locomotive #1	600
____ **01769**	WM 2-8-0 Locomotive #2	600

Retail

01771	2-8-0 Locomotive, DCC sound	600 ___
01772	B&O 2-8-0 Locomotive #1	600 ___
01773	B&O 2-8-0 Locomotive #2	600 ___
01774	ATSF 2-8-0 Locomotive #1	600 ___
01775	ATSF 2-8-0 Locomotive #2	600 ___
01776	C&NW 2-8-0 Locomotive #1	600 ___
01777	C&NW 2-8-0 Locomotive #2	600 ___
01778	Erie 2-8-0 Locomotive #1	600 ___
01779	Erie 2-8-0 Locomotive #2	600 ___
01780	MEC 2-8-0 Locomotive #1	600 ___
01781	MEC 2-8-0 Locomotive #2	600 ___
01782	NYC 2-8-0 Locomotive #1	600 ___
01783	NYC 2-8-0 Locomotive #2	600 ___
01784	Southern 2-8-0 Locomotive #1	600 ___
01786	UP 2-8-0 Locomotive #1	600 ___
01787	UP 2-8-0 Locomotive #2	600 ___
01788	WM 2-8-0 Locomotive #1	600 ___
01789	WM 2-8-0 Locomotive #2	600 ___
01790	GTW USRA Rebuilt Covered Hopper #1	50 ___
01791	2-8-0 Locomotive, DC, no sound	450 ___
01792	B&O 2-8-0 Locomotive #1	450 ___
01793	B&O 2-8-0 Locomotive #2	450 ___
01794	ATSF 2-8-0 Locomotive #1	450 ___
01795	ATSF 2-8-0 Locomotive #2	450 ___
01796	C&NW 2-8-0 Locomotive #1	450 ___
01797	C&NW 2-8-0 Locomotive #2	450 ___
01798	Erie 2-8-0 Locomotive #1	450 ___
01799	Erie 2-8-0 Locomotive #2	450 ___
01800	Chicago Macaroni Wooden Billboard Reefer	53 ___
01801	Hamm Brewing Wooden Billboard Reefer	53 ___
01802	Westcott & Winks Wooden Billboard Reefer	53 ___
01803	Marhoefer Wooden Billboard Reefer #1	53 ___
01804	Flatcar with 2 Stuart tanks	60 ___
01807	Santa Fe Flatcar with trailer, scheme II #1	63 ___
01808	Santa Fe Flatcar with trailer, scheme II #2	63 ___
01809	Reading Flatcar #1 with trailer	63 ___
01810	Reading Flatcar #2 with trailer	63 ___
01811	Flatcar with REA trailer, 2007 Christmas Car	63 ___
01812	SP Flatcar #1 with trailer	63 ___
01813	SP Flatcar #2 with trailer	63 ___
01814	CGW Bulkhead Flatcar with pipes #1	56 ___
01815	CGW Bulkhead Flatcar with pipes #2	56 ___
01816	ACL Bulkhead Flatcar #1 with pipes	56 ___
01817	ACL Bulkhead Flatcar #2 with pulpwood	56 ___
01818	ATSF Standard Flatcar #2, red	50 ___

_____ **01819**	ATSF Standard Flatcar #3, red	50
_____ **01820**	Reading Standard Flatcar #1	50
_____ **01821**	Reading Standard Flatcar #2	50
_____ **01822**	ACL Standard Flatcar #1	50
_____ **01823**	ACL Standard Flatcar #2	50
_____ **01824**	PRR Standard Flatcar #4	50
_____ **01825**	PRR Standard Flatcar #5	50
_____ **01826**	SP Standard Flatcar, scheme II #1	50
_____ **01827**	SP Standard Flatcar, scheme II #2	50
_____ **01828**	Santa Fe Wooden Billboard Reefer #1	53
_____ **01829**	Santa Fe Wooden Billboard Reefer #2	53
_____ **01830**	Carling Black Label Billboard Reefer #3 (Port Lines)	53
_____ **01831**	B&O USRA Single-sheathed Boxcar, scheme II #1	50
_____ **01832**	B&O USRA Single-sheathed Boxcar, scheme II #2	50
_____ **01833**	CNJ USRA Single-sheathed Boxcar #1	50
_____ **01834**	CNJ USRA Single-sheathed Boxcar #2	50
_____ **01835**	MEC USRA Single-sheathed Boxcar #1	50
_____ **01836**	MEC USRA Single-sheathed Boxcar #2	50
_____ **01839**	PRR USRA Single-sheathed Boxcar #3	50
_____ **01840**	PRR USRA Single-sheathed Boxcar #4	50
_____ **01842**	Canada Southern USRA Rebuilt Covered Hopper #1	50
_____ **01843**	Canada Southern USRA Rebuilt Covered Hopper #2	50
_____ **01845**	RFP Express USRA Double-sheathed Boxcar #1	50
_____ **01846**	RFP Express USRA Double-sheathed Boxcar #2	50
_____ **01847**	DCC Interface PCB for Switchers	25
_____ **01848**	B&O USRA Rebuilt Covered Hopper #1	50
_____ **01849**	B&O USRA Rebuilt Covered Hopper #2	50
_____ **01850**	CNJ USRA Rebuilt Covered Hopper #1	50
_____ **01851**	CNJ USRA Rebuilt Covered Hopper #2	50
_____ **01852**	C&O USRA Rebuilt Covered Hopper #1	50
_____ **01853**	C&O USRA Rebuilt Covered Hopper #2	50
_____ **01854**	D&H USRA Rebuilt Covered Hopper #1	50
_____ **01855**	D&H USRA Rebuilt Covered Hopper #2	50
_____ **01856**	LNE USRA Rebuilt Covered Hopper #1	50
_____ **01857**	LNE USRA Rebuilt Covered Hopper #2	50
_____ **01858**	LV USRA Rebuilt Covered Hopper #1	50
_____ **01859**	LV USRA Rebuilt Covered Hopper #2	50
_____ **01861**	MEC USRA Rebuilt Covered Hopper #2	55
_____ **01862**	NYC USRA Rebuilt Covered Hopper #1	50
_____ **01863**	NYC USRA Rebuilt Covered Hopper #2	50
_____ **01864**	NKP USRA Rebuilt Covered Hopper #1	50
_____ **01865**	NKP USRA Rebuilt Covered Hopper #2	50
_____ **01866**	Reading USRA Rebuilt Covered Hopper #1	50
_____ **01867**	Reading USRA Rebuilt Covered Hopper #2	50
_____ **01868**	Cambria & Indiana Offset Hopper #1	50

01869	Cambria & Indiana Offset Hopper #2	50 ____
01870	USRA Rebuilt Covered Hopper, gray	50 ____
01871	PRR Standard Flatcar #4	50 ____
01872	S-Helper Service 35' Trailer, horizontal corrugations	20 ____
01874	ATSF 35' Trailer, horizontal corrugations, scheme II	20 ____
01875	Reading 35' Trailer, vertical ribs	20 ____
01876	Moxie Wooden Billboard Reefer #1 (NASG)	53 ____
01877	Moxie Wooden Billboard Reefer #2 (NASG)	53 ____
01878	REA 35' Trailer, vertical ribs	20 ____
01879	SP 35' Trailer, horizontal corrugations	20 ____
01880	ATSF 35' Trailer, vertical ribs, scheme II	20 ____
01881	Weber Wooden Billboard Reefer #1 (Badgerland)	53 ____
01882	Weber Wooden Billboard Reefer #2 (Badgerland)	53 ____
01883	Weber Wooden Billboard Reefer #3 (Badgerland)	53 ____
01884	Sampson Canning Wooden Billboard Reefer	53 ____
01885	ATSF USRA Double-sheathed Boxcar #1	50 ____
01886	ATSF USRA Double-sheathed Boxcar #2	50 ____
01887	CB&Q USRA Double-sheathed Boxcar #1	50 ____
01888	CB&Q USRA Double-sheathed Boxcar #2	50 ____
01889	CH&D USRA Double-sheathed Boxcar #1	50 ____
01890	CH&D USRA Double-sheathed Boxcar #2 (Miami Valley)	50 ____
01891	NKP USRA Double-sheathed Boxcar #1 (Hoosier)	50 ____
01892	NKP USRA Double-sheathed Boxcar #2 (Hoosier)	50 ____
01893	NKP USRA Double-sheathed Boxcar #3	50 ____
01894	NKP USRA Double-sheathed Boxcar #4	50 ____
01895	NWP Double-sheathed Boxcar, scheme II #1 (O West)	50 ____
01896	NWP Double-sheathed Boxcar, scheme II #2 (O West)	50 ____
01897	NWP USRA Double-sheathed Boxcar, scheme II #3	50 ____
01898	NWP USRA Double-sheathed Boxcar, scheme II #4	50 ____
01899	Frank Fehr Brewery Wooden Billboard Reefer	53 ____
01900	Buffalo Creek & Gauley USRA Rib Side Hopper #1	50 ____
01901	Buffalo Creek & Gauley USRA Rib Side Hopper #2	50 ____
01902	Buffalo Creek & Gauley USRA Rib Side Hopper #3	50 ____
01903	Buffalo Creek & Gauley USRA Rib Side Hopper #4	50 ____
01904	C&O USRA Rib Side Hopper #5	50 ____
01905	C&O USRA Rib Side Hopper #6	50 ____
01906	PRR USRA Rib Side Hopper, scheme II #1	50 ____
01907	PRR USRA Rib Side Hopper, scheme II #2	50 ____
01908	GTW USRA Rebuilt Covered Hopper #2	50 ____
01909	CB&Q NW2 Diesel Freight Set, 5 cars	350 ____
01910	SLSF SW9 Diesel Freight Set, 5 cars	350 ____
01911	MP F7A Diesel Freight Set, 6 cars	430 ____
01912	GN SW1 Diesel Freight Set, 4 cars	315 ____
01913	CRI&P 40' Steel Rebuilt Boxcar #1 (State Line)	50 ____
01914	CRI&P 40' Steel Rebuilt Boxcar #2 (State Line)	50 ____

01915	CRI&P 40' Steel Rebuilt Boxcar #3 (State Line)	50
01916	ATSF "Chief" 40' Steel Rebuilt Boxcar #1	50
01917	ATSF "Chief" 40' Steel Rebuilt Boxcar #2	50
01918	C&O 40' Steel Rebuilt Boxcar #3	50
01919	C&O 40' Steel Rebuilt Boxcar #4	50
01920	P&LE (NYC) 40' Steel Rebuilt Boxcar #2	50
01921	P&LE (NYC) 40' Steel Rebuilt Boxcar #3	50
01922	MP "Eagle" 40' Steel Rebuilt Boxcar #3	50
01923	MP "Eagle" 40' Steel Rebuilt Boxcar #4	50
01941	CNJ USRA Rebuilt Covered Hopper #3	50
01942	CNJ USRA Rebuilt Covered Hopper #4	50
01943	Moxie Wooden Billboard Reefer #3	53
01944	Moxie Wooden Billboard Reefer #4	53
01946	Santa Fe Wooden Billboard Reefer #3	53
01947	Santa Fe Wooden Billboard Reefer #4	53
01951	PFE Wooden Billboard Reefer, scheme IV #1	53
01952	PFE Wooden Billboard Reefer, scheme IV #2	53
01957	PFE Wooden Billboard Reefer, scheme IV #3	53
01958	B&A 40' Steel Rebuilt Boxcar #1 (Daniel Lundy)	50
01959	B&A 40' Steel Rebuilt Boxcar #2 (Daniel Lundy)	50
01960	B&A 40' Steel Rebuilt Boxcar #3 (Daniel Lundy)	50
01961	B&A 40' Steel Rebuilt Boxcar #4 (Daniel Lundy)	50
01962	Sherman Williams PS-2 2-bay Hopper #1 (CVSG)	50
01963	Sherman Williams PS-2 2-bay Hopper #2 (CVSG)	50
01964	Sherman Williams PS-2 2-bay Hopper #3 (CVSG)	50
01965	Sherman Williams PS-2 2-bay Hopper #4 (CVSG)	50
01966	Sherman Williams PS-2 2-bay Hopper #5 (CVSG)	50
01967	Union Carbide "Bakelite" PS-2 3-bay Covered Hopper	50
01968	ATSF PS-2 3-bay Covered Hopper #1	50
01969	ATSF PS-2 3-bay Covered Hopper #2	50
01970	Erie PS-2 3-bay Covered Hopper #1	50
01971	Erie PS-2 3-bay Covered Hopper #2	50
01972	Erie PS-2 3-bay Covered Hopper #3	50
01973	CRI&P 40' Steel Boxcar, scheme II #2 (State Line)	50
01976	GN PS-2 3-bay Covered Hopper #3	50
01977	GN PS-2 3-bay Covered Hopper #4	50
01978	SW8/9 Diesel, DCC sound	290
01979	C&NW (CGW) PS-2 3-bay Covered Hopper #1	50
01980	C&NW (CGW) PS-2 3-bay Covered Hopper #2	50
01981	Marhoefer Wooden Billboard Reefer #2	50
01982	Marhoefer Wooden Billboard Reefer #3	50
01983	CP Stock Car #1	50
01984	CP Stock Car #2	50
01985	CB&Q Stock Car #3	50
01986	CB&Q Stock Car #4	50

		Retail	
01987	UP Stock Car #7	50	____
01988	UP Stock Car #8	50	____
01989	B&O Composite Side Hopper #5	53	____
01990	B&O Composite Side Hopper #6	53	____
01991	PRR Composite Side Hopper, scheme II #5	53	____
01992	PRR Composite Side Hopper, scheme II #6	53	____
01993	Black Fishbelly Hopper	53	____
01994	Red Fishbelly Hopper	53	____
01995	Akron, Canton & Youngstown Fishbelly Hopper #1	53	____
01996	Akron, Canton & Youngstown Fishbelly Hopper #2	53	____
01997	Akron, Canton & Youngstown Fishbelly Hopper #3	53	____
01998	Akron, Canton & Youngstown Fishbelly Hopper #4	53	____
01999	ACL Fishbelly Hopper #1	53	____
02000	ACL Fishbelly Hopper #2	53	____
02001	ACL Fishbelly Hopper #3	53	____
02002	ACL Fishbelly Hopper #4	53	____
02003	B&O Fishbelly Hopper #1	53	____
02004	B&O Fishbelly Hopper #2	53	____
02005	B&O Fishbelly Hopper #3	53	____
02006	B&O Fishbelly Hopper #4	53	____
02007	CNJ Fishbelly Hopper #1	53	____
02008	CNJ Fishbelly Hopper #2	53	____
02009	CNJ Fishbelly Hopper #3	53	____
02010	CNJ Fishbelly Hopper #4	53	____
02011	C&O Fishbelly Hopper #1	53	____
02012	C&O Fishbelly Hopper #2	53	____
02013	C&O Fishbelly Hopper #3	53	____
02014	C&O Fishbelly Hopper #4	53	____
02015	D&H Fishbelly Hopper #1	53	____
02016	D&H Fishbelly Hopper #2	53	____
02017	D&H Fishbelly Hopper #3	53	____
02018	D&H Fishbelly Hopper #4	53	____
02019	LV Fishbelly Hopper #1	53	____
02020	LV Fishbelly Hopper #2	53	____
02021	LV Fishbelly Hopper #3	53	____
02022	LV Fishbelly Hopper #4	53	____
02023	N&W Fishbelly Hopper #1	53	____
02024	N&W Fishbelly Hopper #2	53	____
02025	N&W Fishbelly Hopper #3	53	____
02026	N&W Fishbelly Hopper #4	53	____
02027	NS Fishbelly Hopper #1	53	____
02028	NS Fishbelly Hopper #2	53	____
02029	NS Fishbelly Hopper #3	53	____
02030	NS Fishbelly Hopper #4	53	____
02031	Reading Fishbelly Hopper #1	53	____

____ **02032**	Reading Fishbelly Hopper #2	53
____ **02033**	Reading Fishbelly Hopper #3	53
____ **02034**	Reading Fishbelly Hopper #4	53
____ **02035**	WM Fishbelly Hopper #1	53
____ **02036**	WM Fishbelly Hopper #2	53
____ **02037**	WM Fishbelly Hopper #3	53
____ **02038**	WM Fishbelly Hopper #4	53
____ **02039**	Ballantine Beer Wooden Billboard Reefer #3 (Hoquat)	53
____ **02040**	Ballantine Beer Wooden Billboard Reefer #4 (Hoquat)	53
____ **02043**	DL&W Reefer #1	53
____ **02044**	DL&W Reefer #2	53
____ **02045**	Eatmor Cranberries Wooden Billboard Reefer	53
____ **02046**	Falstaff Wooden Billboard Reefer #1 (NASG)	53
____ **02047**	Falstaff Wooden Billboard Reefer #2 (NASG)	53
____ **02048**	Lemp Falstaff Wooden Billboard Reefer #1 (NASG)	53
____ **02049**	Lemp Falstaff Wooden Billboard Reefer #2 (NASG)	53
____ **02050**	Prima Special Wooden Billboard Reefer	53
____ **02051**	CB&Q NW2 Diesel Freight Set, 6 cars	390
____ **02052**	BN SW8 Diesel Freight Set, 4 cars	346
____ **02053**	CRI&P SW8 Diesel Freight Set, 5 cars	360
____ **02054**	GN 2009 Christmas Boxcar	63
____ **02055**	Toronto, Hamilton & Buffalo Double-sheathed Boxcar #2	50
____ **02056**	3M USRA Double-sheathed Boxcar #1	50
____ **02057**	3M USRA Double-sheathed Boxcar #2	50
____ **02058**	Flatcar with 4 wrapped steel coils	63
____ **02059**	Mine Run Coal Load	7
____ **02060**	Gluek Brewing Billboard Reefer, blue (Hoquat)	53
____ **02061**	Gluek Brewing Billboard Reefer, red (Hoquat)	53
____ **02065**	Gray Steel Coil Loads	63
____ **02066**	Metal Rail Joiners, unweathered, 36 pieces	7
____ **02070**	Laser Cut Reels with rack	75
____ **02071**	PRR 2D-F1 Archbar Truck, code 110, pair	25
____ **02072**	PRR 2D-F1 Archbar Truck, hi-rail, pair	25
____ **02073**	B&O USRA Rib Side Hopper, scheme II #1	53
____ **02074**	B&O USRA Rib Side Hopper, scheme II #2	53
____ **02075**	B&O USRA Rib Side Hopper, scheme II #3	53
____ **02076**	B&O USRA Rib Side Hopper, scheme II #4	53
____ **02077**	Reading USRA Rib Side Hopper #5	53
____ **02078**	Reading USRA Rib Side Hopper #6	53
____ **02079**	ATSF Composite Side Hopper #5	53
____ **02080**	ATSF Composite Side Hopper #6	53
____ **02081**	CB&Q Composite Side Hopper #5	53
____ **02082**	CB&Q Composite Side Hopper #6	53
____ **02083**	LV Composite Side Hopper #9	53
____ **02084**	LV Composite Side Hopper #10	53

		Retail	
02086	C&O Composite Side Hopper #5	53	____
02087	C&O Composite Side Hopper #6	53	____
02109	GN 40' Steel Rebuilt Boxcar, scheme III #3	53	____
02110	GN 40' Steel Rebuilt Boxcar, scheme III #4	53	____
02111	NKP Steel Rebuilt Boxcar #1	53	____
02112	NKP Steel Rebuilt Boxcar #2	53	____
02113	NKP Steel Rebuilt Boxcar #3	53	____
02114	NKP Steel Rebuilt Boxcar #4	53	____
02115	Seaboard "Orange Blossom Special" Rebuilt Boxcar #2	53	____
02116	Seaboard "Orange Blossom Special" Rebuilt Boxcar #3	53	____
02117	SP Steel Rebuilt Boxcar #1 (S Scale West)	53	____
02118	SP Steel Rebuilt Boxcar #2 (S Scale West)	53	____
02119	SP Steel Rebuilt Boxcar #3 (S Scale West)	53	____
02120	SP Steel Rebuilt Boxcar #4 (S Scale West)	53	____
02127	40" SW/NW Wheelset, Code 110	16	____
02128	40" SW/NW Wheelset, AF compatible	16	____
02129	40" F unit Wheelset, Code 110	16	____
02130	40" F unit Wheelset, AF compatible	16	____
02149	WM Fishbelly Hopper, scheme II #1	53	____
02150	WM Fishbelly Hopper, scheme II #2	53	____
ART-5400	DC Power Pack, 24VDC	50	____
20064	Rock Island Boxcar, silver (State-Line S Gaugers)	45	____
20070	Rock Island Boxcar, green (State-Line S Gaugers)	45	____

Unnumbered Items

	Train Pack Lube Set	15	____

			Good (P-5)	Exc (P-7)

1946

			Good	Exc
____	D1451	Consumer Catalog	35	150
____		with red binder	75	450
____	D1455	Dealer Catalog	27	172
____	D1457	Gilbert Scientific Toys	10	26
____	D1458	Appointment Card	1	2
____	M2499	Instruction Sheet		1
____		Envelope for D1451	2	10

1947

			Good	Exc
____	D1462	Catalog Mailer	14	60
____	D1472	Catalog Mailer	14	50
____	D1473	Consumer Catalog	27	75
____	D1482	Dealer Catalog	20	75
____	D1492	Erector Fun and Action	4	13
____	D1495	What Retail Stores Should Know	4	13
____	D1496	Display Suggestions	45	270
____	D1502	Advance Catalog	13	46
____	M2502	Instruction Book	2	5
____		Envelope for D1473	2	4

1948

			Good	Exc
____	D1505	Advance Catalog	10	56
____	D1507	Consumer Catalog	15	50
____	D1508	Superman	17	105
____	D1508	Consumer Catalog	10	24
____		with prepaid postage	5	18
____	D1517	HO Catalog	9	23

1949

			Good	Exc
____	D1524	Gilbert Scientific Toys Catalog	5	9
____	D1525	Bang Bang Torpedo	45	115
____	D1530	Advance Catalog	18	55
____	D1531	Gilbert Scientific Toys Catalog	5	9
____	D1536	Consumer Catalog	9	28
____	D1547	Catalog Envelope	1	4
____	D1552	How to Sell American Flyer	5	18
	M2690	Instruction Booklet		
____		(A) Yellow cover	1	3
____		(B) White cover	2	4

1950

			Good	Exc
____	D1578	Dealer Catalog	13	45
____	D1579	Gilbert Toys	5	16
____	D1581/A	Red/Blue Ad		180
____	D1604	Consumer Catalog	16	40

GILBERT PAPER 1946–1967		Good (P-5)	Exc (P-7)	
D1610	Catalog Envelope	1	4	___
D1629	Dealer Action Displays Sheet		NRS	___
D1631	Dealer TV Ad	9	18	___
	Ready Again Booklet		300	___

1951

D1637	Dealer Catalog	13	50	___
D1637A	Advance Catalog	8	33	___
D1640	Consumer Catalog	15	35	___
D1641	Erector and Gilbert Toys Catalog	2	5	___
D1652	Facts About AF Trains		60	___
D1656	AF and Toys	5	9	___
D1660	Gilbert Electric Eye	5	9	___

1952

D1667	Advance Catalog	10	45	___
D1667A	Advance Catalog	11	45	___
D1668A	Consumer Catalog		40	___
D1670	Single Sheet 200 Series Buildings	2	9	___
D1677	Consumer Catalog	8	27	___
D1678	Facts About AF Trains	7	11	___
M2978	AF Model Railroad Handbook	5	9	___
M2984	Instruction Book	1	3	___
	Advance Catalog		NRS	___
	Consumer Catalog, Spanish		NRS	___

1953

D1699	Consumer Catalog		45	___
D1703	Erector and Other Toys	3	7	___
D1704	Dealer Catalog	9	35	___
D1714	Dealer Catalog, East	8	30	___
D1715	Consumer Catalog, West	11	29	___
D1727	Tips on Selling AF Trains	5	9	___
D1728	Tips on Erector	2	8	___

1954

D1734	Catalog Envelope	1	4	___
D1740	Erector and Gilbert Toys	1	4	___
D1744	AF and Erector Ad Program	4	16	___
D1746	Dealer Catalog			
	(A) Pulp	8	35	___
	(B) Glossy	8	47	___
D1748	Catalog, East			
	(A) Consumer	3	15	___
	(B) Dealer	4	20	___
D1749	Dealer Catalog, West	11	29	___
D1750	Dealer Displays		NRS	___
D1751	Microscope Flysheet	1	2	___
D1760	Consumer Catalog, East	10	44	___
D1761	Consumer Catalog, West	12	37	___
D1762	Boys Railroad Club Letter	1	5	___

GILBERT PAPER 1946–1967

			Good (P-5)	Exc (P-7)
____	D1769	Read All About Ad Campaign		NRS
____	D1774	Erector and Other Gilbert Toys	2	5
____	D1777	Reply Postcard	1	2
____	M3290	Instruction Book	1	4

1955

____	D1782	Dealer Catalog	8	30
____	D1783	Certificate of Registry	5	9
____	D1784	Erector and Other Gilbert Toys		80
____	D1801	Consumer Catalog, East	7	20
____	D1802	Consumer Catalog, West	9	20
____	D1814	Choo Choo Sound Foldout	1	4
____	D1816	Dealer Catalog	9	29
____	D1820	HO Consumer Catalog	1	5
____	D1835	Tips for Selling Erector	1	2
____	D1840	Envelope	1	4
____	M3450	Instruction Book	1	5

1956

____	D1866	Consumer Catalog, East	7	12
____	D1867	Consumer Catalog, West	8	12
____	D1874	Dealer Catalog	14	39
____	D1879	Gilbert and Erector Toys	1	6
____	D1882	AF and Erector Displays	1	7
____	D1892	Store Banner (Dealer)		525
____	D1893	Store Banner		1250
____	D1899	Big Value AF Trestle System Special Set Brochure		100
____	D1904	Gilbert HO Catalog	2	6
____	D1907	Dealer Catalog	6	28
____	D1920	How to Build a Model Railroad	2	15
____	D1922	Miniature Catalog	6	25
____	D1925	Erector Folder	2	7
____	D1926	Envelope for D1922 Catalog	1	4

1957

____	D1937	Dealer Catalog	9	35
____	D1966	Consumer Catalog	2	10
____	D1973	Erector and Other Toys	1	2
____	D1980	Cardboard		35
____	D1981	Same as D1980		35
____	D2006	Consumer Catalog, East	5	15
____	D2007	Consumer Catalog, West	13	20
____	D2008	Erector and Toys	1	4
____	D2022	Dealer Flyer		55
____	D2031	Consumer Catalog		41
____	D2037	Erector and Gilbert Toys	1	5
____	D2045	Gilbert Promotion Kit		NRS
____	M3817	HO Instructions	2	7
____		Same as M3450 (1955) but without number		20

		Good (P-5)	Exc (P-7)	

1958

		Good	Exc	
D2047	Consumer Catalog	21	90	____
D2048	Catalog, West	25	75	____
D2058	Erector and Toys	1	5	____
D2060	Erector and Gilbert Toys	2	10	____
D2073	Advance Catalog	6	17	____
D2080	Smoking Caboose		125	____
D2086	Consumer Folder, East	2	10	____
D2087	Consumer Folder, West	1	10	____
D2088	Consumer Folder	2	11	____
D2101	Career Building Science Toys	1	2	____
D4106	HO Catalog	1	4	____
M4195	Accessory Folder	1	4	____
M4202	Color Billboards		10	____

1959

		Good	Exc	
D2115	Dealer Catalog	12	50	____
D2118	AF No. 20142, Willit		15	____
D2120	Career Building Science Toys	1	12	____
D2125	Overland Express Sheet	1	2	____
D2132	HO Catalog		34	____
D2146	Consumer Catalog	1	10	____
D2148	Consumer Catalog	1	7	____
D2171/-79	Dealer Promotional Set		NRS	____
D2179	Promotional Sheet, Franklin Set	1	5	____
D2180	Gilbert Science Toys	1	4	____
M4225	Train Assembly and Operating Instructions		NRS	____
M4326	Accessory Catalog	1	4	____
M4869	AF Maintenance Manual	1	2	____
	Canadian D2115 Catalog		NRS	____
	Catalog, Gilbert Toys		NRS	____

1960

		Good	Exc	
D2192	Catalog			
	(A) Dealer	5	28	____
	(B) Advance		33	____
D2193	Consumer Catalog	2	9	____
D2193REV	Revised Consumer Catalog	2	7	____
D2196	Dealer Catalog		120	____
D2197	Dealer Display Catalog		85	____
D2198	Action and Fun Catalog	2	6	____
D2205	Gilbert Toys	2	9	____
D2208	Dealer Advance Catalog		75	____
D2223	Gilbert Science Toys	1	4	____
D2224	Consumer Folder	1	5	____
D2225	Consumer Folder	3	6	____
D2226	Consumer Folder	1	4	____
D2230	Consumer Catalog	9	40	____
D2231	Consumer Catalog	2	7	____
	Truscott Set Promotional Sheet		50	____

			Good (P-5)	Exc (P-7)

1961

			Good	Exc
____	D2238	Career Building Science Toys	2	25
____	D2239	Consumer Catalog	4	10
____	D2242REV	Auto Rama Catalog	1	2
____	D2255	1961–62 Retail Display	1	2
____	D2266	Gilbert Science Toys	1	5
____	D2267	Consumer Catalog	4	10
____	D2268	Auto Rama Folder	1	2

1962

			Good	Exc
____	D2277REV	Career Building Science Toys	7	24
____	D2278	Dealer Catalog	2	22
____	D2278REV	Revised Dealer Catalog	2	13
____	D2282	Dealer Catalog		35
____	D2283	HO Trains and Accessories	2	8
____	D2307	Consumer Ad Mats		75
____	D2310	Consumer Catalog	4	15
____	D2329	HO Catalog		45
____	M6874	Instruction Booklet	1	4
____		The Big Ones Come From Gilbert		35

1963

			Good	Exc
____	D2321	Dealer Catalog	1	15
____	D2321REV	Revised Dealer Catalog	5	14
____	D2328	Consumer Catalog		16
____	X863-3	Consumer Catalog	4	31

1964

			Good	Exc
____	X264-6	Consumer Catalog	3	21
____	564-11	Dealer Catalog	2	7
____		Similar to X264-6, 8 pages		NRS
____		Similar to X264-6, black binding		NRS

1965

			Good	Exc
____	X165-12	Dealer Catalog	6	29
____	X165-12REV	Revised Dealer Catalog	6	13
____	X365-10	Consumer Folder	1	5
____	T465-5REV	Dealer Folder	1	2

1966

			Good	Exc
____	T166-6	Dealer Catalog	4	21
____	T166-7	Gilbert Action Toys	6	32
____	X466-1	Consumer Catalog	3	14
____	T1065-11	Dealer Sales Folder		200
____	M6788	All Aboard Instructions	3	8

1967*

			Good	Exc
____		Four-page Folder	1	4

*Gilbert train production ended in 1966; however, an American Flyer Industries Folder was released for 1967.

ABBREVIATIONS

Descriptions

AF	American Flyer
AFL	American Flyer Lines
ART	American Refrigerator Transit Co.
BAAFC	Baltimore Area American Flyer Club
CC	Command Control
CD	Center discharge
CVSG	Cuyahoga Valley S Gauge Association
EMD	Electro-Motive Division
FGE	Fruit Growers Express
FM	Fairbanks-Morse
GP	Diesel locomotive
GM	General Motors
MDT	Merchants Despatch Transportation
MOW	Maintenance-of-way
NASG	National Association of S-Gaugers
NETCA	New England Division, TCA
NMRA	National Model Railroad Association
PA	Alco diesel with cab
PB	Alco diesel without cab
PFE	Pacific Fruit Express
PM	Pike Master
REA	Railway Express Agency
s-i-b	Smoke in boiler
s-i-t	Smoke in tender
TCA	Train Collectors Association
TTOS	Toy Train Operating Society
UFGE	United Fruit Growers Express
USRA	United States Railroad Administration
WFE	Western Fruit Express
1-D	One dome
3-D	Three dome

ABBREVIATIONS
Railroad names

ACL	Atlantic Coast Line
ATSF	Atchison, Topeka & Santa Fe
B&A	Boston & Albany
BAR	Bangor & Aroostook
B&LE	Bessemer & Lake Erie
B&M	Boston & Maine
BN	Burlington Northern
BNSF	Burlington Northern Santa Fe
B&O	Baltimore & Ohio
CB&Q	Chicago, Burlington & Quincy
CMStP&P	Chicago, Milwaukee, St. Paul & Pacific
CN	Canadian National
CGW	Chicago Great Western
CNJ	Central of New Jersey
C&NW	Chicago & North Western
C&O	Chesapeake & Ohio
CP	Canadian Pacific
CRI&P	Chicago, Rock Island & Pacific
C&S	Colorado Southern
CUVA	Cuyahoga Valley Railway
D&H	Delaware & Hudson
D&RGW	Denver & Rio Grande Western
DT&I	Detroit, Toledo & Ironton
DM&IR	Duluth, Missabe & Iron Range
Erie-Lack.	Erie-Lackawanna
FEC	Florida East Coast
FWD	Fort Worth & Denver
GM&O	Gulf, Mobile & Ohio
GN	Great Northern
GN&W	Genesee & Wyoming
GTW	Grand Trunk Western
IC	Illinois Central
ICG	Illinois Central Gulf
IGN	International-Great Northern
KCS	Kansas City Southern

L&N	Louisville & Nashville
LNE	Lehigh New England
LV	Lehigh Valley
MEC	Maine Central
MILW	Milwaukee Road
MKT	Missouri-Kansas-Texas
MNS	Minnesota, Northfield & Southern
MP	Missouri Pacific
M&StL	Minneapolis & St. Louis
NdeM	Nacionales de Mexico Railway
NH	New Haven
NKP	Nickel Plate Road
NOT&M	New Orleans, Texas & Mexico
NP	Northern Pacific
NS	Norfolk Southern
N&W	Norfolk & Western
NWP	Northwestern Pacific
NYC	New York Central
NYO&W	New York, Ontario & Western
NYNH&H	New York, New Haven & Hartford
OSL	Oregon Short Line
P&LE	Pittsburgh & Lake Erie
PC	Penn Central
PRR	Pennsylvania Railroad
PMKY	Pittsburgh, McKeesport & Youghiogheny
PTM	ST Rail System
RFP	Richmond, Fredericksburg & Potomac
SF	Santa Fe
SLSF	St. Louis-San Francisco
SP	Southern Pacific
SSW	St. Louis Southwestern
T&P	Texas & Pacific
TP&W	Toledo, Peoria & Western
UP	Union Pacific
WM	Western Maryland
WP	Western Pacific

Build Your Toy Train Library

Scenery Techniques for Toy Trains

For toy train operators looking to add scenery and dimension to their layouts, this book offers simple solutions. It explains how to use foam as a scenery base and how to shape it into mountains and rivers. Step-by-step photographs and instructions illustrate techniques for adding streets, accessories, and even a working drive-in theater.

10-8400 • $17.95

Trackwork for Toy Trains

This essential guide addresses O gauge trackwork from nearly all of today's major manufacturers. Peter H. Riddle provides an overview of the various lines of sectional and flexible track, then demonstrates with step-by-step photography the basic techniques for cutting, bending, wiring, and layout installation. Also includes tips and tricks fo working with special trackwork, such as switches, crossings, and accessory-activation sections.

10-8365 • $19.95

Realistic Modeling for Toy Trains: A Hi-Rail Guide

Author Dennis Brennan shows step-by-step how various creative elements of a layout fit together using his Sandy Harbor Terminal Railway. Practical building techniques and realistic modeling concepts explain how readers can build a hi-rail toy train layout.

10-8390 • $19.95

Buy now from your local hobby shop! Shop at KalmbachHobbyStore.com